Modern App Deployment with Azure Kubernetes

Dawid Borycki

Modern App Deployment with Azure Kubernetes

Published with the authorization of Microsoft Corporation by:
Pearson Education, Inc.

Copyright © 2026 by Pearson Education, Inc.

Hoboken, New Jersey

All rights reserved. This publication is protected by copyright, and permission must be obtained from the publisher prior to any prohibited reproduction, storage in a retrieval system, or transmission in any form or by any means, electronic, mechanical, photocopying, recording, or likewise. For information regarding permissions, request forms, and the appropriate contacts within the Pearson Education Global Rights & Permissions Department, please visit www.pearson.com/global-permission-granting.html.

No patent liability is assumed with respect to the use of the information contained herein. Although every precaution has been taken in the preparation of this book, the publisher and author assume no responsibility for errors or omissions. Nor is any liability assumed for damages resulting from the use of the information contained herein. Please contact us with concerns about any potential bias at www.pearson.com/report-bias.html.

ISBN-13: 978-0-13-544250-0
ISBN-10: 0-13-544250-8

Library of Congress Control Number: 2025941170

1 2025

Trademarks

Microsoft and the trademarks listed at http://www.microsoft.com on the "Trademarks" webpage are trademarks of the Microsoft group of companies. All other marks are property of their respective owners.

Warning and Disclaimer

Every effort has been made to make this book as complete and as accurate as possible, but no warranty or fitness is implied. The information provided is on an "as is" basis. The author, the publisher, and Microsoft Corporation shall have neither liability nor responsibility to any person or entity with respect to any loss or damages arising from the information contained in this book or from the use of the programs accompanying it.

Editor-in-Chief
Julie Phifer

Executive Editor
Loretta Yates

Associate Editor
Shourav Bose

Development Editor
Songlin Qiu

Technical Editor
Charles Pluta

Managing Editor
Sandra Schroeder

Senior Project Editor
Tracey Croom

Copy Editor
Linda Laflamme

Indexer
Ken Johnson

Proofreader
Barbara Mack

Cover Designer
Twist Creative, Seattle

Compositor
codeMantra

Cover Illustration
Yakov24_Shutterstock

Contents at a Glance

	Introduction	*xix*

PART I   CONTAINERIZATION

CHAPTER 1	Motivation	3
CHAPTER 2	Application	13
CHAPTER 3	Containerization with Docker	21
CHAPTER 4	How to Containerize an Application with Docker	37
CHAPTER 5	Azure Container Registry	55

PART II   CONTAINER ORCHESTRATION

CHAPTER 6	Container Orchestration with Kubernetes	71
CHAPTER 7	Azure Kubernetes Service	83
CHAPTER 8	Azure SQL Database and Azure Key Vault	97
CHAPTER 9	Diagnosing and Monitoring the Cluster	115
CHAPTER 10	Application Rollouts and Rollbacks	127

PART III   AUTOMATION

CHAPTER 11	Automating Image Builds and Deployment Using CI/CD Pipelines	141
CHAPTER 12	Load Testing, Horizontal Pod Autoscaling, and Cluster Autoscaling	161
CHAPTER 13	Deploying and Managing Kubernetes Applications with Helm	181
CHAPTER 14	Infrastructure as Code	205

	Index	*237*

Contents

Introduction .... *xix*

PART I   CONTAINERIZATION

Chapter 1   Motivation   3
    Modern application development and deployment 4
    The advantage of disk images 6
    The advantages of containers for application deployment 6
    Tools 8
        Git 8
        .NET 8 SDK 8
        Docker Desktop 8
        Visual Studio Code 9
        Azure Subscription 9
        Azure Command Line Interface 10
        Notation 10
    Summary 11

Chapter 2   Application   13
    Running the application 14
    Database connection 14
    Web API 15
        Retrieving data using the web browser 16
        Swagger 16
    Summary 19

Chapter 3 Containerization with Docker   21

Why use containers?..21
    Imperative vs. declarative configuration......................21
    What is containerization, and how can it help you?.............22
    Containers vs. virtual machines................................23

What is Docker?..25
    Architecture..25
    How to pull and run a container...............................26
    How to manage containers......................................29
    How to remove a container.....................................30

Running multiple containers..31
    Volumes...32
    Networking..34
    Docker Compose..35

Summary..36

Chapter 4 How to Containerize an Application with Docker   37

Dockerfile...37

Containerize the People.WebApp...38

Building the container image...40

Running a containerized People.WebApp......................................42

Modifying application settings...43

Using Docker Compose to provision a multi-container solution...............46
    Creating a configuration file.................................47
    Adding Microsoft SQL Server...................................48
    Running an app..50
    Testing a solution..51
    Cleaning up...53

Summary..54

Chapter 5 Azure Container Registry   55

What is Azure Container Registry?..56

How do you create the Container Registry in Azure?.........................56

	Azure Portal..56
	Azure CLI..59
	Azure Cloud Shell..64
	Clean up...65

How do you push a local image to the container registry?..............65

Summary...68

PART II CONTAINER ORCHESTRATION

Chapter 6 Container Orchestration with Kubernetes   71

What is Kubernetes?...72

Kubernetes architecture...73

How does Kubernetes work?...74

Local Kubernetes cluster..75

kubectl...77

How do you deploy an application to the Kubernetes cluster?.......................78

Summary...82

Chapter 7 Azure Kubernetes Service   83

How Azure Kubernetes Service can help you...83

	What does it cost?...84
	What resources do you need?..84

Creating a cluster using Azure Kubernetes Service.................................84

	What resources were created with the cluster?.......................88

Connecting to the cluster...90

	Using the local machine..90
	Using the Azure Cloud Shell..92

Deploying an application..92

Summary...95

Chapter 8 Azure SQL Database and Azure Key Vault   97

Azure SQL Database 97
    Creating the database 98
    Configuring the connection 103
    Previewing the Azure SQL Database 106

Azure Key Vault 107
    Creating the key vault 107
    Retrieving the secret 108
    Configuring the key vault permissions 110
    Updating the application 110

Summary 112

Chapter 9 Diagnosing and Monitoring the Cluster   115

Kubernetes resources 115
    Namespaces, workloads, and services 115
    Storage and configuration 117
    Running commands 119

Monitoring 119
    Alerts and metrics 119
    Container Insights 121

Summary 125

Chapter 10 Application Rollouts and Rollbacks   127

How to retrieve the Pod name 127

Rollout 130

Rollout strategies 132

Rollout history and rollbacks 134

Manual scaling 137

Summary 138

PART III AUTOMATION

Chapter 11 Automating Image Builds and Deployment Using CI/CD Pipelines 141

Setting up the workflow 141

Automatically building and pushing a Docker image 143

Configuring the Secret 147

Testing the workflow 151

Updating the deployment in Azure Kubernetes Service 153

Running an updated workflow 157

Automatic updates of the application 159

Summary 160

Chapter 12 Load Testing, Horizontal Pod Autoscaling, and Cluster Autoscaling 161

Load testing with Hey 161

    Automating the load test using Docker 164

    Building and running the containerized load tests 167

Horizontal Pod autoscaling 170

    Configuring horizontal Pod autoscaling? 170

    Applying horizontal Pod autoscaling? 172

    Resource requests and limits for Pods and containers 173

    Performance of the HorizontalPodAutoscaler under load test conditions 177

Summary 179

Chapter 13 Deploying and Managing Kubernetes Applications with Helm 181

Introduction to Helm 182

Creating a Helm chart 182

Rollouts and rollbacks 187

Integration with the CI/CD pipeline 190

Git branch and chart files.......................................190
Chart and values files 191
Deployment...194
Service..196
HorizontalPodAutoscaler 197
Helpers 198
GitHub Actions 199
Testing the workflow..201

Summary 203

Chapter 14 Infrastructure as Code   205

Introduction to Terraform...206

Deploying Azure Container Registry...................................207
Creating Terraform declarations for Azure Container Registry....208
Remote backend 209
Deploying the infrastructure 210

Deploying Azure Kubernetes Cluster 213

Deploying a SQL database 216

Deploying a Key Vault 219

Integration with the CI/CD pipeline...................................221
Declaration files 222
Helm files 227
CI/CD declaration..228
Testing the pipeline..233

Summary 235

Conclusion..236

Index   *237*

About the Author

 **DAWID BORYCKI** is a multifaceted professional known for his significant contributions as a scientist, programmer, author, and conference speaker.

With a robust academic background Dawid has pioneered innovations like interferometric methods for brain and eye imaging. He has authored several books and numerous articles aimed at advancing programming and cloud technologies.

Dawid is also a seasoned consultant and trainer, helping others master a range of technical skills.

Acknowledgments

I would like to express my deepest gratitude to my wife and children for their unwavering patience and support throughout the writing of this book. Their encouragement and understanding have been invaluable, allowing me to dedicate the necessary time and effort to bring this work to fruition. This book would not have been possible without their love and support. Thank you for being my pillars of strength.

Preface

I wrote this book because of my extensive experience delivering trainings on Docker, Kubernetes, and Azure for developers, DevOps teams, and IT professionals. One piece of feedback from those courses particularly stood out:

> Dawid is really good at what he does, he makes something very complicated seem like a stroll in the park. This course is well constructed and very well presented. I finished this course with all the knowledge needed to start a new AKS-based web app or to migrate an existing app to AKS. Which cannot be said for any number of courses I already watched on Udemy/LinkedIn Learning.

This feedback was the direct trigger for writing this book. My goal is to enable others to gain thorough knowledge on Docker, Kubernetes, and Azure for application deployment.

What the book gives you is:

PRACTICAL EXPERIENCE

The book is based on real-world training sessions delivered to developers, DevOps specialists, and IT professionals, ensuring that the content is practical and applicable.

SIMPLIFIED COMPLEX CONCEPTS

The book breaks down complex topics in Docker, Kubernetes, and Azure into easily understandable segments, making advanced topics feel approachable and manageable.

COMPREHENSIVE KNOWLEDGE

It provides all the necessary knowledge to start a new AKS-based web app or migrate an existing app to AKS, addressing a gap that many online courses fail to fill.

STRUCTURED LEARNING PATH

The book offers a well-constructed and logically presented learning path, building on concepts step-by-step to facilitate thorough understanding.

REAL FEEDBACK-DRIVEN CONTENT

The content is directly influenced by feedback from course participants who appreciated the clarity and effectiveness of the teaching methods.

HANDS-ON EXAMPLES

Includes practical, hands-on examples and exercises that mirror real-world scenarios, enabling readers to apply what they learn immediately.

FOCUSED ON APPLICATION DEPLOYMENT

Special emphasis on deploying applications using Docker, Kubernetes, and Azure, making it highly relevant for modern cloud-based development and operations.

Foreword

I've always said, if you can do something twice, it's time to automate it. The advent of containerization along with a renewed focus as an industry on automation has energized the software development community. Containers allow you to ship not an entire operating system like a virtual machine, but to ship only the programming interfaces (syscals) that are needed to support an application and keep it running reliably. Combine this with automation, and a single individual has the power and influence of a team! Just imagine what a whole team could do with these tools and techniques!

Given that containers have become the new "atoms," you can use these atoms to build "molecules" that make up your systems and applications. These powerful building blocks can orchestrate sophisticated interactions between containers with Kubernetes at the center. You can effectively deploy an entire web farm in one go! Imagine bootstrapping your entire company with a single command!

Automated builds and deployment used to be considered eXtreme Programming but are now standard operating procedure in any software engineering best practice. At Microsoft, we used to fly in a team of consultants to consult on setting up a load balancer, and cluster auto scaling was nearly unheard of. Today, open-source software like Kubernetes along with the Azure Cloud and infrastructure as code tools can turn us all into 10X developers.

Dawid has taken his extensive practical experience and poured it into this fantastic book. He breaks down these complex topics in a way that is both approachable while unapologetically detailed and complete. I truly appreciate how thoughtfully organized the learning path is as he builds each chapter on the previous. Just a few pages in and I was following along with actual examples that work great on macOS, Windows, or Linux. By the end, I'd put together a complete solution that was building in GitHub Actions and happily deploying to the cloud.

While *Modern App Deployment with Azure Kubernetes* may seem daunting, you've got the formula for success in your hands. Stick with Dawid and this book, and you'll be a pro in no time!

Scott Hanselman
VP Developer Community, Microsoft

Introduction

Containerization has revolutionized the way software applications are developed, packaged, and deployed, offering a lightweight, portable approach that simplifies application management across diverse environments. By encapsulating applications along with their dependencies into containers, developers achieve consistency and reliability, significantly reducing deployment challenges and enhancing productivity. This approach enables rapid deployment cycles, streamlined updates, and improved scalability, setting a foundation for efficient software delivery.

Azure Kubernetes Service (AKS) builds upon containerization by providing a robust and managed orchestration environment for deploying, scaling, and operating containerized applications in the cloud. AKS simplifies the complexities inherent in managing Kubernetes clusters, seamlessly integrating with essential Azure services, such as Azure SQL Database, Key Vault, and comprehensive monitoring tools. Automation further complements this ecosystem, enabling continuous integration and delivery through powerful tools like GitHub Actions and infrastructure automation via Terraform. This end-to-end automation provides rapid, consistent deployments and empowers teams to effectively scale their applications, maintain high availability, and optimize resource utilization.

Organization of this book

This book is designed to guide you through the essential concepts and practical applications of containerization, Kubernetes, and automation for application deployment.

This book is divided into three comprehensive parts:

- **Part I: Containerization**. This part contains five chapters:
    - Chapter 1: Motivation
    - Chapter 2: Application
    - Chapter 3: Containerization with Docker
    - Chapter 4: How to Containerize an Application with Docker
    - Chapter 5: Azure Container Registry

In Part I of the book, you will learn about the primary motivations for introducing containerization and its relevance to modern application development and deployment. Specifically, Chapter 1 explores how containerization relates to Git, Kubernetes, infrastructure as code, and build/release pipelines. Chapter 2 introduces the starting point: an ASP.NET Core web application called People.WebApp, which stores data in SQL Server. This application represents a typical workload for many companies beginning their transition to the cloud. Chapter 3 covers Docker, explaining what it is and how it functions. You will learn how to use Docker to manage and run containers, as well as how to handle multi-container applications with Docker Compose. Chapter 4 then guides you through containerizing an ASP.NET Core web application. You will learn how to set up a multi-container solution where the app runs in one container and communicates with SQL Server in another. Finally, Chapter 5 introduces container registries. In this chapter, you will create a registry in Azure and push a container image of People.WebApp to the cloud, enabling deployment of the application to a Kubernetes cluster in Part II.

- **Part II: Container Orchestration.** This part contains five chapters:
  - Chapter 6: Container Orchestration with Kubernetes
  - Chapter 7: Azure Kubernetes Service
  - Chapter 8: Azure SQL Database and Azure Key Vault
  - Chapter 9: Diagnosing and Monitoring the Cluster
  - Chapter 10: Application Rollouts and Rollbacks

Part II is about container orchestration, a process that simplifies the running and management of distributed systems composed of hundreds of containers. These containers must run across many virtual machines, either deployed on-premises or in cloud environments. Chapter 6 describes Kubernetes, the open-source and most popular orchestration platform, to demonstrate how to deploy containerized applications with container orchestrators. The goal of this part is to show how to use a local development Kubernetes cluster and then deploy the containerized application from the container registry to a production Kubernetes cluster running in the cloud within the Azure Kubernetes Service (Chapter 7). In Chapter 8, you will learn how to connect the application running in the cluster to other Azure services, such as SQL and KeyVault. Chapter 9 shows how to monitor the containerized application deployed to the cluster. Finally, Chapter 10 explains how to quickly perform application rollouts and rollbacks.

- **Part III: Automation.** This part has four chapters:
  - Chapter 11: Automating Image Builds and Deployment Using CI/CD Pipelines
  - Chapter 12: Load Testing, Horizontal Pod Autoscaling, and Cluster Autoscaling

- Chapter 13: Deploying and Managing Kubernetes Applications with Helm
- Chapter 14: Infrastructure as Code

The aim of Part III is to demonstrate how to automate the application deployment. I will show you how to incorporate continuous integration/continuous delivery (CI/CD) pipelines to gain full control over the application and underlying resource deployment. Specifically, in Chapter 11, you will use GitHub Actions to create the CI pipeline, which will automate the building and pushing of Docker images to Azure Container Registry. This pipeline will be triggered whenever the source code is updated, and a pull request is accepted. In Chapter 12, you will explore how to automatically adjust the application's size (the number of Pods) using the Horizontal Pod Autoscaler (HPA) and adjust the cluster's size depending on the current load. Chapter 13 will delve into deploying applications using Helm charts, enabling you to manage multiple declarations of deployments, services, and accompanying Kubernetes objects, such as HPA. Finally, in Chapter 14, you will learn how to employ Infrastructure as Code (IaC) to deploy and update cloud resources in a declarative way, enabling you to achieve a complete continuous deployment pipeline triggered by changes in the source code.

Audience

This book is intended for readers seeking to deepen their understanding and skills in deploying modern applications on the cloud using Azure's powerful Kubernetes platform. It is an excellent choice for developers, DevOps professionals, and IT experts interested in mastering modern application deployment strategies on Azure.

Companion code

This book includes companion code to enrich your learning experience. The companion code is organized into two repositories:

PEOPLE.WEBAPP Contains the source code of the application that will be containerized and deployed to Azure Kubernetes Service.

github.com/dawidborycki/People.WebApp or *MicrosoftPressStore.com/modernapp/downloads*

PEOPLE.WEBAPP.DECLARATIONS Includes declarations such as Dockerfiles, YAML files with Kubernetes manifests, and Terraform YAML files for infrastructure deployment.

github.com/dawidborycki/People.WebApp.Declarations or *MicrosoftPressStore.com/modernapp/downloads*

Errata, updates, & book support

We've made every effort to ensure the accuracy of this book and its companion content. You can access updates to this book—in the form of a list of submitted errata and their related corrections—at:

MicrosoftPressStore.com/modernapp/errata

If you discover an error that is not already listed, please submit it to us at the same page.

For additional book support and information, please visit *MicrosoftPressStore.com/Support*

Please note that product support for Microsoft software and hardware is not offered through the previous addresses. For help with Microsoft software or hardware, go to *http://support.microsoft.com*

Stay in touch

Let's keep the conversation going! We're on X: *http://x.com/MicrosoftPress*

PART I

Containerization

CHAPTER 1 Motivation 3
CHAPTER 2 Application 13
CHAPTER 3 Containerization with Docker 21
CHAPTER 4 How to Containerize an Application with Docker 37
CHAPTER 5 Azure Container Registry 55

In this part of the book, you will learn about the primary motivations for introducing containerization and its relevance to modern application development and deployment. Specifically, Chapter 1, "Motivation," explores how containerization relates to Git, Kubernetes, infrastructure as code, and build/release pipelines.

Chapter 2, "Application," introduces you to your starting point for the book's exercises: an ASP.NET Core web application called People.WebApp that stores data in SQL Server. This application represents a typical workload for many companies beginning their transition to the cloud.

Chapter 3, "Containerization with Docker," explains what Docker is and how it functions. You will learn how to use Docker to manage and run containers, as well as how to handle multi-container applications with Docker Compose.

Subsequently, Chapter 4, "How to Containerize an Application with Docker," guides you through containerizing an ASP.NET Core web application. You will learn how to set up a multi-container solution where this app runs in one container and communicates with SQL Server in another.

Finally, Chapter 5, "Azure Container Registry," introduces container registries. You will create a registry in Azure, and then push a container image of People.WebApp to the cloud. This will enable you to deploy the application to a Kubernetes cluster in Part II.

CHAPTER 1

Motivation

Modern business applications need to operate continuously without any downtime. Teams rely heavily on mobile and web applications, and any interruptions or errors can dramatically impact their everyday processes and tasks.

Web and mobile applications typically consume services from distributed backend systems. These backends consist of complex meshes of microservices, each utilizing its own datastore and communicating with other microservices, external services and applications to perform business workflows. In such environments, many operations happen concurrently, requiring services to work in tandem to meet ever-increasing user demands and expectations. This complexity makes continuously operating modern applications incredibly challenging, particularly when updating and scaling based on traffic, resource consumption, geographic distribution, and performance metrics.

To address these challenges, you need innovative software development and deployment approaches. Modern teams use tools like Git, containerization, Kubernetes, cloud technologies, infrastructure as code, and monitoring tools, allowing them to implement, test, deploy, and manage each part of the application independently. Furthermore, app deployment can be synchronized with updates to the provisioned cloud infrastructure through a declarative approach provided by infrastructure as code.

Specifically, Git serves as the distributed source control system that can track changes in code or infrastructure declarations. A code commit can trigger an automated build operation, followed by unit tests. Continuous delivery extends this process by allowing deployment of the application after the build, provided the test suite has passed.

Containerization enables independent deployment, testing, updates, and scaling of each microservice. Kubernetes manages these containers and provides a software platform that simplifies running thousands of containers across many machines.

Additionally, the cloud enables quick provisioning of Kubernetes services and the creation of nodes for Kubernetes clusters. It also provides robust data services, file storage, security, and governance.

Finally, modern teams manage resources using infrastructure as code. This approach involves maintaining declarations of cloud resources in a text file of a specific format within a Git repository and applying the same management strategies as in code development. For instance, changes to infrastructure can be reviewed and approved through the Git pull request mechanism.

These tools enable automated builds and deployments to minimize downtimes and accelerate software development cycles. Whenever an application is deployed or updated in production, it is crucial to monitor the system to respond to any events as swiftly as possible, ideally before your customers even notice.

This chapter explores why traditional approaches to software development and deployment fall short in meeting the demands of modern application architectures. Specifically, it highlights the necessity of adopting advanced tools and methodologies such as Git, containerization, Kubernetes, cloud technologies, infrastructure as code, and comprehensive monitoring. By understanding how each of these tools addresses particular challenges, such as ensuring continuous availability, enabling rapid and independent deployment of microservices, automating infrastructure management, and facilitating immediate response to operational issues, you can better appreciate their integral role in maintaining robust, reliable, and scalable applications.

Modern application development and deployment

Figure 1-1 illustrates a typical modern application development and deployment workflow. The workflow comprises two loops:

- **Inner loop** This loop is primarily used by developers to implement, build, and test the application (step 1 in Figure 1-1). Updates within the inner loop are rapid, allowing developers to quickly iterate and validate changes without extensive delays.

- **Outer loop** This loop covers the deployment, operation, and monitoring phases of the application lifecycle (steps 2–7 in Figure 1-1). The outer loop typically involves automated builds, deployments, system monitoring, and responding swiftly to operational events to ensure application stability and availability.

Developers continue to work on app features using their favorite integrated development environments (IDEs), testing and debugging their applications in a development environment that could be either a local PC or a Kubernetes development cluster (step 1). Once satisfied with the code, they push it to a source code control system like Git (step 2). Ideally, this push triggers the continuous integration and delivery (CI/CD) pipelines (step 3). The CI pipeline automatically builds the container image from the source code, which is then pushed to a container registry (step 4). From there, it can be deployed to the Kubernetes production cluster through the CD pipeline (step 6).

When working with multi-container applications, Helm charts are used to automate and simplify application deployment to Kubernetes. As explained in Chapter 13, "Deploying and Managing Kubernetes Applications with Helm," Helm is the package manager for Kubernetes, with Helm charts serving as the Helm packages.

The release (CD) pipeline may include local or cloud infrastructure declarations that need to be deployed or updated along with the application (step 3). This allows for resource management using a declarative approach, where you "code" your environment rather than manually provisioning hardware resources. Consequently, these declarations are kept in the source control system and deployed like any other part of your application. As mentioned above, this approach is known as *infrastructure as code* (IaC).

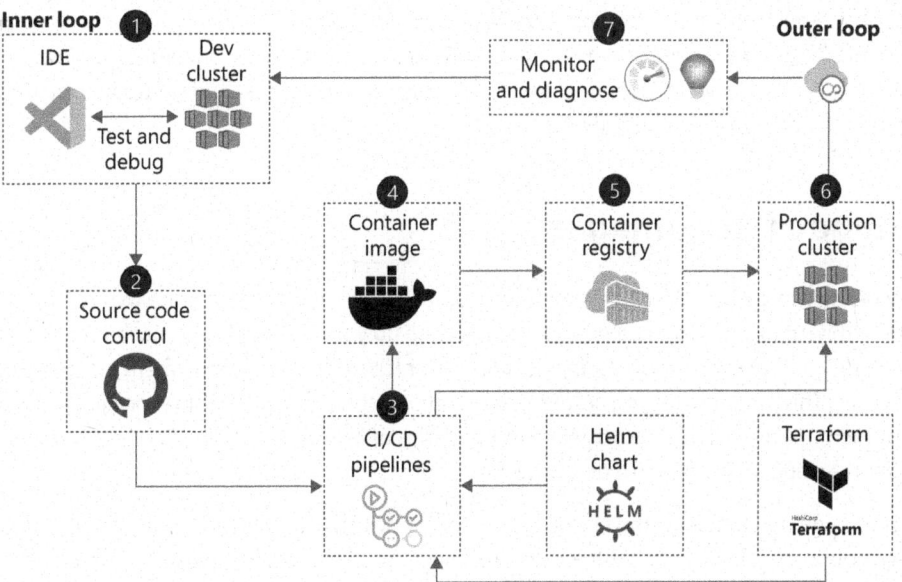

FIGURE 1-1 A typical workflow of modern application development and deployment.

Each cloud provider offers its own IaC tools, such as Azure Resource Manager (ARM) for Microsoft Azure and CloudFormation for AWS. Each tool is specific to its cloud provider. To address this and accelerate IaC adoption, Terraform provides a cross-platform IaC approach. In Terraform, you create template files describing your infrastructure and deploy them using a single command-line tool. This simplifies the use of IaC without the need to master complex, cloud-specific tools. Chapter 14, "Infrastructure as Code," will explore Terraform further.

Once applications are deployed, monitoring is crucial to ensure they operate continuously and without errors (step 7). Tools such as Azure Monitor, application telemetry, container health, and real-time log analytics are utilized. If an issue is detected, it is reported back to developers who then return to the inner loop to address the problem or develop new features. Subsequently, they push the code to the source control system to initiate the outer loop workflow. This loop starts with the push operation, which triggers the CI/CD pipelines, turning the source code into a container image that is pushed to the registry. This image is then used to update the application running in the production cluster. Along the way, CI/CD pipelines can automatically update the underlying hardware resources, such as the number of nodes in the cluster. Post-deployment, the application is monitored for errors or issues.

These inner and outer loops processes are repeated continuously throughout the application lifecycle, defining what we commonly refer to as development and operations (DevOps) cycles. The "Dev" is known as the inner loop, encompassing daily activities of developers, while "Ops" (outer loop) involves tasks related to deploying, scaling, and monitoring the application.

Adopting the practices from Figure 1-1 accelerates these tasks by leveraging best practices and automation, thereby enhancing an organization's agility in software delivery.

In this book, I aim to explain how to utilize these tools to deploy your applications to the Kubernetes cluster. Additionally, you will learn how to automatically scale the app cluster and integrate it with Azure services. Finally, you will discover how to adapt infrastructure as code and set up automated build and deployment pipelines with GitHub.

The advantage of disk images

You might wonder why people adopt the modern application development and deployment approach. To understand this, think back to the old days when setting up your development machine was a task in itself. You had to install every application, including your IDE, software development kits (SDKs), and all dependencies. This process is an *imperative configuration*, where the state of the model (in this case, your development machine) is defined by executing a series of instructions (installing applications). Everything worked fine until your hard drive crashed.

After a crash, you had to repeat the entire setup process, which was typically time-consuming and during which you were offline and couldn't work. To save time after a crash, a new practice arose: Create an image of the disk containing all your tools—a snapshot of your reference drive–so you could quickly restore the state of your development machine. This method is known as a *declarative configuration*, because you declare the desired state of your system. Specific software then automatically compares the desired state (the disk image) to the actual state and updates it if needed.

Importantly, this disk image can also be deployed to other machines, whether they are physical or virtual. This ability is particularly crucial for IT operators who might need to prepare hundreds or thousands of machines for employees. Using a declarative configuration is more efficient than an imperative one, where IT operators must manually install the same applications on all machines. With a declarative configuration, IT operators can prepare one machine, then take a drive snapshot to create a disk image. Using dedicated software, they can deploy this image to other machines, even utilizing network boot capabilities to deploy disk images from distributed devices.

Hardware manufacturers recognized this issue and provided recovery drives containing a default disk image. Thus, in the event of a crash, you could automatically recover your computer.

This approach also serves as a foundation for cloud deployments. For instance, you can package your application with its dependencies into a virtual machine (VM) image and then rapidly deploy it to cloud infrastructure. Once it's deployed, you can scale your application horizontally by starting additional virtual machine instances from the same VM image.

The advantages of containers for application deployment

In traditional deployment, applications are installed on top of the operating system running on physical hardware (see Figure 1-2). Each application is instantiated from underlying binaries and libraries and functions as a process within the operating system. To update an application, you need to provide a new version of these binaries. Similarly, to scale the application, you spin up new processes using these binaries. The running applications share hardware and software resources and are isolated by the operating system.

Following the great success of disk images, a question arose: Why not package application binaries and all dependencies by using images? This allows for a more granular use of images. Instead of packaging the entire operating system with all apps and dependencies, you package only the application and its dependencies in the form of a container image. Then, to start the app, you create a container instance using the given image, similar to how traditional apps are instantiated from binaries. Thus, the running container instance functions like a process in the operating system.

The rationale for using containers becomes evident when you consider the inefficient use of resources during the horizontal scaling of VM images, where each new app instance includes the entire operating system. Modern applications, however, are often composed of many components, typically architected using microservices. Each microservice, developed independently using different, problem-specific tools and programming languages (AI components in Python, APIs in Java or .NET, for example), can be packaged as a separate container image and scaled independently to better match actual traffic and application specifics.

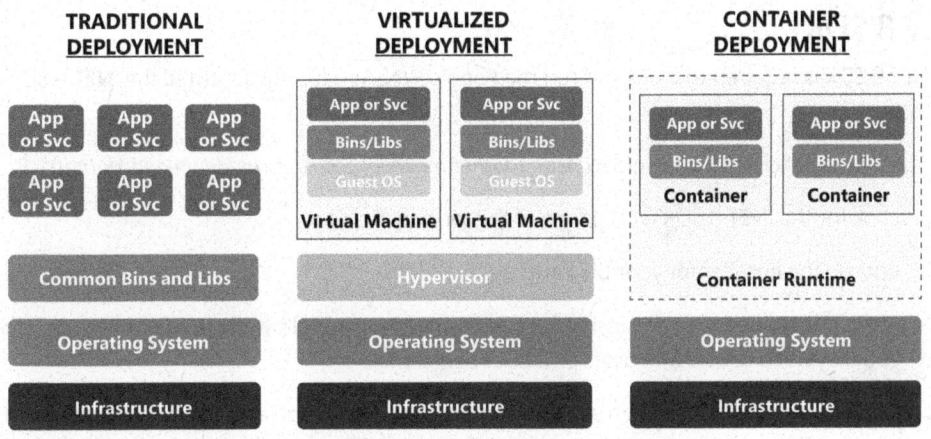

FIGURE 1-2 A comparison of the application deployment models.

Consider a typical e-commerce application with several microservices providing such features as a product catalog, a basket, ordering, and payment. Users spend significantly more time browsing the product catalog than using the payment microservice. In practice, this means you would need many more instances of the catalog service than the payment service. Scaling such a solution using virtual machines would require scaling the entire application, including the operating system and all dependencies, leading to excessive use of hardware resources. Using containers allows you to overcome this issue with scaling at the app or service level. In this approach, you horizontally scale individual services, maintaining perhaps 10 instances of the catalog and only two of the payment service, and can deploy and update them independently. However, there is still some overhead due to deploying app or service dependencies within each container.

CHAPTER 1 Motivation   7

Tools

To practice the processes described above, ensure you have all the necessary tools.

Git

You will use Git to clone repositories and to automate container building and deployment to the cloud. To download the Git Installer, follow these steps:

1. Visit the official Git downloads page (*git-scm.com/downloads*), and select the appropriate installer for your operating system (Windows, macOS, or Linux).

2. Once the installer is downloaded, run it and follow the on-screen prompts. You can use the default installation settings.

3. After installation, open a terminal or command prompt and run **git --version**.

You should see the installed version number.

.NET 8 SDK

The .NET 8 SDK is required to build and run the People.WebApp locally. To install the .NET 8 SDK, follow these steps:

1. Visit the official .NET download page (*dotnet.microsoft.com/en-us/download/dotnet*)

2. Look for the .NET 8 SDK (at the time of this writing, 8.0.0).

3. Choose the installer for your platform

4. After it downloads, run the installer on your machine and follow the guided steps. On Linux, you may need to add Microsoft package repositories.

5. Verify your installation: Open a terminal or command prompt, and run **dotnet --version**

6. Confirm that the version displayed matches the one you installed.

Docker Desktop

Docker Desktop is essential for building and managing Docker images locally. To get started with Docker Desktop and set up your local Docker environment, follow these steps:

1. Go to the official Docker Desktop page (*www.docker.com/products/docker-desktop*), and choose the installer for Windows, macOS, or Linux.

2. Run the downloaded installer and follow the on-screen steps. On Windows and macOS, this is a straightforward graphical installer. On Linux, follow the instructions for adding Docker's official repositories and installing from them.

3. After installation, launch Docker Desktop. On first run, you may need to sign in with a Docker Hub account or create one if you do not have an account already.

4. Open a terminal or command prompt and run:

```
docker --version
docker run hello-world
```

If the hello-world container runs successfully and prints a greeting, your Docker environment is set up correctly.

Visual Studio Code

Follow these steps to install Visual Studio Code and configure it with the necessary extensions for Docker, Kubernetes, Azure, and C# development:

1. Visit the official the official Visual Studio Code page (*code.visualstudio.com/download*), and choose the correct installer for your operating system (Windows, macOS, or Linux).

2. After the download completes, run the installer and follow the on-screen instructions. On Linux, you may alternatively install via your distribution's package manager or a .deb/.rpm package if provided.

3. Open Visual Studio Code.

4. To set up your development environment for this project, navigate to the Extensions view by clicking Extensions in the Activity Bar or pressing Ctrl+Shift+X (Windows)/Command+Shift+X (macOS). In this view, install each extension:

    a. Search for "Docker," and click Install.

    b. Search for "Azure Kubernetes Service," and click Install.

    c. Search for "Azure Tools," and click Install.

    d. Search for "C#," and click Install.

5. After installing the extensions, reload Visual Studio Code if prompted.

Azure Subscription

To complete the exercises in this book, you'll need an Azure subscription. If you don't already have one, follow these steps to set up a subscription:

1. Visit the official Azure free account page (*azure.microsoft.com/en-us/pricing/purchase-options/azure-account?icid=azurefreeaccount*), and sign up. New users typically receive $200 in credit for the first 30 days, sufficient to complete the tutorials in this book.

2. Ensure that you have proper billing and permissions configured for any services you plan to use.

Azure Command Line Interface

You will use the Azure Command-Line Interface (Azure CLI) to interact with Azure services from the command line, specifically to push local Docker images to the Azure Container Registry. To install the Azure CLI, go to the official Azure CLI site (*learn.microsoft.com/en-gb/cli/azure/install-azure-cli*).

That's all. You should now be ready to follow all the examples in this book.

Notation

While learning, you will perform many operations, such as invoking commands from the command line, creating and editing configuration files, and working with code. Throughout the book, I will use the following notation to help you navigate between these operations and easily identify the type of information you are working with.

Commands you need to type will be marked in **bold**. For example:

docker images

Configuration files (Docker, YAML, or JSON files) will be presented using a screened style:

```
version: '3.4'

services:
  peoplewebapp:
    image: peoplewebapp
    build:
      context: .
      dockerfile: ./Dockerfile
    ports:
      - 5000:5000
```

Code blocks will appear as follows:

```
public class PeopleController : Controller
{
    private readonly PeopleDbContext context;

    public PeopleController(PeopleDbContext context)
    {
        this.context = context;
    }
}
```

Also, the symbol ↵ in a command indicates that the command should be continued. This symbol is used in text to fit long commands within the page width.

Summary

This chapter introduced modern application deployment and highlighted the motivations behind adopting advanced development practices. It discussed how such tools as Git, Docker, Kubernetes, and cloud services enhance agility and streamline the deployment, scaling, and monitoring of applications. Finally, I demonstrated how combining these technologies enables automated, reliable, and efficient application deployment in today's dynamic environments.

In subsequent chapters, you will put the modern application development approach described here into practice. Specifically, you'll use a sample application implemented in C# to investigate how tools such as Git, Docker, Kubernetes, and various cloud services can be integrated into real-world scenarios, enabling automated deployments and streamlined workflows.

CHAPTER 2

Application

To demonstrate how to deploy and maintain modern applications with Docker and Kubernetes in Azure, I will use an ASP.NET Core application running on .NET 8. The application, named People.WebApp, consumes data persisted in SQL Server and resembles a simplified but typical workload many companies already have in production. This application also includes a web API, acting as the microservice with the underlying CRUD (create, read, update, delete) datastore.

Figure 2-1 shows an example of the running app. The application features three tabs: Home, Privacy, and People. The People tab allows you to interact with the underlying data: a model containing a list of hypothetical individuals. For example, you can get, create, update, and delete items after navigating to the People tab.

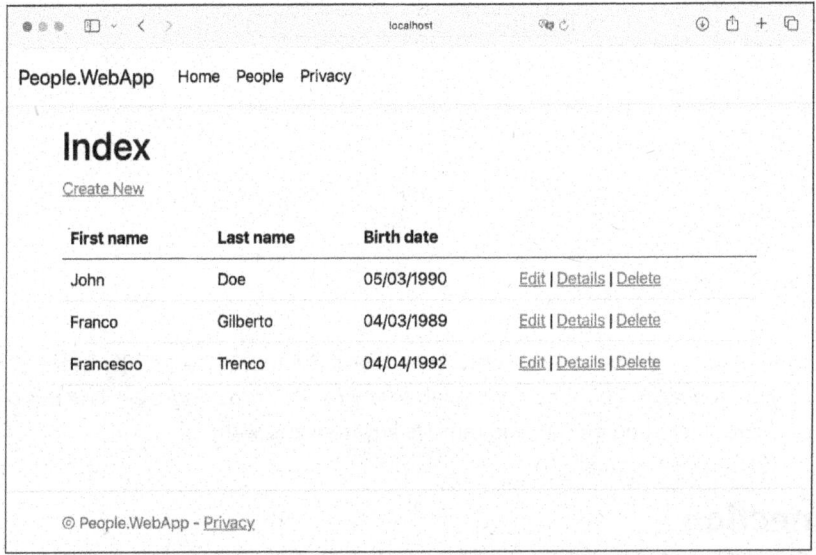

FIGURE 2-1 The People.WebApp running with the People tab open and the underlying data accessible.

The application uses the .NET Entity Framework Core as a relational object mapper to implement data access, which converts C# objects and statements into database operations, and vice versa. You will be using People.WebApp for all the book's examples. For now, take a look at how to clone and run the application locally.

Running the application

You can find the complete source code of the application in the repository *github.com/dawidborycki/People.WebApp*.

To clone the application, open the terminal or Command Prompt, and type the following commands:

```
git clone https://github.com/dawidborycki/People.WebApp.git
cd People.WebApp
git checkout net8
dotnet run
```

The output generated by those commands looks like Figure 2-2.

```
% git clone https://github.com/dawidborycki/People.WebApp.git
Cloning into 'People.WebApp'...
remote: Enumerating objects: 640, done.
remote: Counting objects: 100% (268/268), done.
remote: Compressing objects: 100% (168/168), done.
remote: Total 640 (delta 125), reused 205 (delta 66), pack-reused 372
Receiving objects: 100% (640/640), 1.01 MiB | 5.79 MiB/s, done.
Resolving deltas: 100% (277/277), done.
%
% cd People.WebApp
%
% git checkout net8
branch 'net8' set up to track 'origin/net8'.
Switched to a new branch 'net8'
%
% dotnet run
Building...
info: Microsoft.Hosting.Lifetime[14]
      Now listening on: http://localhost:5000
info: Microsoft.Hosting.Lifetime[0]
      Application started. Press Ctrl+C to shut down.
info: Microsoft.Hosting.Lifetime[0]
      Hosting environment: Development
info: Microsoft.Hosting.Lifetime[0]
```

FIGURE 2-2 Cloning and running the People.WebApp.

To see the application running, open a web browser and navigate to *localhost:5000*. There, you will see the welcome page. Afterwards, go to the People tab to see results from Figure 2-1. Use this page to add a new record, update an existing record, and remove any item you want.

Database connection

Launching the application for the first time automatically creates the underlying database using Entity Framework Core. This framework retrieves the database connection string from the appsettings.json file. Specifically, People.WebApp uses the `PeopleDbConnection` string under the `Connection-Strings` group:

```
{
  "Logging": {
```

```
    "LogLevel": {
      "Default": "Information",
      "Microsoft": "Warning",
      "Microsoft.Hosting.Lifetime": "Information"
    }
  },
  "AllowedHosts": "*",
  "UseInMemoryDatabase": "True",
  "ConnectionStrings": {
    "PeopleDbConnection": "Server=(localdb)\\mssqllocaldb;Database=People;"
  }
}
```

The `PeopleDbConnection` string points to the local SQL Server hosting the People database. Recognizing that the local SQL Server may not be available on every platform, I added the capability to use an in-memory database, which will function on all platforms, such as Mac or Linux.

Depending on the `UseInMemoryDatabase` setting, the application will use either the in-memory database or SQL Server. In the former case, the application creates a volatile in-memory database named People, which means every time you restart the app, the database will be recreated and previous data will be lost. In the latter case, the app connects to the local SQL Server and creates a persistent database, where data remains even after restarting the application. This flexibility allows you to launch the app locally on platforms where the local SQL Server is unavailable.

Note When using the in-memory database, remember that all data will be lost every time the application restarts. This option is useful for development and testing purposes but should not be used in production scenarios.

Web API

The People.WebApp contains a web API implemented by the `PeopleApiController`, which resembles a typical CRUD microservice. Therefore, you can access records in the database through the front end or the web API. However, the web API does not expose views.

There are several ways to access the web API:

- Command-line tools, such as HttpRepl and curl, or desktop applications like Postman.
- A web browser with a dedicated extension, like the Advanced REST client.
- Swagger, which is an open-source suite of tools for testing web APIs. Under the hood, it uses curl to interact with the web API.

The following section demonstrates how to access the list of people using a web browser. Then, I will explain how to use Swagger to test the web API.

Retrieving data using the web browser

To retrieve data through the web API, simply append /api/people to the application URL. For example, navigating to localhost:5000/api/people displays the list of people as a JSON-formatted string, as illustrated in Figure 2-3. The JSON formatting might be automatically color-coded and formatted depending on your web browser and any installed packages. Here, I used Safari with the JSON Peep extension, which automatically formats the JSON to be more human-readable.

```
[
  {
    "id": "13398c8c-c0f1-4dc8-8d60-712a47e3704f",
    "firstName": "John",
    "lastName": "Doe",
    "birthDate": "1990-05-03T00:00:00",
    "age": 33
  },
  {
    "id": "8f695c67-07f0-4b34-94a3-b8ec1150b596",
    "firstName": "Franco",
    "lastName": "Gilberto",
    "birthDate": "1989-04-03T00:00:00",
    "age": 34
  },
  {
    "id": "72f4e65a-43ba-4d0a-b8d7-7b89ee6c6611",
    "firstName": "Francesco",
    "lastName": "Trenco",
    "birthDate": "1992-04-04T00:00:00",
    "age": 31
  }
]
```

FIGURE 2-3 Retrieving a list of people using the web API.

Swagger

Swagger was automatically included in the ASP.NET MVC project template used to create People. WebApp through the Swashbuckle.AspNetCore NuGet package. In the Program.cs file of the People. WebApp project, you will notice a Swagger-related statement:

```
builder.Services.AddSwaggerGen();
```

This statement activates the Swagger generator to create an OpenAPI document describing your web APIs. Specifically, the Swagger generator analyzes the structure of the code, including route configurations, models, and web API controllers, to create the OpenAPI file, which is a JSON-formatted document.

Then, Swashbuckle.AspNetCore exposes an OpenAPI file as an endpoint using the following statement in Program.cs:

```
app.UseSwagger();
```

By default, this command exposes an OpenAPI file under the link *localhost:5000/swagger/v1/swagger.json*.

The last Swagger-related statement configures the Swagger UI:

```
app.UseSwaggerUI();
```

This command activates the web-based UI, which uses the specification from the OpenAPI file and the actual web APIs to provide an easy-to-use tool for testing web API controllers.

To access the Swagger UI, run the app and then open *localhost:5000/swagger*. It will appear as shown in Figure 2-4.

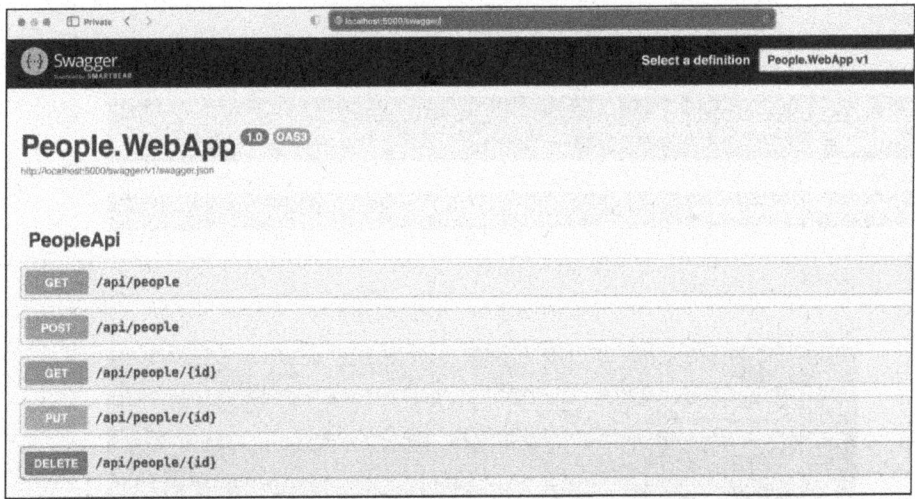

FIGURE 2-4 A Swagger UI.

The Swagger UI displays a list of web API controllers and their exposed methods (like GET). Each item in the list has an associated button and a label showing the route. You can click a list item to expand it and display an extended group of controls (buttons, text boxes), which you use to test specific methods and preview results. For example, if you click the GET list item, you will see another button: Try It Out. After clicking this button, another set of two buttons appears (Execute and Clear). Clicking the Execute button retrieves the list of people in the database. It returns a JSON-formatted object containing the list of people, as you can see in the Response Body section of Figure 2-5. The results are the same as when using the web browser.

Although accessing the data through the GET method is not as straightforward as using the web browser, the Swagger UI offers several advantages, as illustrated in Figure 2-6. First, it displays the complete curl command that you can execute directly from the command line. Second, it clearly shows the server's response code. Third, it enables you to test other web API controller methods interactively. For example, by expanding the POST method and clicking Try It Out you can easily add new items to the database.

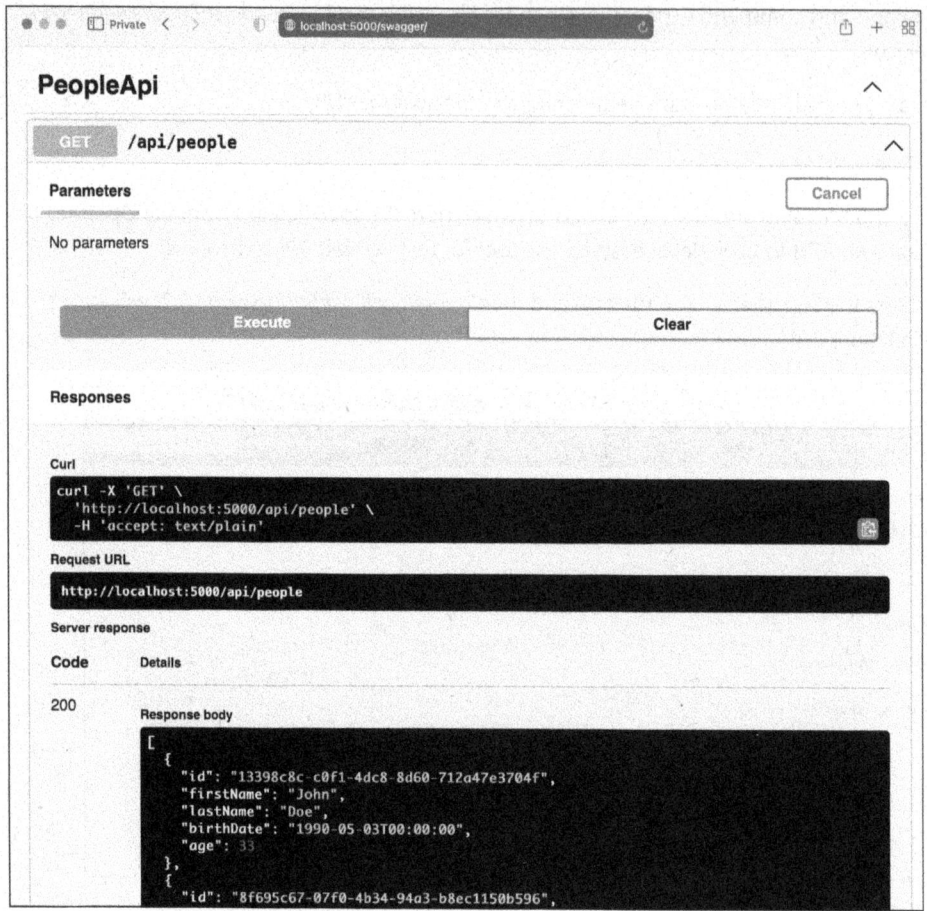

FIGURE 2-5 Accessing the GET method of the PeopleApi controller using the Swagger UI.

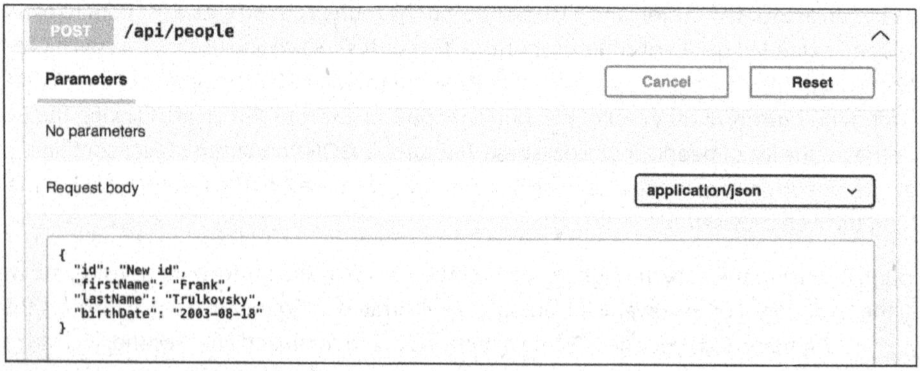

FIGURE 2-6 Adding people to the database through the *POST* method accessed using the Swagger UI.

To test the POST method, simply modify the JSON code shown in the Request Body section and click the Execute button. Interestingly, Swagger recognizes the model used to represent a person and, based on that, prepares an object with four properties: `id`, `firstName`, `lastName`, and `birthDate`:

```
{
  "id": "string",
  "firstName": "string",
  "lastName": "string",
  "birthDate": "2023-08-22"
}
```

You'll need to modify the values, for example:

```
{
  "id": "New id",
  "firstName": "Frank",
  "lastName": "Trulkovsky",
  "birthDate": "2003-08-18"
}
```

Then, click the Execute button to add the new item. You can confirm this by sending another GET request. You can test other methods of the web API (DELETE and PUT) in a similar way.

> **Note** Swagger UI not only helps test your APIs interactively but also provides automatically generated documentation, which is valuable for developers and integration teams to understand the structure and behavior of your API endpoints.

Summary

In this chapter, you prepared your tools and learned how the application stores data (the list of people) in the database on SQL Server or in memory. The chapter also demonstrated that this data can be accessed and modified through the web user interface or the web API. Additionally, you learned how to access the web API using Swagger UI. In the next step, you will learn how to containerize the application and push the container image to the Azure Container Registry so that it can be deployed to a Kubernetes cluster running within the Azure Kubernetes Service. You will use the web API to test the auto-scaling capabilities of the applications running in the Kubernetes service.

CHAPTER 3

Containerization with Docker

This chapter provides an overview of containerization and Docker, delving deeper into the motivation for using containers in application development and deployment. You will learn how to use Docker to create and manage containers and put the People.WebApp to work.

Why use containers?

Containers have become a critical technology with many advantages over traditional approaches to managing development environments and deploying applications. Contrasting these advantages with the limitations of traditional methods will clarify why containers, and specifically Docker, have gained widespread adoption in the industry.

Imperative vs. declarative configuration

Remember the old days of preparing your development machine? You'd install every application individually, from your integrated development environment (IDE) to dependencies, in a process called *imperative configuration*. The state of your development machine was defined by executing a series of installation steps. If your hard drive crashed, you had to replace it and reinstall everything, a time-consuming process that left you unable to work during the restoration.

Hardware manufacturers and software companies proposed a better solution based on hard drive images. After installing all your tools, you could take a drive snapshot to create an image containing all your applications, dependencies, and data. In the event of a crash, you could quickly restore your machine using this image and dedicated software to replicate the image to a new hard drive. As you may remember from Chapter 1, "Motivation," this method is called *declarative configuration*; you declare a desired system state (defined as the image), and the software automatically updates it if necessary.

Declarative configuration using drive images has two advantages:

- **Disaster preparedness and rapid deployment** After you prepare your computer and take a snapshot of the drive, you can deploy this image to hundreds of devices in your company, even over a network, preparing for disaster and enabling rapid deployment of cloned systems.

- **Physical and virtual machines** You can use drive images to set up environments on both physical and virtual machines. In the cloud, you can use an image to create a virtual machine (VM) instance, which can differ from the host's operating system.

What is containerization, and how can it help you?

Given the success of disk and VM images, the next logical step was to apply this concept to application deployment. By packaging an application with all its dependencies into a container image, you can deploy the application as a container instance in local, virtual, or cloud environments. This process, known as *containerization*, allows for the creation and versioning of various container images to fully control deployment. Containerization packages together an application or service, its dependencies, and its configuration (abstracted as deployment manifest files) all into a single container image. This enables you to test and deploy the containerized application as a unit to any host operating system (OS).

In practice, containerization addresses multiple challenges. For instance, if a hypothetical application requires a specific runtime like the Visual C++ redistributable, it may work fine on your development machine but fail on a customer's machine due to missing dependencies. Containers package the application with all necessary runtimes and configurations, ensuring it functions identically everywhere.

Containers simplify application distribution by encapsulating the application, all its dependencies, configurations, and necessary data into a container image. You then distribute this image to end-users, who need to have only a container runtime installed on their machines. This ensures that everything you tested on your development machine works the same way on any other device, provided both machines use the same container runtime.

Another significant advantage of containerization is its ability to support applications or services developed using different programming languages and technologies, all running under the same container runtime. What does this mean? In modern application development, you select the right tool for each job, using dedicated tools to address specific challenges. Specifically, you might use:

- Python for machine learning and AI
- JavaScript, HTML, and CSS for frontends
- Java, Go, PHP, or .NET for backends

Furthermore, all containers can run under the same container runtime. This is similar to how multiple virtual machines, each powered by different guest operating systems, can run simultaneously on a single host machine using the same virtualization software. This is feasible because each container image encapsulates a specific part of the entire software solution—along with all the dependencies (like runtimes), configurations, and data. After the container image is created, the container runtime does not concern itself with the programming language or technology used to develop the app or service.

To better understand software containers and containerization, think of the transportation industry. Teams pack items—cars, electronics, clothing, tools, and more—into physical containers. Trucks and container ships then transport these physical containers (Figure 3-1). Because the containers conform to standard dimensions, they're easy to transfer from train cars to trucks to ships, which are all designed to be compatible with that standard. Importantly, the vehicles do not concern themselves with the contents of the containers, or other items.

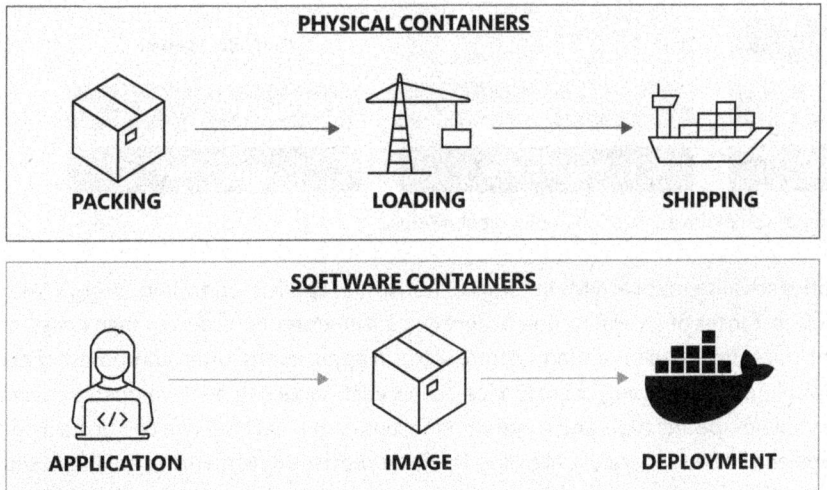

FIGURE 3-1 An analogy between physical and software containers.

The same principle applies to software containers. The container runtime is indifferent to the programming tools used to implement an application or service packaged within a container image. You only need to adhere to specific standards when creating the container image, ensuring the container runtime can correctly initiate one or more container instances from your image as shown in Figure 3-2.

Containers vs. virtual machines

Containers are often explained using their similarity to virtual machines (VMs), as shown in Figure 3-2. While containers are somewhat akin to VMs, there are key differences: VMs require more resources because they include the entire guest operating system (OS), applications, and their dependencies. Containers, on the other hand, encapsulate only the applications and their direct dependencies, without an entire guest OS. Therefore, containers are quicker to deploy and start but provide less isolation compared to VMs. The primary goal of a container image is to ensure consistency across different deployments, eliminating the "it works on my machine" issue.

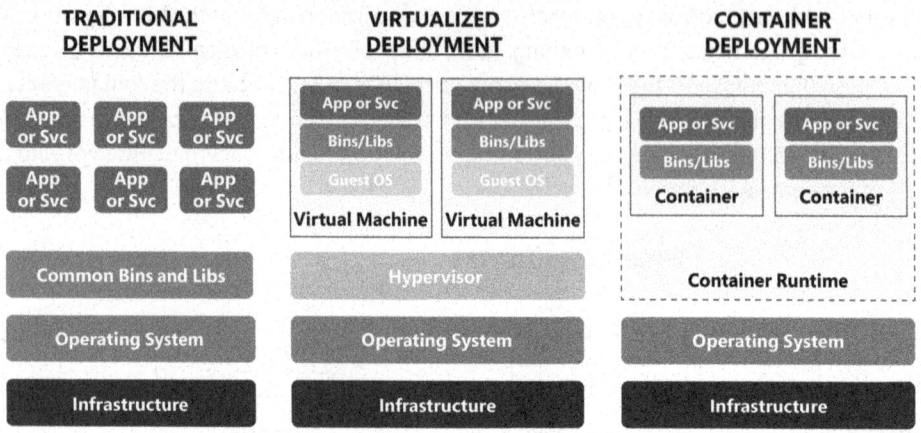

FIGURE 3-2 A comparison of the application deployment models.

Containers offer advantages over VMs in terms of horizontal application scaling. Using VMs to provision multiple instances of an application or service consumes more resources than necessary, as each instance includes the entire operating system. Modern applications, often composed of many components typically designed using microservices, allow each service to be developed independently with different, problem-specific tools and programming languages. Each service can be packaged as a container image and scaled separately, allowing for more precise adjustments to scaling based on actual traffic and application-specific needs.

For example, a typical media streaming platform might include several microservices responsible for user authentication, content browsing, media playback, and recommendation engines. Users typically spend much more time browsing or watching content than logging in. Therefore, in practice, more instances of the browsing and playback services are needed compared to the login or user profile services.

Scaling such an application using VMs would involve scaling the entire application along with the OS and all dependencies, thereby using more hardware resources than necessary. This challenge can be addressed at the app or service level by scaling using containers. In this approach, individual services are scaled horizontally, allowing, for example, for 15 instances of the media playback service and only two of the authentication service. Furthermore, these services can be deployed and updated independently. Although there is still some overhead due to the deployment of app or service dependencies in each container, this overhead is significantly smaller than that associated with VMs.

> **Note** Containers provide a lighter, faster alternative to virtual machines because they do not require an entire guest operating system. This results in quicker startup times and more efficient resource utilization, especially when scaling microservices individually.

PART I Containerization

What is Docker?

Docker is a renowned open platform for automating and deploying applications as portable, self-sufficient containers that can run either in the cloud or on-premises. The only requirement is that the given machine must provide a Docker host, which serves as the containerization manager and runtime. Docker is also the name of the company that promotes and develops this containerization technology.

Developers can use Docker Desktop on Windows, Linux, or macOS. This tool includes a single-node Kubernetes cluster, which developers can use for local deployments and testing.

Docker is implemented in the Go programming language and employs namespaces technology to provide an isolated workspace, the container. These namespaces are used to isolate running containers. Specifically, a running container has access only to its associated set of namespaces and cannot access the namespaces of other containers. In virtual machines, such isolation is achieved with a hypervisor.

Architecture

The Docker architecture, depicted in Figure 3-3, uses a client-server approach in which a Docker client communicates with the Docker daemon running on the server (Docker Host). The Docker daemon is a background process (server) that listens to requests from the client. These requests are usually sent using the Docker Command Line Interface (Docker CLI) or the remote API.

The major Docker CLI commands include:

- **docker pull** Downloads a container image from a container registry, which is a service that can contain multiple repositories for container images, like Git. There are local and remote repositories, so the **docker pull** command (like **git pull**) downloads an image from a remote repository.

- **docker push** Sends a local container image to a remote repository.

- **docker build** Builds a container image by turning the application, its dependencies, and its configuration into a self-sufficient container image, which can then be sent to a remote repository or used to run the container locally.

- **docker run** Creates and runs a container instance from the specified container image. This command first tries to locate the selected container image in the local repository. If the container is unavailable locally, the command pulls the image from the remote repository hosted by the container registry.

By default, Docker uses Docker Hub as the container registry, where you can create public or private repositories. Private repositories are used for images that you do not want to share with others.

Notably, the Docker client and daemon can run on the same machine, as is the case when Docker Desktop is installed.

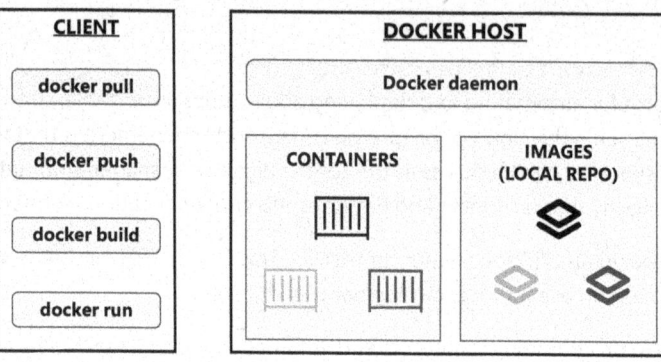 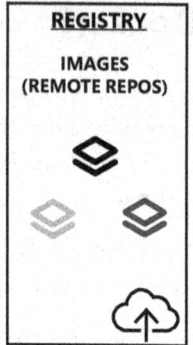

FIGURE 3-3 Docker architecture.

How to pull and run a container

To use the Docker CLI to pull a container image and run it on a local Docker host, you must first ensure that Docker Desktop is running (see Figure 3-4).

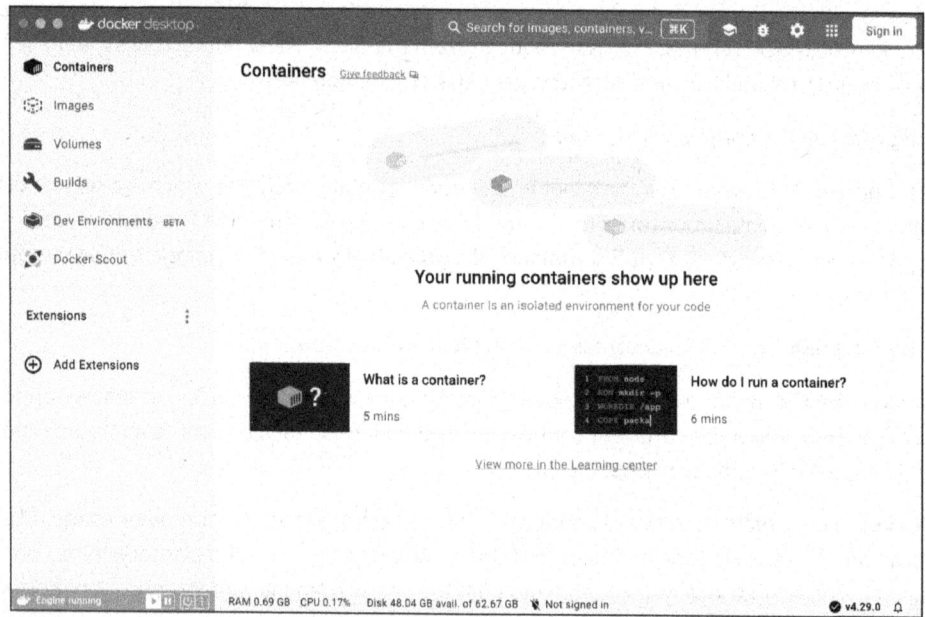

FIGURE 3-4 Docker Desktop.

The icon in the bottom-left corner indicates the status of the Docker Engine (which includes both the daemon and client). The icon should be green. If it is red, you might want to restart the engine or troubleshoot using the Docker documentation.

After ensuring that Docker is up and running, it is helpful to familiarize yourself with the available tabs in Docker Desktop:

- **Containers** Shows the list of running containers. When you start Docker Desktop for the first time, this list will be empty. The Containers tab will display instructions on how to run a container.

- **Images** Includes the list of images in your local and remote repositories.

- **Volumes** Displays the list of volumes, which can be attached to containers to provide non-volatile storage.

- **Builds** Contains the list of builds and builder configurations.

- **Dev Environments** Enables you to manage Dev Environments, which you can use to create reusable environments for developers that contain all the tools they need.

- **Docker Scout** Enables advanced analysis of Docker images.

You can access the same lists through the Docker CLI.

Now, back to the task at hand: To pull the container image with the ASP.NET Core sample app, open the command line or terminal, and then type:

`docker pull mcr.microsoft.com/dotnet/samples:aspnetapp`

The command downloads the Docker image from the .NET repository hosted on Microsoft's public container registry (see Figure 3-5). Note the last string after the colon (**aspnetapp**). This is the image tag, an additional label you can apply to images and use for versioning. Docker will use the most recent version of the tag if you do not specify an explicit tag.

```
% docker pull mcr.microsoft.com/dotnet/samples:aspnetapp
aspnetapp: Pulling from dotnet/samples
bca4290a9639: Pull complete
17d2a7d981b9: Pull complete
efe110e27a85: Pull complete
6da8b764e0f9: Pull complete
865ec80fbac4: Pull complete
4516858e824c: Pull complete
0c895121d435: Pull complete
Digest: sha256:9eff28ca884ba26647500affe757c4c888f977132a09de82387fd71564d66625
Status: Downloaded newer image for mcr.microsoft.com/dotnet/samples:aspnetapp
mcr.microsoft.com/dotnet/samples:aspnetapp

What's Next?
  1. Sign in to your Docker account → docker login
  2. View a summary of image vulnerabilities and recommendations → docker scout quickview mcr.mic
rosoft.com/dotnet/samples:aspnetapp
%
% docker images
REPOSITORY                          TAG         IMAGE ID       CREATED       SIZE
mcr.microsoft.com/dotnet/samples    aspnetapp   4effeeb11734   9 days ago    125MB
%
```

FIGURE 3-5 Pulling a Docker image.

By analyzing the output of the **docker pull** command, you can see that the pull operation is composed of several steps, because this specific image contains multiple layers. Docker uses layers to optimize container builds and transfers, as detailed in the Dockers Layers Guide (*docs.docker.com/build/guide/layers*).

To verify that the image was downloaded, type:

```
docker images
```

The command lists the images available in your local repository. If you return to Docker Desktop and click the Images tab, you will see the same image (as shown in Figure 3-6).

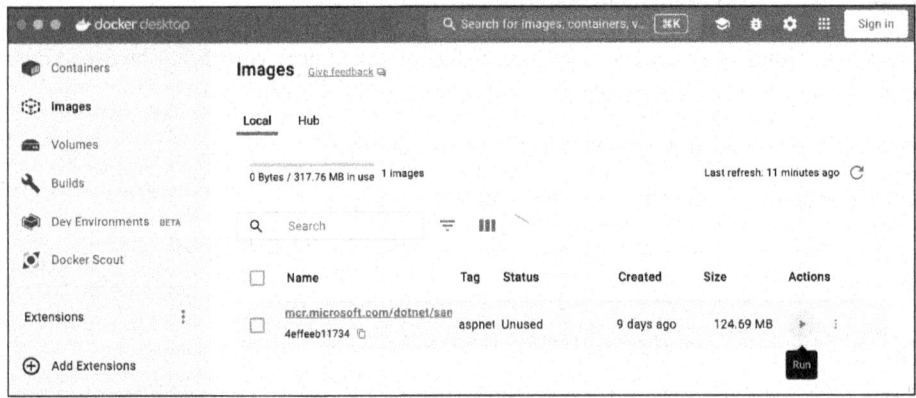

FIGURE 3-6 A list of local images.

To run a container, use the Docker CLI. In the command line or terminal, type (see Figure 3-7):

```
docker run -p 80:8080 --name aspnet-sample-app mcr.microsoft.com/dotnet/↵
    samples:aspnetapp
```

```
● ● ●   People.WebApp — com.docker.cli • docker run -p 80:8080 --name aspnet-sample-app mcr.microsoft.com/dotnet/samples:...
% docker run -p 80:8080 --name aspnet-sample-app mcr.microsoft.com/dotnet/samples:aspnetapp
warn: Microsoft.AspNetCore.DataProtection.Repositories.FileSystemXmlRepository[60]
      Storing keys in a directory '/root/.aspnet/DataProtection-Keys' that may not be persisted o
utside of the container. Protected data will be unavailable when container is destroyed. For more
 information go to https://aka.ms/aspnet/dataprotectionwarning
warn: Microsoft.AspNetCore.DataProtection.KeyManagement.XmlKeyManager[35]
      No XML encryptor configured. Key {3d2ed1a6-1ae7-42eb-8775-cea731e03408} may be persisted to
 storage in unencrypted form.
info: Microsoft.Hosting.Lifetime[14]
      Now listening on: http://[::]:8080
info: Microsoft.Hosting.Lifetime[0]
      Application started. Press Ctrl+C to shut down.
info: Microsoft.Hosting.Lifetime[0]
      Hosting environment: Production
info: Microsoft.Hosting.Lifetime[0]
      Content root path: /app
```

FIGURE 3-7 Running a container.

This command runs the container named aspnet-sample-app using the **--name** parameter. If you omit this parameter, Docker will assign a random name to the container. The running container will be accessible from the host on port 80, which will be mapped to port 8080 inside the container. This mapping is configured using the **-p** parameter. The first value is the host port, and the second is the container port. Finally, you provide the image to spin up the container. If the image was not pulled beforehand, the **docker run** command will pull it for you as shown earlier in Figure 3-6.

The container is up and running in the background. To access the application, open a web browser and type **localhost** in the address bar. The application will appear as shown in Figure 3-8.

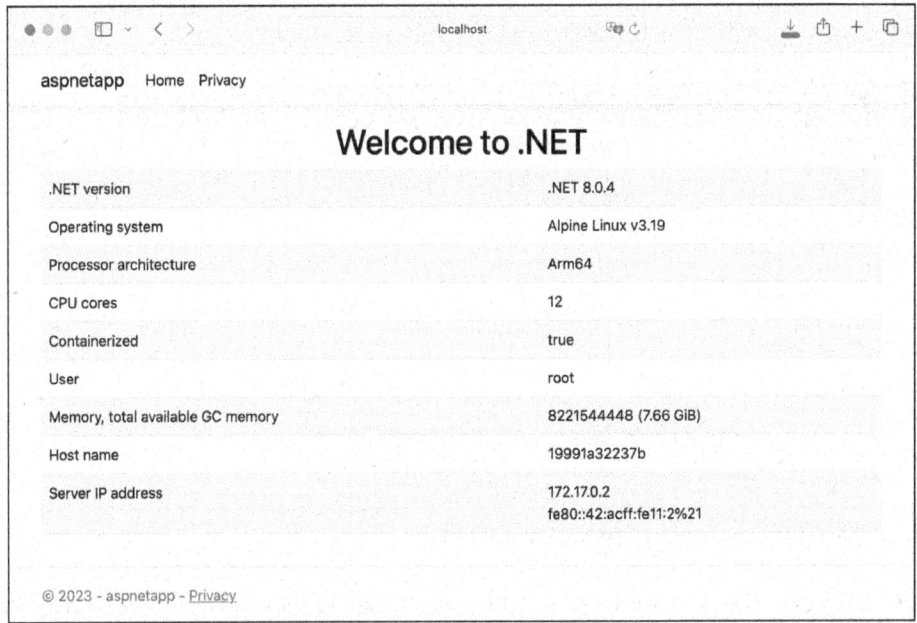

FIGURE 3-8 Running a containerized ASP.NET Core application.

How to manage containers

To see a list of running container instances, go to Docker Desktop and click Containers. The Containers tab lists each running container's name (aspnet-sample-app) and identifier (19991a32237b), as shown in Figure 3-9. It also displays the name of the image used to spin up the container, the container's status, port mapping, uptime, and additional actions. You can use these actions to stop, pause, or restart the container.

Additionally, if you click the ellipsis under Actions and select View Details, you will see the app's output and the container's stats, such as CPU and memory usage. From this view, click Exec to access the terminal inside the running container. From here, you can invoke any command available in the container, for example, *top* (see Figure 3-10). The available commands will depend on the base image used to create the container and the tools installed within it.

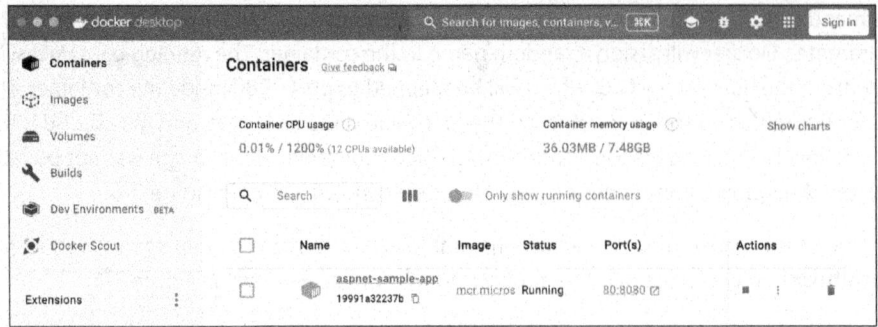

FIGURE 3-9 Docker Desktop showing a containerized ASP.NET Core application.

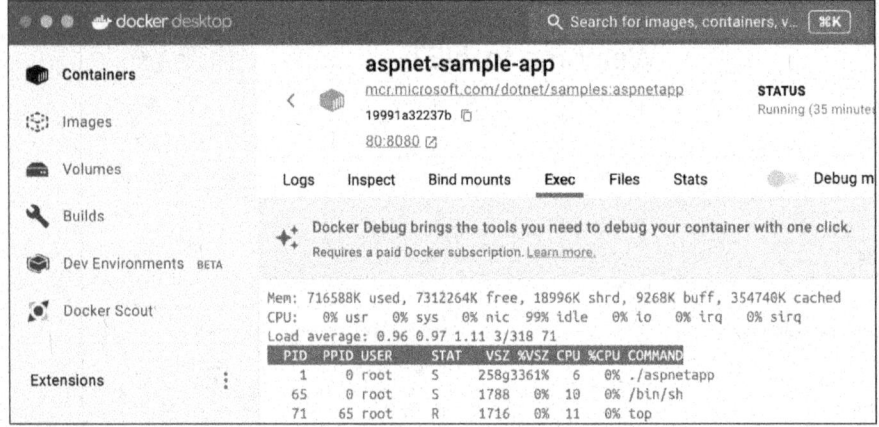

FIGURE 3-10 Connecting to a terminal of the running container.

Importantly, you can achieve similar results using the Docker CLI. Specifically, to get a list of running containers, use the command:

`docker ps`

To connect to a terminal inside a running container named aspnet-sample-app, you can use the following command:

`docker exec -it aspnet-sample-app /bin/sh`

This command executes **/bin/sh** inside the running container. Note the usage of the **-it** flag, which indicates that the command should be invoked in interactive mode, giving you access to the standard input for the container (here, a command line or terminal).

How to remove a container

When you launch a container, the command line displays the app's output running in the container. If you close the output by pressing Ctrl+C (Windows) or Command+C (macOS), the application running in the container will stop and the container's status will change to Exited. Consequently, you cannot re-run the container with the same name. Therefore, you need to delete the aspnet-sample-app container, either by clicking the Trash icon in Docker Desktop or by typing:

```
docker rm aspnet-sample-app
```

Finally, Docker Desktop enables you to run a local image using the UI. To do this, open the Images tab of Docker Desktop, select a container image, and click its Run icon under Actions (Figure 3-6). In the Run A New Container window that appears, you configure the container's name, port mapping, volumes, and more, as shown in Figure 3-11.

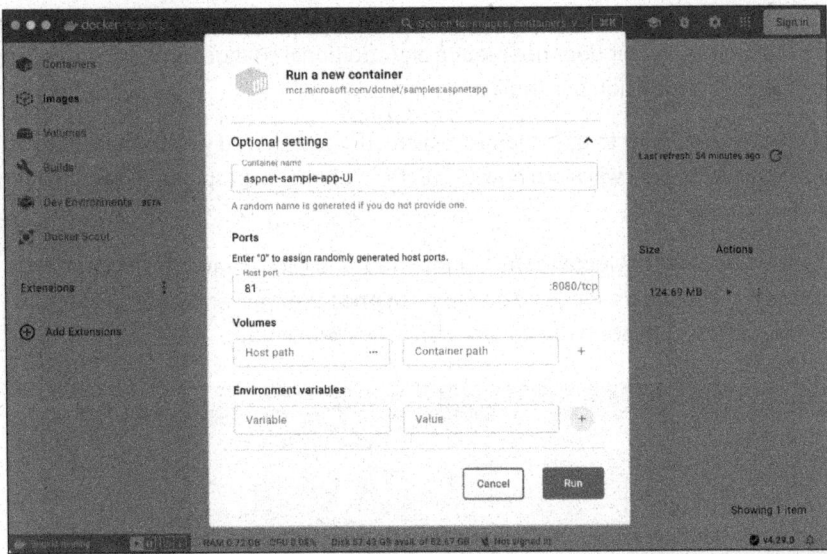

FIGURE 3-11 Running a container.

Running multiple containers

Consider the processes (instances of applications) in the operating system. Typically, multiple applications run in parallel. The applications can use the system's storage to persist files or data, interact with the system services, or use the network to communicate with external applications and services. For example, an application can consume a database in the Microsoft SQL Server running as a system service. Also, the same application can save photos to a drive and synchronize its local data with the remote service provisioned in the cloud. Of course, multiple applications can run on the same computer, communicating with the same Microsoft SQL Server but accessing different databases.

To achieve a similar functionality with multiple containerized applications, you simply need to extend what you now know about running and managing an individual container. Docker offers some additional tools to help you, including container networking, volumes, and Docker Compose.

As you remember, a container is created from a container image. The container then acts as a self-contained unit. It can process and store data, but when you close the container, the data stored in it is lost. To preserve this data, you can keep it on the host disk or in a database. You can use *volumes* to allow the container to persist the data on the Docker host. The database can run inside the container or in another container. For the latter case, you need to *network* multiple containers. Finally, the *Docker Compose tool* enables you to run and manage multiple containers, their networks, and volumes using a declarative approach. Take a closer look at each tool in the following sections.

Volumes

Docker provides several mechanisms for sharing data between containers, all of which are detailed in the official Docker documentation. One common feature of these approaches is that the data becomes available inside the container as any other element of the container's file system. Therefore, the app or service running inside the container does not require any additional changes and can use the same data access methods as it would outside of containerization.

In this section, I will show you how to use volumes, which offer a preferred way to share data between containers. Specifically, you will learn how to create a volume, then spin up two containers that access the same volume.

To start, open Docker Desktop, navigate to the Volumes tab, and click Create (top-right corner). In the New Volume window that appears, name your volume **aspnet-volume**, and click Create (see Figure 3-12). A new volume will appear on the Volumes list in Docker Desktop.

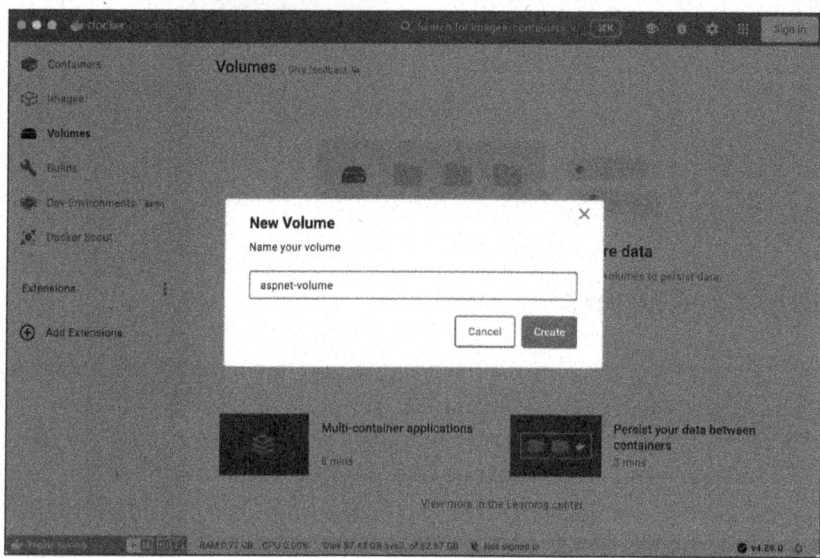

FIGURE 3-12 Creating a volume using Docker Desktop.

Alternatively, you could create the new volume with a Docker CLI command:

```
docker volume create --name aspnet-volume
```

To show the list of volumes using Docker CLI, type:

```
docker volume ls
```

With your volume ready, you can spin up the first container. Use the same container image as before and supplement the **docker** command with two additional parameters: **-d** to run the container in detached (background) mode and **-v** to attach aspnet-volume such that it will be accessible inside the container from the /etc/data folder:

```
docker run -dp 80:8080 --name aspnet-sample-app -v aspnet-volume:/etc/data ↵
    mcr.microsoft.com/dotnet/samples:aspnetapp
```

The command outputs the container identifier, as shown in Figure 3-13.

```
% docker run -dp 80:8080 --name aspnet-sample-app -v aspnet-volume:/etc/data mcr.microsoft.com/do
tnet/samples:aspnetapp
f6b1b4a40e3951ddc353f37b3e0c1e28142a2ce266ea28c778f4fb161eed9bfa
%
```

FIGURE 3-13 Attaching a volume to a container.

You can now go back to Docker Desktop, click the Containers tab, and then open the Terminal of the running container (under Actions select the ellipsis, View Details, then Exec). Then, in the container's Terminal, type the following commands:

```
ls -la /etc/data

echo "Hello from container 1">> /etc/data/test.file

cat /etc/data/test.file
```

The first command lists the contents of the /etc/data folder to confirm that the volume is initially empty. The second creates a new text file inside that folder. The last command displays the contents of the new file.

To view the items in the volume, you can use Docker Desktop. Click Volumes, select a volume, and then click Data.

One done, one to go. Spin up another container using the same container image as before. This new container will use the same volume (aspnet-volume) and port 81 on the host. To avoid a name conflict, name the second container aspnet-sample-app2:

```
docker run -dp 81:8080 --name aspnet-sample-app2 -v aspnet-volume:/etc/data ↵
    mcr.microsoft.com/dotnet/samples:aspnetapp
```

Again, the command outputs a container identifier. You now have two containers running, both with the same volume attached. In particular, the second container, aspnet-sample-app2, can access the test.file created from the aspnet-sample-app container. To see this, open the Terminal of the second container (aspnet-sample-app2) and type:

```
cat /etc/data/test.file
```

The message "Hello from container 1" displays as shown in Figure 3-14.

You've just learned how to use volumes to persist data. The file you created will be available to other containers until the volume is removed.

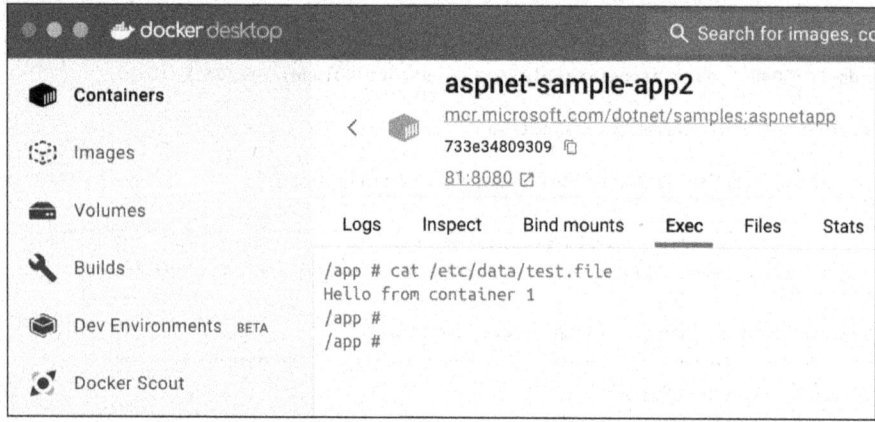

FIGURE 3-14 Accessing a file created by another container.

Networking

In the previous section, you spun up two containers. Both containers joined the default Docker network (bridge), which Docker creates along with two other default networks. This setup allows both containers to communicate with each other. To confirm this, use the Terminal of the first container (aspnet-sample-app) to type:

```
hostname -i
```

The command will output the local IP address of the first container within the Docker network (172.17.0.2, in my case). Open the Terminal of the second container (aspnet-sample-app2), and type the following commands:

```
hostname -i
```

```
ping 172.17.0.2
```

The first command displays the local IP address of the second container (172.17.0.3, in my case). The second command sends a ping to the first container, and you should see a response similar to what is shown in Figure 3-15. This confirms that both containers are inside the same network and can communicate with each other.

The practical implication of this communication capability is that you can create multi-container solutions where, for example, one container runs a web application, and another container runs a database server that the application consumes.

Moving forward, you can even create a more advanced network architecture where some containers are isolated within their own networks, so they cannot be reached by containers running in other networks.

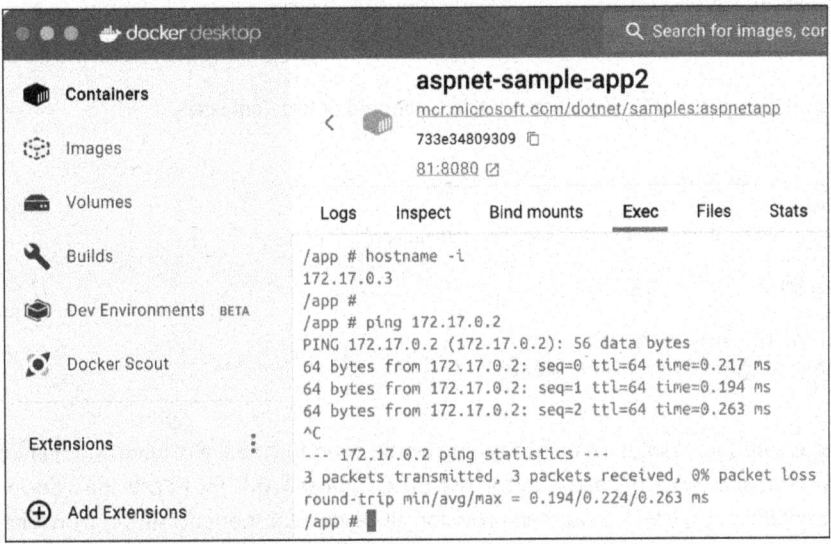

FIGURE 3-15 Communication Between Containers.

To create a new network, use the **docker network create** command. Once the network is created, you can instruct Docker to have a new container join that network using the **--network** parameter of the **docker run** command. Additionally, you can connect a running container to a specified network with the **docker network connect** command. For specific scenarios, you can refer to various Docker networking tutorials available in the official Docker documentation.

> **Note** Containers use declarative configuration, allowing consistent, reproducible deployment by packaging applications and dependencies into images. This is a significant improvement over traditional, imperative setup methods, simplifying deployment and disaster recovery.

Docker Compose

Although your new containers can share data and communicate with each other, you had to create the volume and spin up the containers manually. Such manual management of Docker components is fine initially, but as your solution grows and becomes more complicated, you might prefer a more automated solution. To address this, Docker provides Compose.

Compose enables you to define, run, and manage Docker applications composed of multiple containers. To define a multi-container Docker application, you use a dedicated YAML file similar to Listing 3-1.

The file defines two application services: `people.webapp` and `sql-server`. The first corresponds to a hypothetical frontend, and the second is a database server. Thus, the compose creates two containers. It creates the first, `people.webapp`, using the container image with the sample ASP.NET Core app. It spins up the second container using an official containerized version of SQL Server.

The definition of the first service also includes port mapping (equivalent to the **-p** parameter of the **docker run** command) and volume creation and attachment.

LISTING 3-1 A Docker Compose YAML File Defines an App Composed of Two Containers.

```
services:
  people.webapp:
    image: "mcr.microsoft.com/dotnet/samples:aspnetapp"
    ports:
      - "8080:8080"
    volumes:
      - .:/usr/data sql-server:
    image: "mcr.microsoft.com/mssql/server"
```

If you were to create such a solution manually, you would need to create a volume and then invoke the **docker run** command twice. Instead, you can use the Compose YAML file to provide a declaration for the manual container application and then provision all Docker components simply by issuing a single command:

`docker compose up`

To shut down the entire application, you use:

`docker compose down`

Notably, the containers created with Compose will join the same network and see each other by the hostnames set based on the service name. This means that `people.webapp` can reach `sql-server` via the service name on port 1433: sql-server,1433.

> **Tip** Use Docker Compose to simplify multi-container application management. With a single YAML file, you can easily define, launch, and manage complex applications composed of multiple interconnected containers, significantly streamlining your workflow.

Summary

In this chapter, you learned how to use Docker for running and managing single and multi-container applications. In the next chapter, you will apply this knowledge to containerize and run People.WebApp. Then, you will learn how to use Docker Compose to launch a multi-container application consisting of People.WebApp and a containerized SQL Server. Before proceeding, clean up your Docker environment by closing both containers and removing a volume with the following commands:

`docker rm -f aspnet-sample-app`

`docker rm -f aspnet-sample-app2`

`docker volume rm aspnet-volume`

CHAPTER 4

How to Containerize an Application with Docker

In this chapter, you will learn how to create a Docker container image from the existing application, People.WebApp. You will then start this container to demonstrate that the containerized version of People.WebApp functions exactly as it did previously. Finally, you will learn how to create and run a multi-container solution composed of the People.WebApp and a containerized instance of Microsoft SQL Server, which will make your solution portable, enabling it to be launched anywhere Docker is installed.

Although the examples use specific technologies (ASP.NET Core and Microsoft SQL Server), the instructions in this chapter are also applicable to other technologies. The primary difference lies in the Dockerfile, which contains instructions for Docker on how to build a container image. Naturally, this file will vary for applications built with Java or Python. However, as you will see, the Dockerfile can be automatically generated based on your project using dedicated tools.

Dockerfile

To containerize an application, you need to create a *Dockerfile*, a text file comprising a series of commands that instruct Docker on how to build an image. The goal of building is to convert the application's source code or binaries into a standalone, self-sufficient container image. This process involves either copying the source code from your computer to a container and building it there or copying the binaries and their dependencies directly into the container image. Additionally, to run the application within a container, you need a runtime, data, and a configuration, which all depend on the technology used to implement the application.

For this reason, the Dockerfile typically starts with the FROM instruction, which specifies a base Docker image. This base image usually provides the basic functionality and software development kits (SDKs) needed to build your application from the source code, or the runtimes required to launch the application. Generally, the Dockerfile may rely on several base images in a *multi-stage build*. This approach uses the first base image with an SDK to build the application from sources. Then, a second FROM instruction can point to another parent image that contains only the runtime. This second image is used to create the final container image. The idea is to optimize the final size of the container image, as in most cases, an SDK-based image is much larger than a runtime-only image.

Then, the Dockerfile includes a COPY instruction, which, as the name implies, copies the required files and dependencies. Alternatively, the source code can be cloned from a repository, and dependencies can be fetched from various remote package repositories, similar to how you would prepare dependencies for a non-containerized application. Each command needed to prepare the application is executed using the RUN instruction.

Once you have the binaries, dependencies, and configuration in place, you must instruct Docker on how to expose and launch your application. Use the EXPOSE command to specify the ports on which your application listens for incoming requests. You use a RUN or ENTRYPOINT instruction to select the application entry point, which can be optionally configured using CMD instructions.

Given the above, you can think of the Dockerfile as an automated application installation script. For most scenarios, you do not need to write a Dockerfile from scratch, and tools like Visual Studio Code extensions can even generate a Dockerfile for you.

Containerize the People.WebApp

You can use Visual Studio Code to create a Dockerfile for the People.WebApp. Open Visual Studio Code, click Open Folder, and select the People.WebApp folder (see Figure 4-1). Then, from the View menu, select Command Palette. Alternatively, you can press Ctrl+Shift+P (Windows) or Command+Shift+P (macOS) to activate this palette.

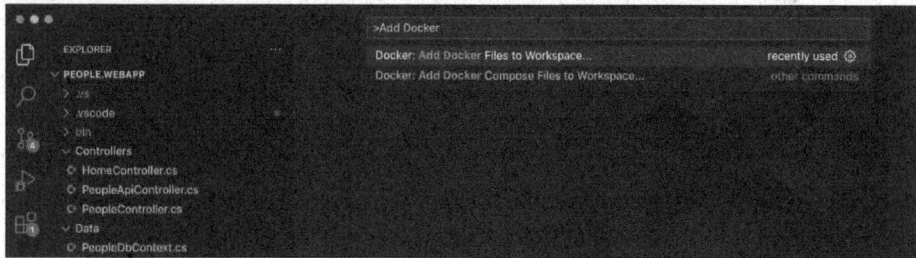

FIGURE 4-1 Visual Studio Code with the Command Palette activated.

The Command Palette initially appears as a text box at the top of Visual Studio Code. In this text box, start typing **Add Docker** to display a list of matched commands. Select Docker: Add Docker Files To Workspace from the list (see Figure 4-1) to activate the Add Docker Files wizard. In the wizard, choose the following:

- Application Platform: **.NET: ASP.NET Core**
- Select Operating System: **Linux**
- Port: **5000**
- Include optional Docker Compose files: **No**

Next, Visual Studio Code will add two files: .dockerignore and Dockerfile. The first file, similar to .gitignore, instructs Docker which files and folders should be ignored during copy operations. The generated Dockerfile (Listing 4-1) is an ASP.NET Core–specific script for converting People.WebApp sources into a self-sufficient container image.

LISTING 4-1 A Dockerfile of the People.WebApp.

```
FROM mcr.microsoft.com/dotnet/aspnet:8.0 AS base
WORKDIR /app
EXPOSE 5000

ENV ASPNETCORE_URLS=http://+:5000

USER app
FROM --platform=$BUILD
PLATFORM mcr.microsoft.com/dotnet/sdk:8.0 AS build
ARG configuration=Release
WORKDIR /src
COPY ["People.WebApp.csproj", "./"]
RUN dotnet restore "People.WebApp.csproj"
COPY . .
WORKDIR "/src/."
RUN dotnet build "People.WebApp.csproj" -c $configuration -o /app/build

FROM build AS publish
ARG configuration=Release
RUN dotnet publish "People.WebApp.csproj" -c $configuration -o /app/publish
/p:UseAppHost=false

FROM base AS final
WORKDIR /app
COPY --from=publish /app/publish .
ENTRYPOINT ["dotnet", "People.WebApp.dll"]
```

Take a closer look inside the Dockerfile generated for People.WebApp. The first instruction (FROM) specifies the base image: mcr.microsoft.com/dotnet/aspnet:8.0. This specialized image, optimized for running ASP.NET Core apps, contains only the ASP.NET Core runtime and libraries. In the Dockerfile, this image is labeled as base. Note that the image is tagged with the .NET version (8.0). Microsoft distributes images with various .NET versions for different platforms (x86, x64, arm64) and operating systems such as Alpine, Debian Bookworm, Nano Server, and Windows Server Core.

The WORKDIR instruction sets the working directory to /app inside the container. Any subsequent RUN instructions will be executed from the /app folder.

The Dockerfile contains an EXPOSE instruction, exposing port 5000. Hence, any application listening on this port will be reachable.

The Dockerfile then uses an ENV instruction to configure the environment variable ASPNETCORE_URLS. This variable is used by ASP.NET Core applications to indicate an IP address and ports on which the application should listen for requests. Here, this variable is configured such that any unbound IP address or localhost will be directed to the underlying ASP.NET Core server (Kestrel) on port 5000.

The Dockerfile then uses a USER instruction to set the user to app (this user was previously created within the base Docker image). The USER instruction ensures that the container does not run with root privileges unless explicitly defined. Running containers as a non-root user is a best practice in Docker security because it reduces the risks associated with potential vulnerabilities in the application or container.

Another FROM instruction indicates a different base image, `mcr.microsoft.com/dotnet/sdk:8.0`, labeled in the Dockerfile as `build`. This image, used for building, contains the .NET SDK, including commands (`dotnet build`, `dotnet run`, and `dotnet publish`) and `dotnet restore` for downloading the app's project dependencies.

Next, the Dockerfile includes an ARG instruction, setting the Docker build variable configuration to `Release`.

The directory is then changed to /src inside the container, and a COPY instruction is used to copy the project file (`People.WebApp.csproj`) to the container (`/src` folder). The RUN instruction invokes dotnet restore to install all the project's dependencies. Subsequent files from the working folder on your computer (the so-called build context) are copied to the container's working directory (COPY . .). The `dotnet build` command is then invoked to build the People.WebApp inside the container, with the build's output directed to the `/app/build` folder.

After the application is built, Docker prepares the People.WebApp for deployment using another RUN instruction, which invokes the `dotnet publish` command. The deployment folder is set to `/app/publish`. Note that build and publish phases use the `mcr.microsoft.com/dotnet/sdk:8.0` image.

Afterward, the parent image is switched back to the runtime only (FROM base), and the contents of the publish folder (generated by the build/publish image) are copied to the `/app` folder. Finally, the ENTRYPOINT instruction runs the application using the `dotnet People.WebApp.dll` command, equivalent to the `dotnet run` command used to launch People.WebApp in Chapter 2.

Building the container image

You're now ready to build the Docker container image using the Dockerfile you just created. First, open the terminal or command-line interface. Change the working directory to the folder containing the sources of the People.WebApp (the folder into which you cloned the application in Chapter 2), then type the following command:

```
docker build -t people.webapp:v1 --platform linux/amd64 .
```

The **-t** option specifies the image name and tag as **people.webapp:v1**. The period (.) at the end of the command sets the build context to the current directory, which is the folder of the People.WebApp.

After invoking the above **docker build** command, you will see output similar to Figure 4-2.

```
% docker build -t people.webapp:v1 .                              docker:desktop-linux
[+] Building 6.7s (5/17)
 => => sha256:c04e0e4f9f307e8be86a2759e3827b19942e15a6a 27.26MB / 30.81MB    6.3s
 => => sha256:1b910ce5bd5c1aed9cd519579c0c89fbb16bc528e7 7.34MB / 30.96MB    6.3s
 => => sha256:b95bdc54d5fd0e83a82a179169cdc493321188a6d  6.29MB / 184.23MB   6.3s
 => => extracting sha256:22d97f6a5d13532e867231d23d92620a81874d51a456196b    1.6s
 => => extracting sha256:8474cb22b524eaa32d1bf34ddbacae7a02a6088577c51df8    0.8s
 => => extracting sha256:d4e713c155f9f296769923004f0fa54d0f5133119152d809    0.0s
 => [internal] load build context                                            0.1s
 => => transferring context: 8.16MB                                          0.0s
 => [base 1/2] FROM mcr.microsoft.com/dotnet/aspnet:8.0@sha256:acb8f8e836    6.3s
 => => resolve mcr.microsoft.com/dotnet/aspnet:8.0@sha256:acb8f8e836ae3ba    0.0s
 => => sha256:41e28f6dfcfcec01866dcc22df713c1af8d1c893a15  1.58kB / 1.58kB   0.0s
 => => sha256:d4e713c155f9f296769923004f0fa54d0f513311915  3.33kB / 3.33kB   0.1s
 => => sha256:acb8f8e836ae3ba350d37edcfdfafb7bb6e58363067  1.08kB / 1.08kB   0.0s
 => => sha256:848ea71a7179384e47ca9a1ab98837fb53a479d10a9  2.72kB / 2.72kB   0.0s
 => => sha256:8474cb22b524eaa32d1bf34ddbacae7a02a608857   18.48MB / 18.48MB  2.9s
 => => sha256:22d97f6a5d13532e867231d23d92620a81874d51a   29.18MB / 29.18MB  4.7s
 => => sha256:c04e0e4f9f307e8be86a2759e3827b19942e15a6a   28.31MB / 30.81MB  6.3s
 => => sha256:317e4da1b5bd68dfce4d331fcbff0879878d2805133b9c1  164B / 164B   3.1s
 => => sha256:e02af66865dc287ab349ae259865da57a7305847f  10.70MB / 10.70MB   4.8s
 => => extracting sha256:22d97f6a5d13532e867231d23d92620a81874d51a456196b    0.8s
 => => extracting sha256:8474cb22b524eaa32d1bf34ddbacae7a02a6088577c51df8    0.2s
 => => extracting sha256:d4e713c155f9f296769923004f0fa54d0f5133119152d809    0.0s
```

FIGURE 4-2 Building a Docker image.

The Docker builder will invoke instructions from the Dockerfile one by one to generate a Docker image. As shown in the output of the **docker build** command, the build operation is partitioned into four stages (a multi-stage build): base, build, publish, and final. These stages correspond to parent images and their labels from the Dockerfile. Each stage comprises ordered build instructions, which translate to image layers. For example, three layers are generated during the base stage by the FROM, WORKDIR, and RUN instructions. The final stage contains only two layers (from the FROM and WORKDIR instructions).

Docker tends to cache and reuse those layers from earlier builds. Therefore, if you re-invoke the **docker build -t people.webapp:v1 .** command, the output will appear almost immediately because all layers are cached. To clear the cache, you can use the **docker builder prune** command.

After the build operation, you can view the new image in the local repository by typing **docker images** or by opening the Images tab of Docker Desktop (see Figure 4-3).

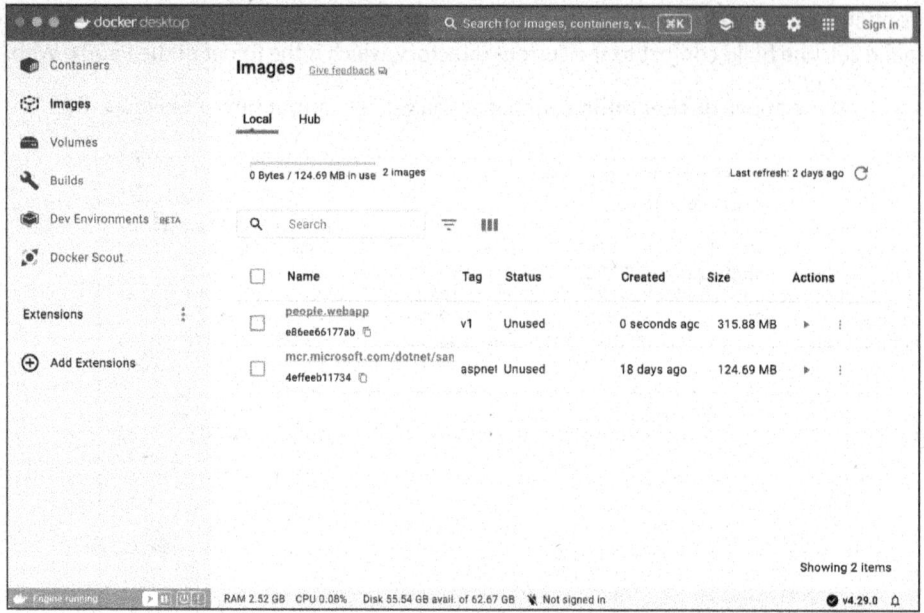

FIGURE 4-3 The People.WebApp image Is now available in the local container image repository.

Running a containerized People.WebApp

You can now run a container using the newly created image of the People.WebApp. To do so, proceed as you did for the ASP.NET Core sample application (using **docker run**). The only difference will be that your application will listen on port 5000 inside the container. Therefore, you will need to account for this during port mapping. To begin, type the following command in the terminal:

```
docker run -dp 80:5000 --name people-webapp people.webapp:v1
```

This command spins up the container in detached (background) mode and responds with the container identifier. To see the app running, open your web browser and type **localhost** in the address bar. People.WebApp appears the same as in Chapter 2 (Figure 4-4).

You can also get the list of people using an underlying web API by typing the following URL into your web browser: **localhost/api/people**. However, when you try to access Swagger at localhost/swagger, you will not see anything because Swagger is disabled in the Release configuration, which is set in the Dockerfile (`dotnet build` and `dotnet publish` commands). Later, you will learn how to enable Swagger using a Docker environment variable.

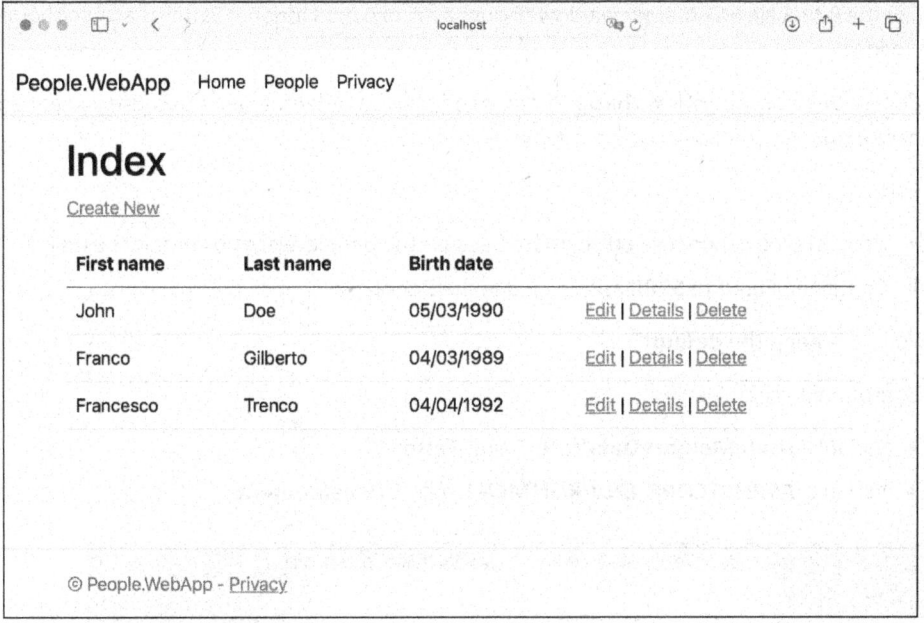

FIGURE 4-4 The containerized version of the People.WebApp functions the same as before.

> **Note** By default, People.WebApp is configured to use an in-memory database, as described in Chapter 2. You can change this configuration by setting `UseInMemorySetting` to `True` in appsettings.json. However, when multiple settings are changed or updated, the Docker image must be rebuilt each time.

For now, ASP.NET Core provides a solution to this problem. Specifically, each configuration item stored in appsettings.json can be overridden by modifying the environment variables in the Dockerfile or when spinning up a container. Take a look how this works in the next section.

Modifying application settings

In the Docker Desktop, go to the Images tab and click the Run icon of the people.webapp:v1 image (as seen in Figure 4-5).

Name	Tag	Status	Created	Size	Actions
people.webapp e86ee66177ab	v1	In use	7 minutes ago	315.88 MB	▶ ⋮
mcr.microsoft.com/dotnet/san 4effeeb11734	aspnet	Unused	18 days ago	124.69 MB	Run ⋮

FIGURE 4-5 Running a container in Docker Desktop.

CHAPTER 4 How to Containerize an Application with Docker   43

Then, in the Run A New Container window (Figure 4-6), expand Optional Settings and configure them as follows:

- Container name: **people-webapp-2** (You need to use a different name because you already have a running container named people-webapp.)

- Ports:
  - Host: **81** (You cannot use 80 anymore because the people-webapp container uses it.)
  - Container: **Fixed to 5000** as specified in the Dockerfile

- Volumes: **Keep the default**

- Environment variables:
  - Variable: **UseInMemoryDatabase**, Value: **False**,
  - Variable: **ASPNETCORE_ENVIRONMENT**, Value: **Development**.

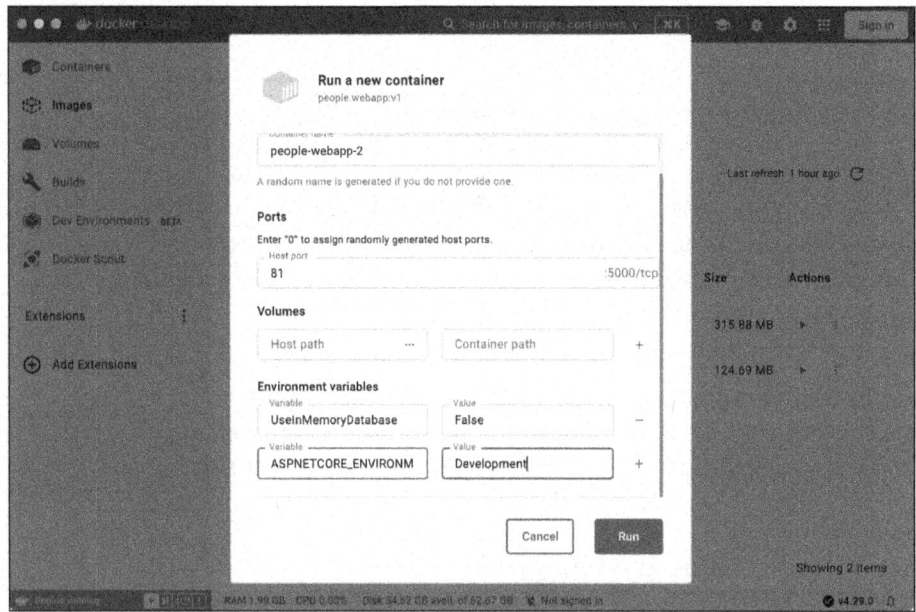

FIGURE 4-6 Configuring container settings.

Click the Run button, and the new container appears under the Containers list in Docker Desktop (see Figure 4-7).

If you now click the hyperlink labeled 81:5000, the app will automatically open in your web browser. You can then access Swagger (see Figure 4-8). When you try to open the People tab, however, you will encounter a problem: The People.WebApp attempts to connect to a local SQL Server, but no instance of SQL Server is running in Docker. Consequently, you will see the following exception: "PlatformNot-SupportedException: LocalDB is not supported on this platform" (see Figure 4-9).

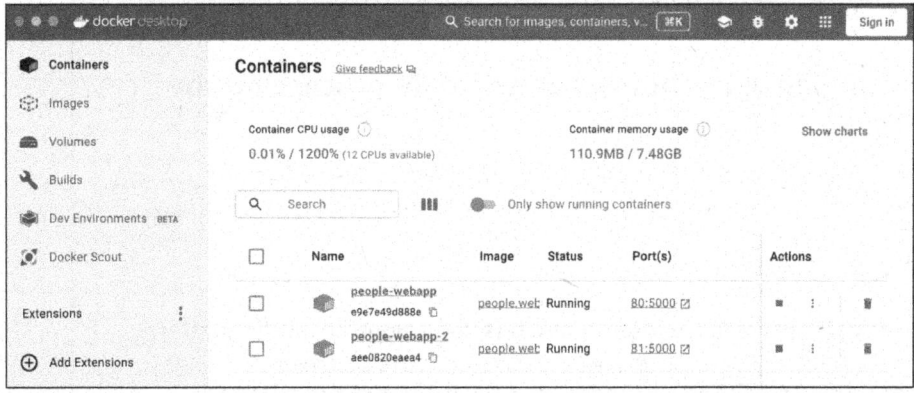

FIGURE 4-7 A list of running containers.

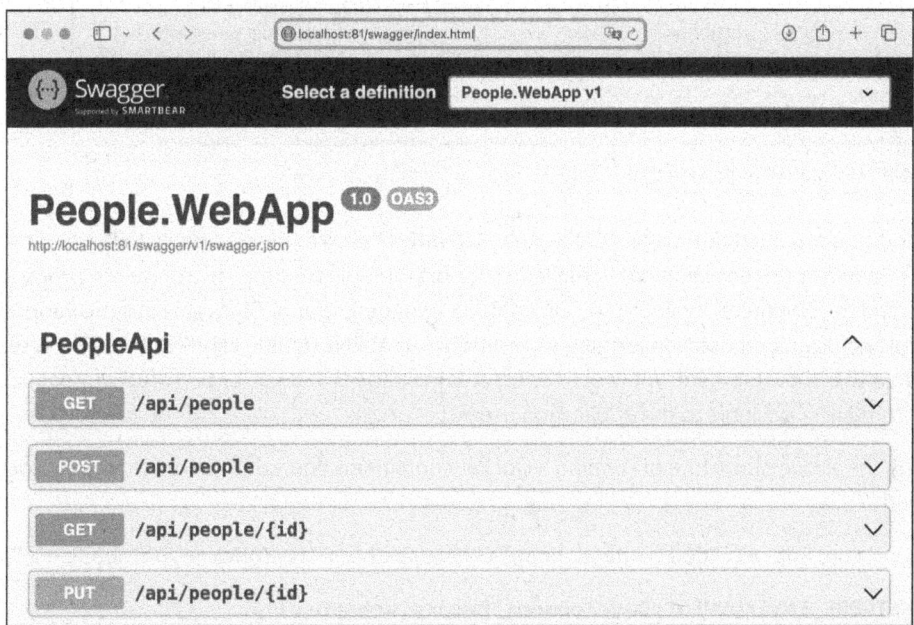

FIGURE 4-8 A Swagger UI in the containerized People.WebApp.

You can solve this problem using Docker Compose. First, however, let me summarize what happened when you launched the new container, people-webapp-2.

First, you changed the UseInMemoryDb setting by configuring an environment variable of the same name to False. This instructed the ASP.NET Core app to override the UseInMemoryDb setting in Appsettings.json. There was no need to manually change this file and then rebuild the Docker image.

CHAPTER 4 How to Containerize an Application with Docker   45

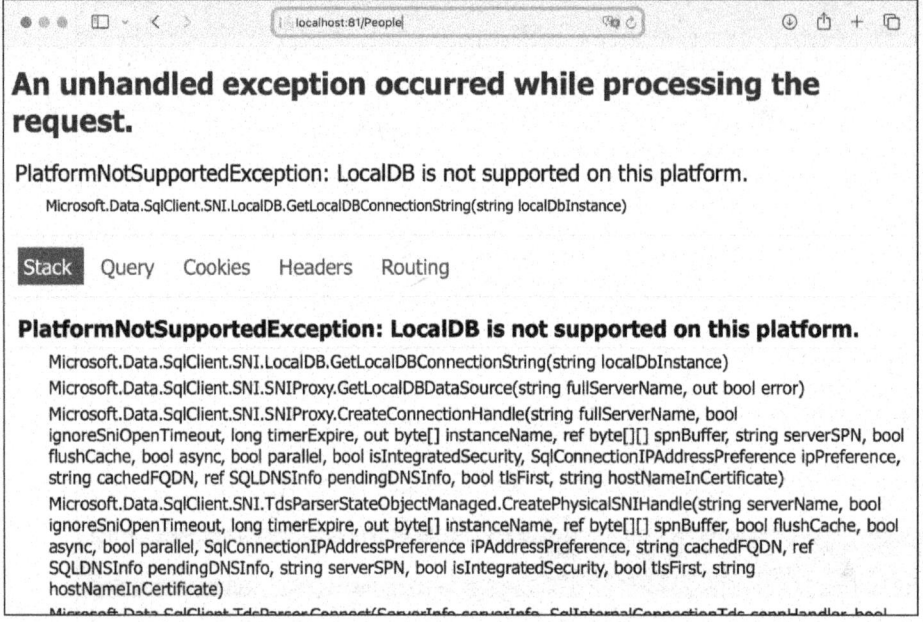

FIGURE 4-9 Information Indicating that LocalDB is not supported in Docker.

Second, you modified the ASPNETCORE_ENVIRONMENT environment variable to Development. ASP.NET Core uses this environment variable to support multiple runtime environments: production, staging, and development. By doing so, you enabled Swagger (refer to Program.cs of the People.WebApp) and facilitated detailed logging of exceptions. If ASPNETCORE_ENVIRONMENT was set to a value other than Development, you would only see a message that an error occurred without additional information available to the application user.

Finally, the above procedure of running a Docker container is equivalent to the following **docker** command:

```
docker run -dp 81:5000 --name people-webapp-2 -e UseInMemoryDatabase=False -e
ASPNETCORE_ENVIRONMENT=Development people.webapp:v1
```

It shows that to set the environment variable, you use the **-e** flag (or **--env**). This command can be helpful for automation.

Using Docker Compose to provision a multi-container solution

Although the People.WebApp cannot use the LocalDB feature of SQL Server, you can overcome this problem by using Docker Compose to provision a multi-container solution. To do so, you will run two containers—one hosting SQL Server and the other hosting the People.WebApp—then modify the People.WebApp's database connection settings with environment variables to point to a SQL Server database.

As discussed in Chapter 3, you first must create a configuration file to use Docker Compose. This YAML-formatted text file declares a multi-container application's services, volumes, port mappings, and environment variables.

Creating a configuration file

To supplement the People.WebApp with the Docker Compose configuration file, proceed as follows: In Visual Studio Code, open the Command Palette (View > Command Palette), and start typing **Docker Compose**. From the filtered list of commands that appears, select Docker: Add Docker Compose Files To Workspace (see Figure 4-10).

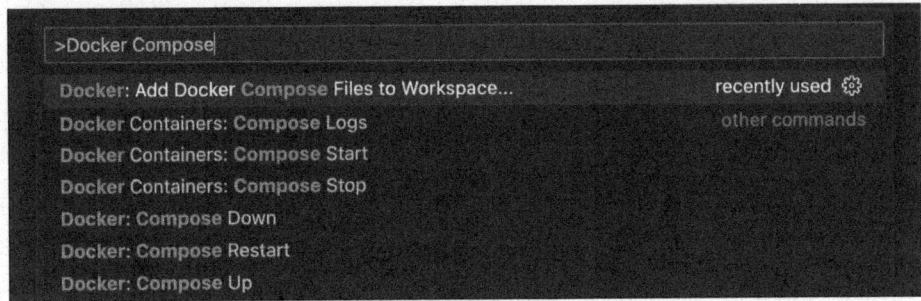

FIGURE 4-10 Adding Docker Compose files to a workspace.

When the Add Docker Compose Files wizard activates, select the following options, and then press Enter (Windows) or Return (macOS):

- Select Application Platform: **.NET: ASP.NET Core**

- Select Operating System: **Linux**

- Port: **5000**

The project's folder will be supplemented with docker-compose.debug.yml and docker-compose.yml. Listing 4-2 shows the contents of the first file. This Docker Compose file uses just one service named peoplewebapp. The service will use the Docker container image of the same name, which will be built using a Dockerfile. The build operation will include one argument named configuration, which is set to Debug. As shown in Listing 4-2, you can list arguments under the args section. Docker Compose will analyze each item on this list and use them to override arguments in the Dockerfile (ARG instructions). Specifically, in the Dockerfile from Listing 4-1, you have just one ARG instruction, which sets the configuration to Release.

The peoplewebapp service will use host-to-container port mapping (5000:5000). The environment variable ASPNETCORE_ENVIRONMENT is set to Development.

Finally, the peoplewebapp service defines a volume, which maps a local.vsdbg folder (inside the People.WebApp folder) to the /remote_debugger folder inside the container with read-write (rw).

LISTING 4-2 A Default docker-compose.debug.yml.

```yaml
version: '3.4'

services:
  peoplewebapp:
    image: peoplewebapp
    build:
      context: .
      dockerfile: ./Dockerfile
      args:
        - configuration=Debug
    ports:
      - 5000:5000
    environment:
      - ASPNETCORE_ENVIRONMENT=Development
    volumes:
      - ~/.vsdbg:/remote_debugger:rw
```

Adding Microsoft SQL Server

Now, try modifying the default docker-compose.debug.yml to include another service (sql-server) as shown in Listing 4-3. Note that when editing the Docker Compose file, you must conform to the YAML specification. The most important rule is that you cannot use tabs for indentation; instead, you must use two spaces.

LISTING 4-3 A docker-compose.debug.yml for the People.WebApp Working with the Database Hosted by the Containerized Microsoft Azure SQL Server.

```yaml
services:
  sql-server:
    image: "mcr.microsoft.com/azure-sql-edge:latest"
    container_name: compose.sql-server
    environment:
      - MSSQL_SA_PASSWORD=P@ssw0rD
      - ACCEPT_EULA=Y
    ports:
      - 1433:1433

  peoplewebapp:
    image: people.webapp
    container_name: compose.people.webapp
    build:
      context: .
      dockerfile: ./Dockerfile
      args:
        - configuration=Debug
    ports:
      - 83:5000
```

PART I Containerization

```
environment:
  - ASPNETCORE_ENVIRONMENT=Development
  - UseInMemoryDatabase=False
  - ConnectionStrings__PeopleDbConnection=Server=sql-server,1433;
      User=SA;Password=P@ssw0rD;Database=People-DB;TrustServerCertificate=True;
volumes:
  - ~/.vsdbg:/remote_debugger:rw
```

Comparing Listing 4-3 to 4-2, you'll notice I removed the `version` statement; it is now obsolete. Also, I supplemented the declaration of the multi-container solution by adding another service, `sql-server`. This service uses the latest version of the Docker image `mcr.microsoft.com/azure-sql-edge`, which is the official container image of Microsoft Azure SQL Edge. I chose this image because it is compatible with Apple Silicon (the architecture I am using to write this book). Additionally, this image is an optimized version of Microsoft SQL Server for Edge and IoT devices. Alternatively, if you are not using Apple Silicon, you can use mcr.microsoft.com/mssql/server instead.

In the above declaration, the container name is explicitly set to `compose.sql-server`. The `container_name` setting used for this purpose functions analogously to the --name option of the docker run command.

Next, the Microsoft Azure SQL Server container is configured using two environment variables: MSSQL_SA_PASSWORD and ACCEPT_EULA. The first variable allows you to set the database engine's system administrator (SA) password, which must be at least eight characters long and include at least one uppercase letter, one digit, or a symbol; otherwise, the container will not set up a database. The second environment variable (ACCEPT_EULA) is set to Y to confirm acceptance of the End-User Licensing Agreement (EULA).

The `sql-server` service maps the host's 1433 port to the container's 1433 port. Port 1433 is the default port on which SQL Server listens for requests.

With these settings in place, I modified the declaration of the `peoplewebapp` service by:

1. Changing the image name to `people.webapp`. Note that the listing does not explicitly use the image tag, so Docker will use the `latest` tag.

2. Setting the container name to `compose.people.webapp`.

3. Modifying the port mapping so that the People.WebApp, which listens on port 5000 inside the container, will be accessible on host port 83 (previous containers already use ports 80–82).

4. Updating the `PeopleDbConnection` string to point to the `sql-server service` with the line:

```
Server=sql-server,1433;User=SA;Password=P@ssw0rD;Database=People-DB;
    TrustServerCertificate=True;
```

The last step requires further discussion. Importantly, `PeopleDbConnection` is a nested JSON object under the `ConnectionStrings` key in `appsettings.json`. To modify the `PeopleDb Connection` using an environment variable, use the following construct: `ConnectionStrings__ PeopleDbConnection`. Nested objects are separated by a double underscore symbol.

To configure a connection string, you need to use the standard Connection String Syntax. For example, I used the Server property to point to the `sql-server` service on port 1433. (Remember, the database container is available to other containers by its service name.) Then, I specified the user as SA (System Administrator) and provided the SA's password, which was set earlier using the environment variable `MSSQL_SA_PASSWORD`. Subsequently, I specified the database name as `People-DB`. Finally, I used the `TrustServerCertificate` keyword to enable encrypted connections with the database server and to bypass certificate verification for validating server trust.

Running an app

Now, you can spin up the multi-container solution by typing (see Figure 4-11):

```
docker compose -f docker-compose.debug.yml up -d
```

This command uses a declaration from the docker-compose.debug.yml file to create both containers: one with the database server and the other with the People.WebApp. Note that the command explicitly indicates a declaration file using the **-f** option. If you omit this option, Docker Compose will look for the following configuration files in the local folder: compose.yaml, compose.yml, docker-compose.yaml, or docker-compose.yml. So, in this case, that would be docker-compose.yml, which Visual Studio Code automatically generated.

Then, the **up** command with an additional **-d** flag indicates that the containers should be instantiated in detached (background) mode. If you skip the **-d** flag, you will see the output of the containers in the command line.

```
● ● ●     People.WebApp — docker-compose · docker compose -f docker-compose.debug.yml up -d — 80×24
% docker compose -f docker-compose.debug.yml up -d
[+] Running 7/13
 ! peoplewebapp Warning    pull access denied for ...                    1.5s
 ⠋ sql-server [████ ██▒▒░] Pulling                                      10.3s
   ✔ c58359f0ed07 Pull complete                                          3.5s
   ✔ f9c126982b5c Pull complete                                          0.2s
   ✔ 589ba23f4d73 Pull complete                                          8.6s
   ⠋ 0c037bc6ac64 Downloading   35.67MB/470.5MB                         10.1s
   ✔ ce1f004ff642 Download complete                                      5.7s
   ✔ 4e0b1d630a9d Download complete                                      6.2s
   ⠋ cf712679c0f8 Downloading   36.75MB/64.58MB                         10.1s
   ✔ 7f5ed2ab3c5b Download complete                                      9.0s
   ⠋ 56e4c7793de3 Downloading   4.585MB/31.16MB                         10.1s
   ⠋ 89f8b7dcee44 Waiting                                               10.1s
   ⠋ 82fa393cf611 Waiting                                               10.1s
```

FIGURE 4-11 Running a multi-container solution.

When you invoke the **docker compose** command, you'll see Docker start by pulling the SQL Server container image (see Figure 4-11). Once this is done, Docker will begin building the people.webapp:latest image using a previously created Dockerfile. However, most build stages will be reused from the previous build as the People.WebApp source code didn't change.

When both images are ready, Docker will create a new network peoplewebapp_default, into which it deploys two containers: compose.people.webapp and compose.sql-server (see Figure 4-12).

```
                         People.WebApp — -zsh — 80×24
 => => transferring context: 383B                                          0.0s
 => [peoplewebapp build 1/7] FROM mcr.microsoft.com/dotnet/sdk:8.0@sha256   0.0s
 => [peoplewebapp base 1/2] FROM mcr.microsoft.com/dotnet/aspnet:8.0@sha2   0.0s
 => [peoplewebapp internal] load build context                             0.0s
 => => transferring context: 7.40kB                                        0.0s
 => CACHED [peoplewebapp build 2/7] WORKDIR /src                           0.0s
 => CACHED [peoplewebapp build 3/7] COPY [People.WebApp.csproj, ./]        0.0s
 => [peoplewebapp build 4/7] RUN dotnet restore "People.WebApp.csproj"    18.3s
 => [peoplewebapp build 5/7] COPY . .                                      0.1s
 => [peoplewebapp build 6/7] WORKDIR /src/.                                0.0s
 => [peoplewebapp build 7/7] RUN dotnet build "People.WebApp.csproj" -c D  3.5s
 => [peoplewebapp publish 1/1] RUN dotnet publish "People.WebApp.csproj"   1.3s
 => CACHED [peoplewebapp base 2/2] WORKDIR /app                            0.0s
 => CACHED [peoplewebapp final 1/2] WORKDIR /app                           0.0s
 => [peoplewebapp final 2/2] COPY --from=publish /app/publish .            0.1s
 => [peoplewebapp] exporting to image                                      0.1s
 => => exporting layers                                                    0.1s
 => => writing image sha256:5ca98000c1ceb4c1667713180a3587fa5aef2f7a73873  0.0s
 => => naming to docker.io/library/people.webapp                           0.0s
[+] Running 3/3
 ✓ Network peoplewebapp_default       Crea...                              0.0s
 ✓ Container compose.sql-server       Star...                              0.0s
 ✓ Container compose.people.webapp    S...                                 0.0s
%
```

FIGURE 4-12 Final output of the Docker Compose command.

Using the **docker network ls** command, you can verify that the new bridge network was created. Also, if you open the Images tab in Docker Desktop or type **docker images**, you will see two new images: mcr.microsoft.com/azure-sql-edge and people.webapp:latest. Finally, by going to the Containers tab of Docker Desktop (see Figure 4-13) or typing **docker ps**, you will see two additional containers running.

Testing a solution

To ensure that the multi-container solution works, open a web browser and navigate to localhost:83. You will then see the People.WebApp. Navigate to the People tab to verify that the application has successfully accessed SQL Server, created a database, and populated it with three records. Additionally, you can create new items (see Figure 4-14). Then, go to localhost:83/swagger to confirm that you can also access the web API (see Figure 4-15).

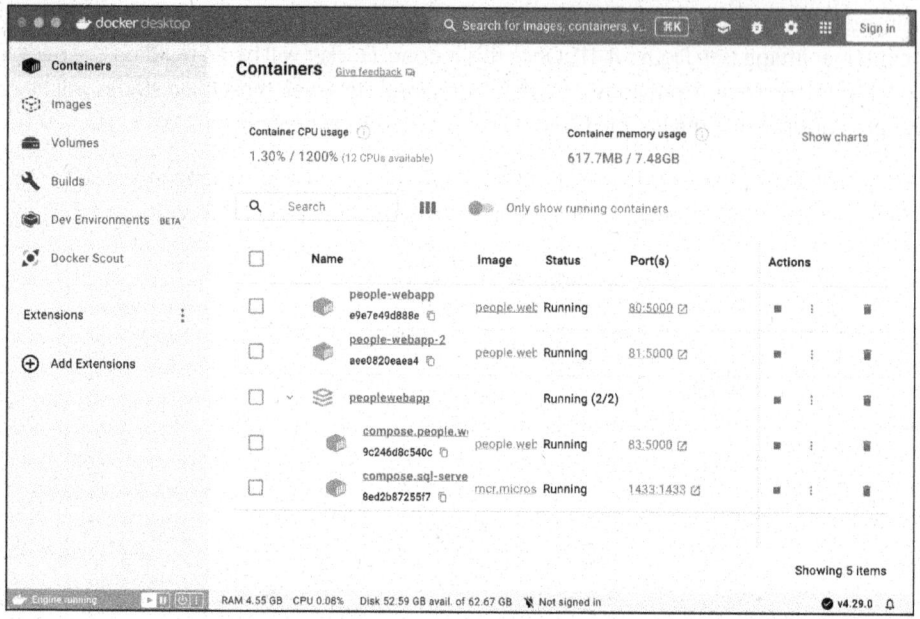

FIGURE 4-13 A list of running containers.

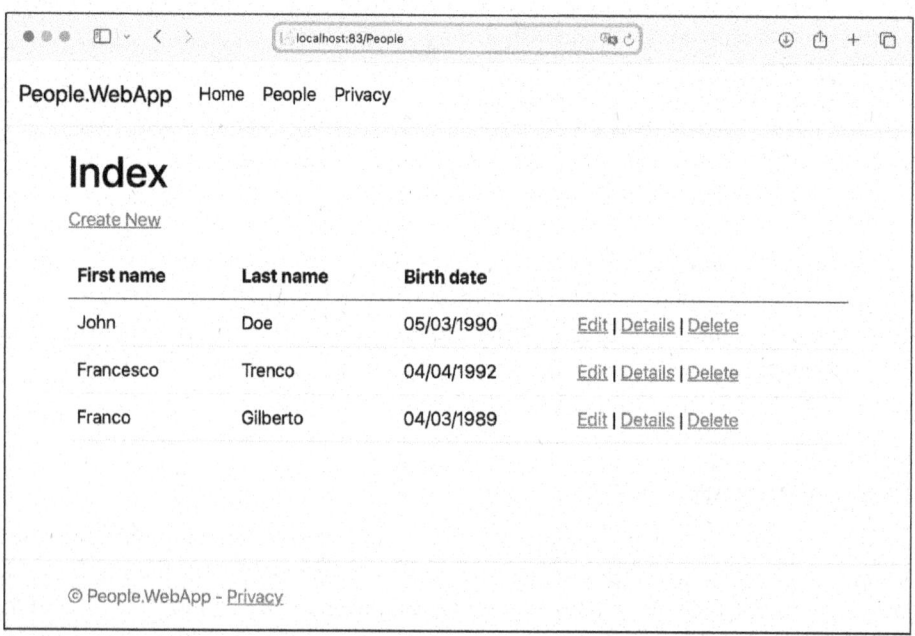

FIGURE 4-14 People.WebApp can now access the SQL Server database running in another container.

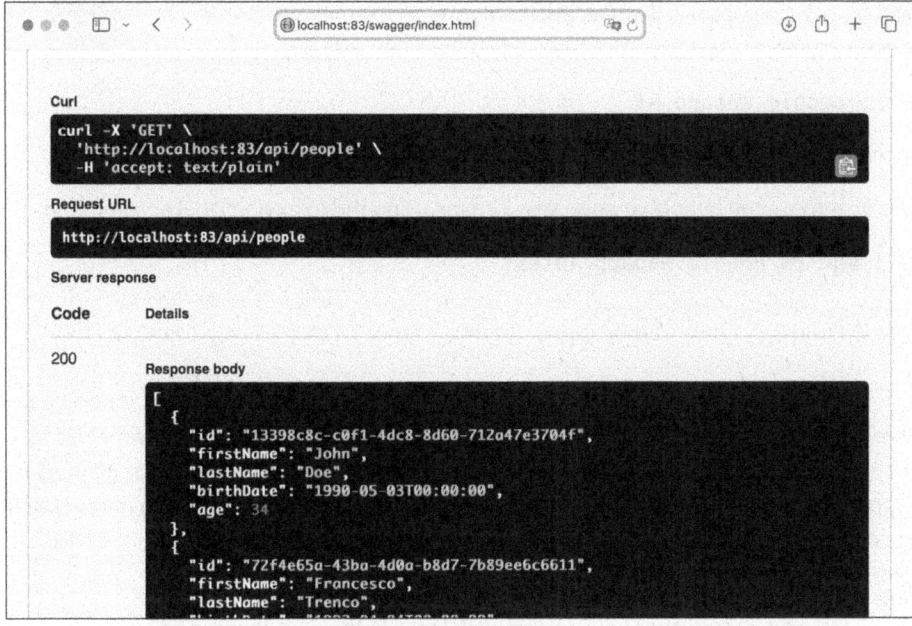

FIGURE 4-15 Retrieving the List of People Using a Web API.

Cleaning up

You just learned how to create and run a multi-container application using Docker Compose. The application comprised two containers (compose.people.webapp and compose.sql.server), which run in the background along with other containers you created in this chapter (people-webapp, people-webapp-2).

One advantage of spinning up multiple containers using Docker Compose is that you can stop them all with a single command:

```
docker compose -f docker-compose.debug.yml down
```

This command will stop and remove both containers and will also remove the network peoplewebapp_default (see Figure 4-16). Docker Compose provides much more control over your running solutions, which can be tailored to the specific needs of your project. For further customization, check the Docker Compose documentation.

```
% docker compose -f docker-compose.debug.yml down
[+] Running 3/3
 ✓ Container compose.sql-server        Remo...          10.1s
 ✓ Container compose.people.webapp     R...               0.1s
 ✓ Network peoplewebapp_default        Remo...            0.0s
```

FIGURE 4-16 Retrieving the list of people using a web API.

After removing the compose.sql-server and compose.people.webapp containers, also remove the other running containers to get ready for the next chapter. Simply type:

```
docker rm people-webapp -f
```

```
docker rm people-webapp-2 -f
```

Additionally, remove the people.webapp:latest image using the following Docker command:

```
docker image rm people.webapp:latest
```

Summary

In this chapter, you learned how to containerize an application and use environment variables to parameterize an app. You explored how environment variables can modify the settings of an ASP.NET Core application. Moreover, you learned how to use Docker Compose to create a multi-container application composed of a web application and a database server. You should now have a solid understanding of the most common Docker commands and feel confident in using Docker.

However, all the container images you created were local. In the next chapter, you will learn how to push them to a remote container repository hosted in the Azure Container Registry. By doing so, you will be able to deploy the People.WebApp to various services, including the Azure Kubernetes Service.

CHAPTER 5

Azure Container Registry

In the previous chapter, you created a Docker image of the People.WebApp, which is available in the local image repository. You will now learn how to push this image to a registry hosted in Azure Container Registry (ACR). By pushing the image to the container registry, you will enable two capabilities: You will be able to share the image with others, and you will be able to run the containerized People. WebApp application on other machines and in the cloud using various services, including Azure Container Instances, Azure App Service, or Azure Kubernetes Service.

The process you will learn in this chapter is a key element of the modern application development workflow (see Figure 5-1). Specifically, you'll learn how to push the container image to the container registry, which is step 5 of the outer loop in the DevOps cycles (discussed in Chapter 1, "Motivation").

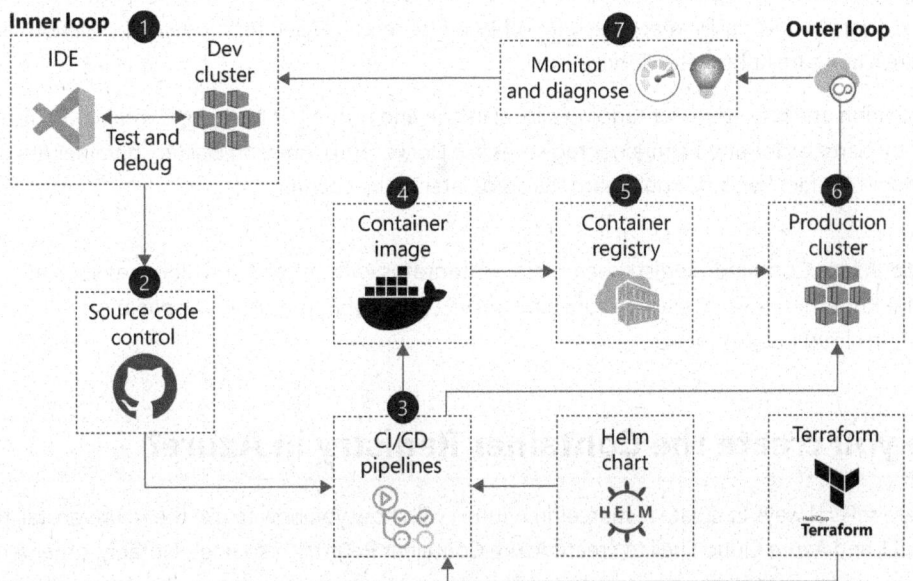

FIGURE 5-1 A workflow of modern application deployment.

In this chapter, you will manually push the container image. In Part III, "Automation," you will combine the push operation with container building and automate this procedure with the CI pipeline. Now, it's time to get to know the Azure Container Registry.

55

What is Azure Container Registry?

Azure Container Registry is a managed service that works with Docker, OCI images, and related components (like Helm charts) in Azure. When you provision an instance of the Azure Container Registry service, you create a container registry—a service for storing and distributing container images. Specifically, this service can contain several repositories, which are collections of images with the same name but different tags. A repository is created when you push a local image to a registry. To push an image to a registry, you need to tag your local image to include the fully qualified name of your domain name and a repository. In Azure Container Registry, the default domain names are formatted as **<acr-name>.azurecr.io**, where **<acr-name>** is the name of the provisioned container registry instance. An example of a fully qualified image tag (which includes the registry domain name and repository) is:

<acr-name>.azurecr.io/people.webapp:v1

Including a registry name in an image tag instructs Docker where to push your image.

Azure Container Registry includes all the necessary features for a container registry and provides additional tooling to manage a registry and repositories, including the Azure Command-Line Interface (Azure CLI). You can integrate Azure Container Registry with Entra ID to manage permissions and use ACR Tasks for automated builds of your images. Most importantly, Azure Container Registry provides a container registry that easily integrates with other Azure services used for modern application deployment, such as Azure Kubernetes Service.

In addition, the procedure for tagging a local image and pushing it to Azure Container Registry is almost the same as for other container registries like Docker Hub, Amazon Elastic Container Registry, and Google Artifact Registry. You'll learn the steps later in the chapter.

> **Note** Azure Container Registry seamlessly integrates with other Azure services such as Azure Kubernetes Service and Azure App Service, simplifying modern application deployment in cloud environments.

How do you create the Container Registry in Azure?

There are several ways to create resources in Azure. I will show you how to use the Azure portal, the Azure CLI, and Azure Cloud Shell to create Azure Container Registry resources. Notably, other Azure resources can be created in a similar manner. Thus, everything you learn here will serve as a foundation for creating other Azure resources in subsequent chapters.

Azure Portal

When you start working with Azure, you typically perform all your tasks in the Azure portal. It's a UI-based web application that provides quick access to various Azure services, video tutorials, and documentation. However, you may find that you need to perform many repetitive tasks. Consequently, you might prefer to switch to command line tools (like the Azure CLI or Azure Cloud Shell) to accelerate and automate your work.

To begin, I'll show you how to use the Azure portal to create an Azure Container Registry. Start by logging into the Azure portal at *portal.azure.com*. Then, in the search box, start typing **container registries**. When the filtered list of items appears, select Container Registries (see Figure 5-2).

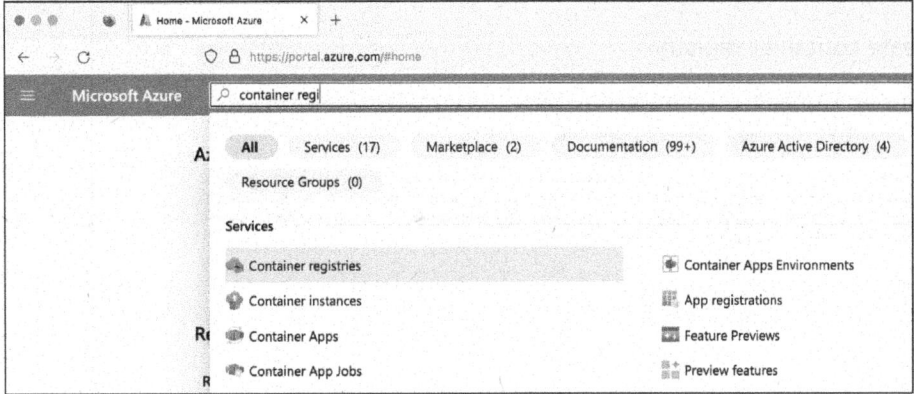

FIGURE 5-2 Looking up the Azure Container Registry service.

In the Container Registries window that appears, click the + Create hyperlink (see Figure 5-3) to open the Create Container Registry wizard.

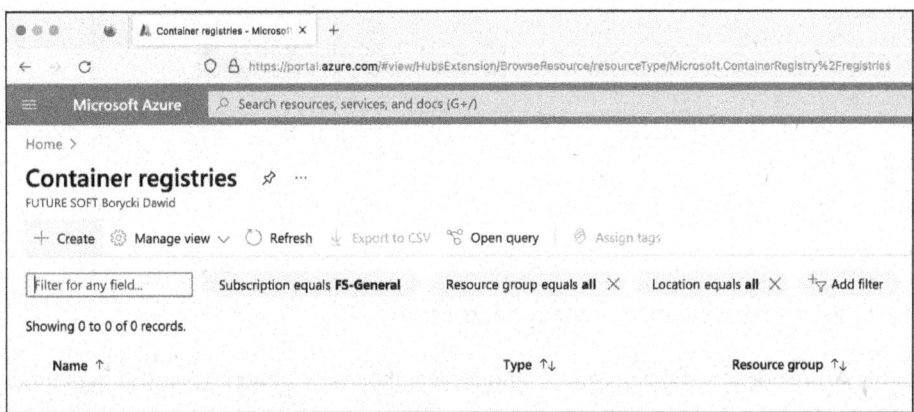

FIGURE 5-3 A list of container registries is initially empty.

In the wizard, perform the following steps (see Figure 5-4):

1. Use the Subscription dropdown list to select your subscription.

2. Click Create New, then create a new resource group named **rg-aks-people**.

3. For Registry Name, enter **people**. Note that this name must be globally unique as it is used to create a domain people.azurecr.io.

4. For Location, select East US (this is a suggested value; you can choose another Azure region).

5. For Pricing Plan, select Basic.

6. Click the Review + Create button.

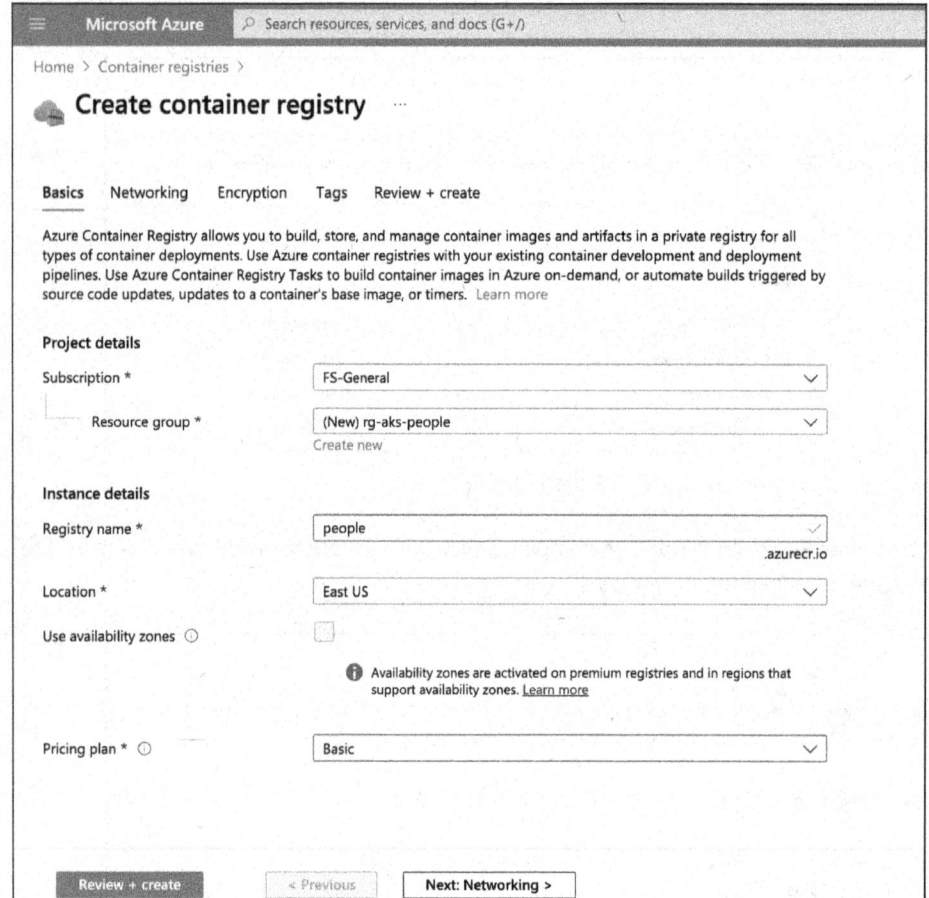

FIGURE 5-4 Provisioning an instance of the Azure Container Registry.

Wait for the Azure portal to validate your configuration, then click Create. This will initiate the process of creating your Azure Container Registry instance. After a few seconds, the new resource should be ready (see Figure 5-5).

Configuring the Azure resource was relatively straightforward. All you needed was a few configuration controls to specify the subscription, resource group, Azure region (the location of the data centers where the resource will be deployed), and additional service-specific parameters like the registry name and pricing plan tier.

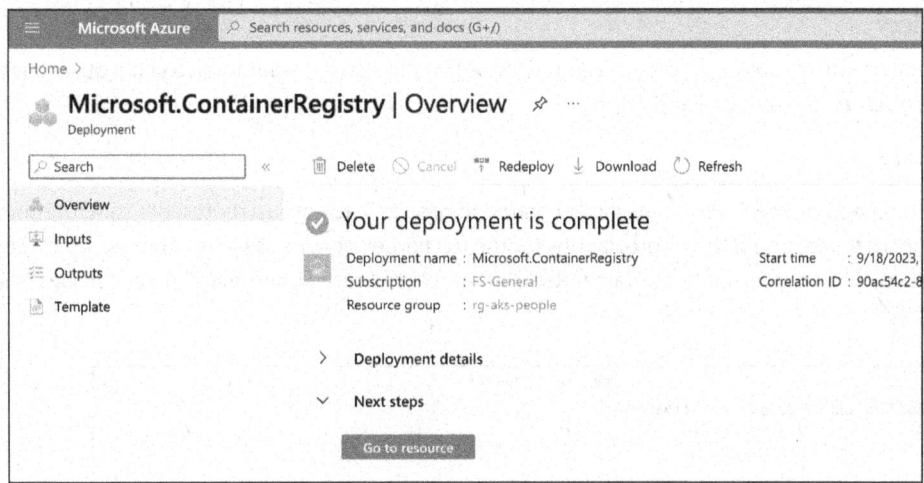

FIGURE 5-5 Confirmation of the successful creation of the container registry in Azure.

To create other Azure resources, you would follow a similar approach. Specifically, for almost all Azure services, you need to provide information about the subscription, resource group, and Azure region (see Figure 5-6).

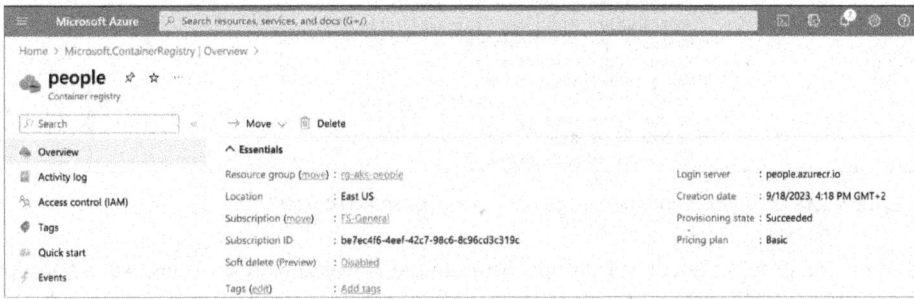

FIGURE 5-6 An overview of the people container registry.

Return to the container registry you just created and click the Go To Resource button on the resource creation confirmation page (Figure 5-5). An overview of this resource will be displayed (see Figure 5-6). This overview presents essential information about the resource, including its location, resource group, creation date, and more. For the following steps, you only need the login server containing the registry domain name required to tag a local image.

Azure CLI

Now that you know how to use the Azure portal to create Azure resources, take a look at how to achieve the same using the Azure CLI.

Overview

Before you use the Azure CLI to create a container registry in Azure, I want to give you a quick overview of this tool. Open the terminal and type:

az help

The command displays a list of available command groups. Each group represents an Azure service. The names of these groups are abbreviations for the full names of Azure services and resources. For example, you will see acr (Azure Container Registry) and aks (Azure Kubernetes Service) groups (see Figure 5-7).

```
Last login: Tue Sep 19 08:54:18 on ttys000
% az help

Group
    az

Subgroups:
    account             : Manage Azure subscription information.
    acr                 : Manage private registries with Azure Container Registries.
    ad                  : Manage Azure Active Directory Graph entities needed for Role Based
                          Access Control.
    advisor             : Manage Azure Advisor.
    afd        [Preview] : Manage Azure Front Door Standard/Premium. For classical
                          Azure Front Door, please refer https://docs.microsoft.com/en-
                          us/cli/azure/network/front-door?view=azure-cli-latest.
    aks                 : Manage Azure Kubernetes Services.
    ams                 : Manage Azure Media Services resources.
    apim                : Manage Azure API Management services.
    appconfig           : Manage App Configurations.
    appservice          : Manage App Service plans.
    aro                 : Manage Azure Red Hat OpenShift clusters.
    backup              : Manage Azure Backups.
    batch               : Manage Azure Batch.
    bicep               : Bicep CLI command group.
```

FIGURE 5-7 The Azure CLI enables you to manage Azure services and resources.

Some command groups contain subgroups. For example, the aks group includes two subgroups: command and nodepool (see Figure 5-8). After you specify the group and any optional command groups, you type the command (like **browse** or **create** as shown in Figure 5-8) along with any optional parameters. What does this mean in practice? I'll show you next.

```
% az aks --help

Group
    az aks : Manage Azure Kubernetes Services.

Subgroups:
    command             : See detail usage in 'az aks command invoke', 'az aks command
                          result'.
    nodepool            : Commands to manage node pools in Kubernetes kubernetes cluster.

Commands:
    browse              : Show the dashboard for a Kubernetes cluster in a web browser.
    check-acr           : Validate an ACR is accessible from an AKS cluster.
    create              : Create a new managed Kubernetes cluster.
    delete              : Delete a managed Kubernetes cluster.
```

FIGURE 5-8 Azure CLI Help.

First, you need to log in to Azure. To do so, use the following command to open a web browser where you can authenticate:

az login

After a successful login, you will see an output—a JSON-formatted string describing your subscription and containing user information. If your Azure account has more than one subscription, you must also invoke

azure account --set-subscription <subscription-id>

where ***<subscription-id>*** is the identifier of the subscription you want to use. To get a list of available subscriptions with their identifiers, type:

az account list -o table

Now, create a new resource group using the Azure CLI (see Figure 5-9):

az group create -n rg-cli -l eastus

The command creates a new resource group named rg-cli (specified by the **-n** parameter) and associates it with the default location of East US (specified by the **-l** parameter). The full command is structured such that **az** is followed by the command group related to resource groups (**group**), and the actual command (**create**). Then, it includes two parameters: **-n** for name and **-l** for location.

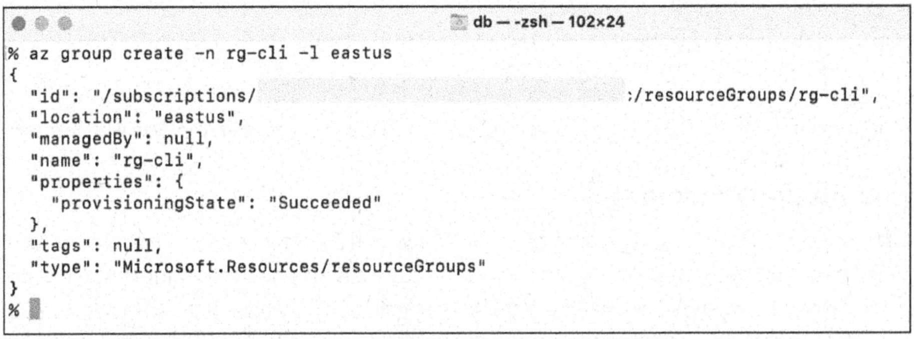

```
% az group create -n rg-cli -l eastus
{
  "id": "/subscriptions/                                    :/resourceGroups/rg-cli",
  "location": "eastus",
  "managedBy": null,
  "name": "rg-cli",
  "properties": {
    "provisioningState": "Succeeded"
  },
  "tags": null,
  "type": "Microsoft.Resources/resourceGroups"
}
%
```

FIGURE 5-9 Creating a resource group using the Azure Command-Line Interface.

Output format

The command output will be a JSON-formatted string containing the provisioning state, as shown in Figure 5-9. Although this format is convenient for machines, it is not easily readable for humans. Fortunately, the Azure CLI enables you to control the output format using the additional --output or -o parameter. To learn how to use this parameter, first list the resource groups by typing:

az group list

This command generates a JSON-formatted string representing a collection of JSON objects, each describing a resource group. In my case, the list contained two objects: one named rg-aks-people and the other named rg-cli.

To change the output to a more human-readable form, use the **-o** parameter and set it to table:

```
az group list -o table
```

The output will be much more concise and easily readable, as shown in Figure 5-10.

```
% az group list
[
  {
    "id": "/subscriptions/b                           319c/resourceGroups/rg-aks-people",
    "location": "eastus",
    "managedBy": null,
    "name": "rg-aks-people",
    "properties": {
      "provisioningState": "Succeeded"
    },
    "tags": null,
    "type": "Microsoft.Resources/resourceGroups"
  },
  {
    "id": "/subscriptions/b                           319c/resourceGroups/rg-cli",
    "location": "eastus",
    "managedBy": null,
    "name": "rg-cli",
    "properties": {
      "provisioningState": "Succeeded"
    },
    "tags": null,
    "type": "Microsoft.Resources/resourceGroups"
  }
]
%
% az group list -o table
Name           Location    Status
-------------  ----------  ---------
rg-aks-people  eastus      Succeeded
rg-cli         eastus      Succeeded
%
```

FIGURE 5-10 The output of the Azure CLI command without using the -o parameter (top) and with (bottom).

Querying the command output

The tabular format is suitable for getting a quick overview of the resources. However, JSON-formatted output is still beneficial for many automation scripts. In tutorials and documentation, you will often see Azure CLI commands supplemented by the **--query** parameter. This parameter executes a JMESPath query against the JSON-formatted output of the Azure CLI commands. Such JSON traversal enables you to efficiently extract relevant information from the entire command output. This information is typically passed to subsequent commands, building a chain of commands that help automate your deployment workflows.

To demonstrate how such JSON traversal works, try supplementing the **az group list** command with a query parameter that retrieves the second element from the JSON collection:

```
az group list --query "[1]"
```

The output is a single JSON object consisting of a collection of key-value pairs. To extract selected value or values, we use the following construct: "*.[key1,key2,...]*". For example, to extract only the name and location fields, type the following command:

```
az group list --query "[1].[name,location]"
```

This command outputs a two-dimensional array. You can further convert this output to a raw string with the **-o tsv** parameter:

```
az group list --query "[1].[name,location]" -o tsv
```

Queries can also contain filter operators. For instance, to display the locations of resource groups whose name contains the substring **'cli'**, you would use the following statement:

```
az group list -o table --query "[?contains(name, 'cli')].location"
```

All the above steps are summarized in Figure 5-11.

```
% az group list --query "[1]"
{
  "id": "/subscriptions/                              /resourceGroups/rg-cli",
  "location": "eastus",
  "managedBy": null,
  "name": "rg-cli",
  "properties": {
    "provisioningState": "Succeeded"
  },
  "tags": null,
  "type": "Microsoft.Resources/resourceGroups"
}
%
% az group list --query "[1].[name,location]"
[
  "rg-cli",
  "eastus"
]
%
% az group list --query "[1].[name,location]" -o tsv
rg-cli  eastus
%
```

FIGURE 5-11 The default output of the Azure CLI command is complex for humans to parse.

Create a container registry

You can now use what you've just learned about the Azure CLI to create a container registry with the same settings as the one you created via the Azure portal. To do so, use the following command:

```
az acr create -n peoplecli -g rg-cli --sku Basic -l eastus
```

This command creates a new container registry named peoplecli (specified by the **-n** parameter) in the resource group rg-cli (specified by the **-g** parameter). Additionally, the command deploys the resource to the East US Azure region (**-l** parameter) and sets the pricing tier to Basic (**--sku** parameter).

Similarly, as with listing the resource groups, you can retrieve a list of created container registries (see Figure 5-12):

```
az acr list -o table
```

This is helpful as you can quickly retrieve all the information you'll need to push your local Docker image to the remote repository hosted by the container registry.

```
% az acr list -o table
NAME        RESOURCE GROUP   LOCATION   SKU     LOGIN SERVER              CREATION DATE           ADMIN ENABLED
----------  ---------------  ---------  ------  ------------------------  ----------------------  -------------
people      rg-aks-people    eastus     Basic   people.azurecr.io         2023-09-18T14:18:08Z    False
peoplecli   rg-cli           eastus     Basic   peoplecli.azurecr.io      2023-09-21T12:22:45Z    False
%
```

FIGURE 5-12 A list of container registries.

Azure Cloud Shell

The third way to create registries is with Azure Cloud Shell, a convenient terminal available within the Azure portal. The significant advantage of Azure Cloud Shell is that it is browser-based, making it particularly useful if you cannot install the Azure CLI on your machine.

You use Azure Cloud Shell in the same way as the Azure CLI. However, you do not need to invoke az login anymore. Azure Cloud Shell uses the same credentials you use to log in to the Azure portal.

Azure Cloud Shell can be used with either Bash or PowerShell. Here, I will show you how to use Bash, so all the commands you used previously for the Azure CLI will be the same.

To begin, return to the Azure portal and click the Cloud Shell icon in the top-right corner (see Figure 5-13).

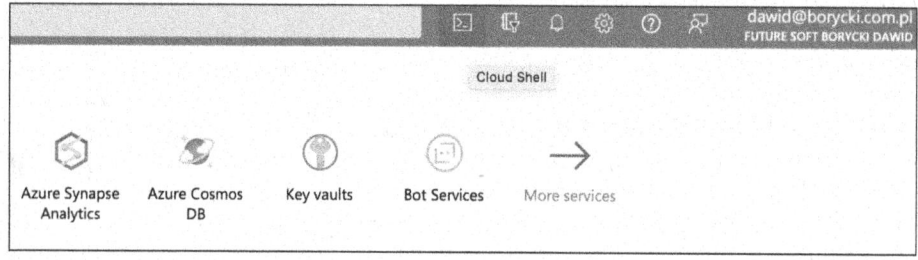

FIGURE 5-13 Accessing Azure Cloud Shell.

After you click the Cloud Shell icon, a new window titled You Have No Storage Mounted appears. Here you can configure the Azure storage account that will be used to persist files and command history. Select your subscription, and then click Create Storage. Next, select the Bash interpreter using the dropdown list in the top-left corner of the Azure Cloud Shell window. Then, you can start typing any command.

First, display the list of resource groups (see Figure 5-14) by typing:

`az group list -o table`

You now have an additional resource group, cloud-shell-storage-<location>, that was created automatically while Azure Cloud Shell was provisioning the underlying Azure Storage Account. You can experiment with other commands in Azure Cloud Shell to verify that everything you used previously for the Azure CLI will work the same way in Azure Cloud Shell. Try using commands with the **--query** parameter.

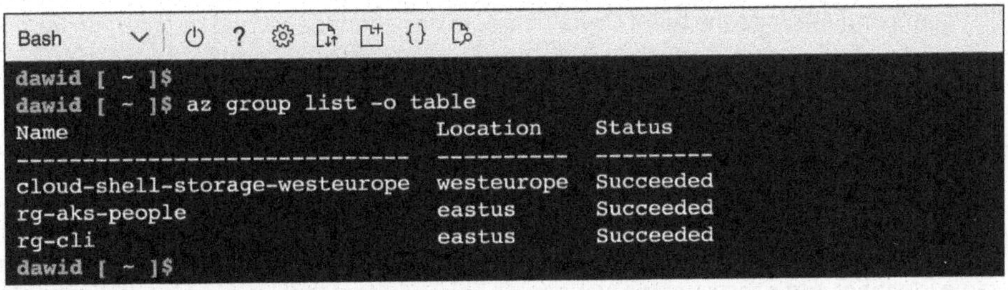

```
Bash           ⌄   ⏻  ?  ⚙  ⎘  ⎗  {}  ⎙
dawid [ ~ ]$
dawid [ ~ ]$ az group list -o table
Name                                Location      Status
----------------------------------  ------------  ---------
cloud-shell-storage-westeurope      westeurope    Succeeded
rg-aks-people                       eastus        Succeeded
rg-cli                              eastus        Succeeded
dawid [ ~ ]$
```

FIGURE 5-14 Azure Cloud Shell can invoke Azure CLI commands from a web browser.

Clean up

While learning about the Azure portal, the Azure CLI, and Azure Cloud Shell, you created two resource groups (the third one was created automatically) and two container registries. For the next steps, you will only need one container registry, so you can remove the peoplecli container registry. This container was deployed to the second resource group named rg-cli. Removing that resource group automatically removes all resources associated with this group (including peoplecli as shown in Figure 5-15).

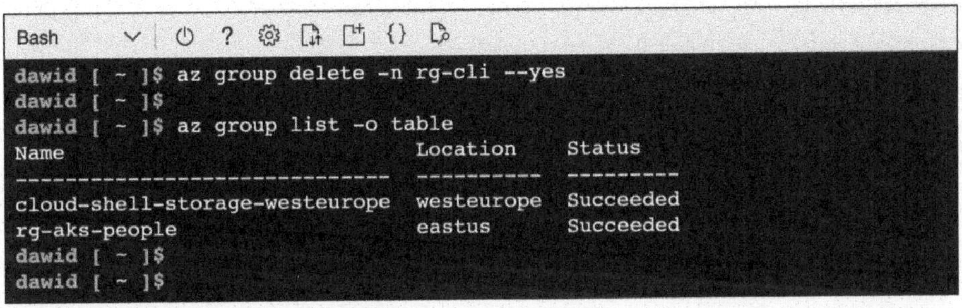

```
Bash           ⌄   ⏻  ?  ⚙  ⎘  ⎗  {}  ⎙
dawid [ ~ ]$ az group delete -n rg-cli --yes
dawid [ ~ ]$
dawid [ ~ ]$ az group list -o table
Name                                Location      Status
----------------------------------  ------------  ---------
cloud-shell-storage-westeurope      westeurope    Succeeded
rg-aks-people                       eastus        Succeeded
dawid [ ~ ]$
dawid [ ~ ]$
```

FIGURE 5-15 Removing a resource group.

To remove the rg-cli group, use either Azure Cloud Shell or the Azure CLI, where you type:

az group delete -n rg-cli --yes

The **--yes** (**-y**) parameter enables you to bypass the confirmation prompt. Sometimes resource deletion can take a while. In such cases, you may prefer to supplement the delete command with the **--no-wait** parameter.

How do you push a local image to the container registry?

You're now ready push the local image of the People.WebApp to the container registry. This requires accessing the local image using the login server of the container registry you created above, followed by a **docker push** command. To do so, open the terminal or command prompt and type:

az acr list -o table

docker images

The first command retrieves the list of container registries, then the second displays the list of local Docker images (see Figure 5-16). To facilitate subsequent commands in which you need to tag the people.webapp:v1 local image with the login server of the people container registry, type:

```
docker tag people.webapp:v1 people.azurecr.io/people.webapp:v1
```

This command does not yield any output. To confirm that you added the tag, re-display the list of local images using docker images. You will see a new item, people.azurecr.io/people.webapp:v1, which has the same identifier and size as people.webapp:v1. This indicates that both refer to the same Docker image. However, to let Docker know where it should push the local image, you need a fully qualified image name, which includes the container registry login server, container name, and a version label.

```
% az acr list -o table
NAME     RESOURCE GROUP   LOCATION   SKU     LOGIN SERVER        CREATION DATE           ADMIN ENABLED
------   --------------   --------   -----   ------------------  ----------------------  -------------
people   rg-aks-people    eastus     Basic   people.azurecr.io   2023-09-18T14:18:08Z    False
%
% docker images
REPOSITORY                            TAG         IMAGE ID        CREATED        SIZE
people.webapp                         v1          332880fd5c9f    4 days ago     285MB
mcr.microsoft.com/dotnet/samples      aspnetapp   f576507b938d    5 weeks ago    91.2MB
mcr.microsoft.com/azure-sql-edge      latest      9d0e27694fc9    7 months ago   1.84GB
%
% docker tag people.webapp:v1 people.azurecr.io/people.webapp:v1
%
% docker images
REPOSITORY                            TAG         IMAGE ID        CREATED        SIZE
people.webapp                         v1          332880fd5c9f    4 days ago     285MB
people.azurecr.io/people.webapp       v1          332880fd5c9f    4 days ago     285MB
mcr.microsoft.com/dotnet/samples      aspnetapp   f576507b938d    5 weeks ago    91.2MB
mcr.microsoft.com/azure-sql-edge      latest      9d0e27694fc9    7 months ago   1.84GB
%
%
```

FIGURE 5-16 Preparing a local image to be pushed to a remote repository.

To push the image, use the **docker push** command as follows:

```
docker push people.azurecr.io/people.webapp:v1
```

However, you will likely see the following message: "unauthorized: authentication required," as shown in Figure 5-17.

Before you can push an image, you need to log in to the container registry. There are several ways to authenticate to a container registry, as described in the Microsoft documentation. Here, you'll use an individual Entra ID identity—the same user you use to log in to the Azure portal and Azure CLI.

First, you need to configure role assignments for the container registry. To add a role assignment, use the following commands (see Figure 5-18):

```
USER_ID=$(az ad user show --id "<TYPE_YOUR_USER_NAME>" --query "id" -o tsv)

ACR_ID=$(az acr list --query "[?contains(name, 'people')].id" -o tsv)

az role assignment create --assignee $USER_ID --role AcrPush --scope $ACR_ID
```

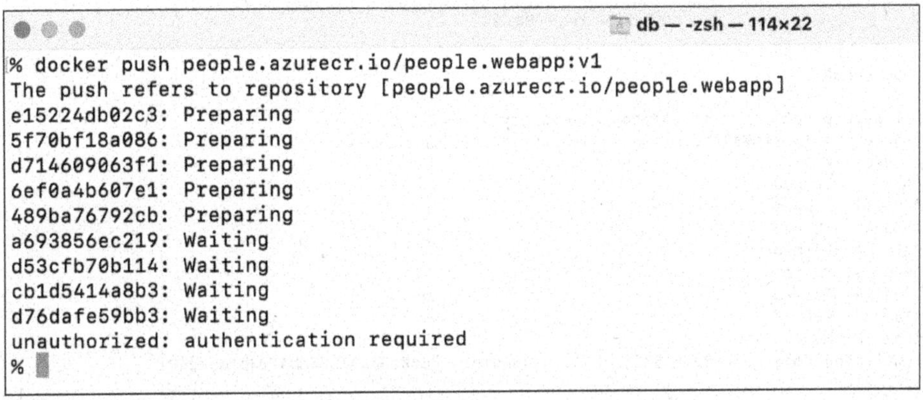

```
% docker push people.azurecr.io/people.webapp:v1
The push refers to repository [people.azurecr.io/people.webapp]
e15224db02c3: Preparing
5f70bf18a086: Preparing
d714609063f1: Preparing
6ef0a4b607e1: Preparing
489ba76792cb: Preparing
a693856ec219: Waiting
d53cfb70b114: Waiting
cb1d5414a8b3: Waiting
d76dafe59bb3: Waiting
unauthorized: authentication required
%
```

FIGURE 5-17 Pushing an image requires authentication.

The first command retrieves the unique identifier (ID) of an Entra ID user. It uses the Azure CLI command az ad user show to display properties of a specific user identified by **--id**, which should be replaced by the actual username or user ID. The **--query "id"** option filters the output to show only the user ID. The **-o tsv** option formats the output as plain text, without headers, and stores this value in the **USER_ID** variable.

The second command lists all Azure Container Registries and filters them to find a registry whose name contains the substring '**people**'. It extracts the ID of this registry using the **--query** option, which is then formatted as plain text and stored in the **ACR_ID** variable.

The last command assigns the built-in role **AcrPush**, which allows the user to push images to the container registry. This setup ensures that the specified user now has push permissions for the designated Azure Container Registry.

The output of the last command will look like Figure 5-18.

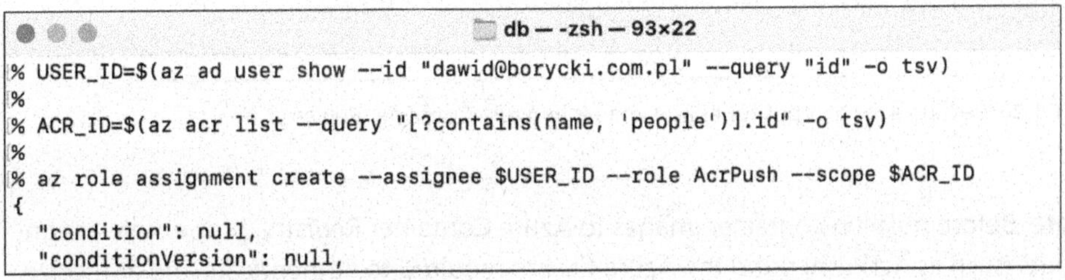

```
% USER_ID=$(az ad user show --id "dawid@borycki.com.pl" --query "id" -o tsv)
%
% ACR_ID=$(az acr list --query "[?contains(name, 'people')].id" -o tsv)
%
% az role assignment create --assignee $USER_ID --role AcrPush --scope $ACR_ID
{
  "condition": null,
  "conditionVersion": null,
```

FIGURE 5-18 Creating the role assignment.

You can now invoke the **az acr login** command to log in to the container registry:

```
az acr login -n people
```

This command invokes the Docker login command, and you should see the "Login Succeeded" message (see Figure 5-19):

```
docker push people.azurecr.io/people.webapp:v1
```

```
% az acr login -n people
Login Succeeded
%
% docker push people.azurecr.io/people.webapp:v1
The push refers to repository [people.azurecr.io/people.webapp]
e15224db02c3: Pushed
5f70bf18a086: Pushed
d714609063f1: Pushed
6ef0a4b607e1: Pushed
489ba76792cb: Pushed
a693856ec219: Pushed
d53cfb70b114: Pushed
cb1d5414a8b3: Pushed
d76dafe59bb3: Pushed
v1: digest: sha256:67903ec87f4987265cb46ea4fc34dfdf4c36c0c86a51225db47e3bfd5ed49
d00 size: 2203
%
%
```

FIGURE 5-19 Pushing a local docker image to Azure Container Registry.

You also created a new repository, people.webapp, in the people container registry by pushing an image. To see the list of repositories, use the following Azure CLI command:

az acr repository list -n people -o table

To retrieve a list of container images in the given repository type the following command (see Figure 5-20):

az acr repository show -n people --repository people.webapp -o table

```
% az acr repository list -n people -o table
Result
--------------
people.webapp
%
%
% az acr repository show -n people --repository people.webapp -o table
CreatedTime                    ImageName       LastUpdateTime                 ManifestCount    Registry             TagCount
-----------------------------  --------------  -----------------------------  ---------------  -------------------  ----------
2023-09-26T21:02:25.5341057Z   people.webapp   2023-09-26T21:02:25.6186937Z   1                people.azurecr.io    1
%
%
%
```

FIGURE 5-20 Getting a list of repositories and images in Azure Container Registry.

> **Note** Before pushing container images to Azure Container Registry, proper role assignments (such as AcrPush) using the Azure CLI are required to authenticate and authorize users securely.

Summary

In this chapter, you learned how to use the Azure portal, the Azure CLI, and Azure Cloud Shell to create and manage resources in Microsoft Azure. Then, you used this knowledge to create a container registry, into which you pushed a local Docker image of the People.WebApp.

PART II

Container Orchestration

CHAPTER 6 Container Orchestration with Kubernetes 71
CHAPTER 7 Azure Kubernetes Service 83
CHAPTER 8 Azure SQL Database and Azure Key Vault 97
CHAPTER 9 Diagnosing and Monitoring the Cluster 115
CHAPTER 10 Application Rollouts and Rollbacks............. 127

In Part I, you learned why containers are necessary for modern application development and deployment. This part of the book takes you to the next level, where you'll learn about container orchestration. A *container orchestration tool* is a software platform that simplifies the running and management of distributed systems composed of hundreds of containers. These containers must run across many virtual machines, either deployed on-premises or in cloud environments.

I will use Kubernetes, the open-source and most popular orchestration platform, to demonstrate how to deploy containerized applications with container orchestrators. Specifically, you will learn how to use a local Development Kubernetes cluster (step 1 in Figure 5-1) and then how to deploy the containerized application from the container registry to the production Kubernetes cluster running in the cloud within the Azure Kubernetes

Service (steps 5 and 6 from Figure 5-1). Finally, you'll learn to monitor the containerized application deployed to the cluster (step 7 in Figure 5-1). Steps 2–4 from the diagram in Figure 5-1 will still be manual for now, but you can look forward to learning how to automate them in Part III.

CHAPTER 6

Container Orchestration with Kubernetes

You already know how to containerize applications, run, and manage Docker containers. You also understand the advantages of using containers for application bundling. However, running containers can be subject to the same problems you face with non-containerized applications. Specifically, containers can become unresponsive or even crash. In such cases, you must kill and restart the Docker containers. Currently, Docker doesn't provide a built-in solution for automatic container restarts, so you would need to monitor and restart them manually.

Additionally, if demand increases, you need to scale the application yourself by starting additional containers. Another practical challenge is updating an application or service. Updates should be performed in a way that ensures no downtime. You could achieve this by spinning up containers using a new image version, redirecting your users to the newly created containers, and then shutting down the unnecessary ones. However, this would require many manual operations.

This is where Kubernetes comes into play. It provides a framework for running containerized distributed applications resiliently. Kubernetes can automatically distribute containers among available compute nodes, scale the application's components (by controlling the number of container instances), update your applications, monitor the state of your containers, and restart them when needed.

For these reasons, Kubernetes is sometimes called "the operating system of the internet." It acts like an operating system by assigning hardware resources to containers, starting and stopping them, and providing shared services (like access to shared volumes or a secret store) to containers running in the cluster. These features are foundational to all modern operating systems.

Kubernetes is an open-source platform that helps manage and run containerized workloads and services. Kubernetes was initially developed by Google, because it was deploying many containerized distributed systems and needed a tool for automating and managing these deployments.

The name "Kubernetes" originates from the Greek, meaning "helmsman" or "pilot." This name underscores that Kubernetes serves as the helmsman steering the ship that carries the containers.

What is Kubernetes?

Kubernetes (also called k8s) is a container orchestrator created to simplify running a vast number of containers on many physical or virtual machines. To achieve this goal, Kubernetes automates the manual tasks typically required to deploy and manage containerized applications.

A Kubernetes *cluster* is created upon deployment. At a high level, the cluster comprises the control plane and nodes. The *control plane* makes global decisions about the cluster, such as scheduling containers on specific nodes and responding to cluster events, like replicating a container to scale the application. *Nodes* are the physical (on-premises) or virtual machines (in the cloud) that run the containers using a container runtime, such as Docker.

Using a declarative approach, you can instruct Kubernetes to deploy specific containers on designated machines (for example, instructing k8s to run a container on a GPU-powered machine) and monitor containers for failover. Kubernetes also enables you to define health checks for containers—known as readiness and liveness probes. A *readiness probe* specifies whether a container is ready to serve clients, while a *liveness probe* indicates whether the container is still functioning. Kubernetes does not route client requests to non-ready containers, which might require more time to initiate. It will automatically restart containers that fail the liveness probes.

Kubernetes efficiently manages the scaling of your deployed application by adjusting the actual state of your deployment to the desired state. For instance, if you specify that you want 10 instances of a specific container, Kubernetes will launch and maintain them until you modify the desired state. If two of those 10 containers fail, Kubernetes will automatically restart them. If you decide to reduce the number of desired container replicas to five, Kubernetes will adjust accordingly.

Kubernetes enables application updates without downtime. In a manual update scenario, you would spin up a container using an updated image, redirect traffic to the new container, and then shut down the old container. This process requires manual effort, especially for applications with many services or frequent updates. Kubernetes automates this with a single command for automated rollout and provides automated rollback to revert to previous versions if needed.

Furthermore, Kubernetes allows you to specify the CPU and memory (RAM) requirements for each container. Based on this information, it automatically deploys containers across available nodes, effectively managing resources.

Kubernetes also offers service discovery and load balancing. If you were running multiple instances of the same application manually using Docker, you would need to configure port mappings for each container instance and inform clients of these ports. Kubernetes simplifies this by exposing containers via DNS names or their IP addresses within the cluster. It provides a service that treats a group of containers as a single entity, enabling clients and dependent services to access your horizontally scaled application via a DNS name or IP address. Kubernetes also balances and distributes network traffic across available containers to ensure deployment stability.

In terms of storage, Kubernetes facilitates storage orchestration. You can mount a storage system of your choice to make it available to containers within the cluster. Like Docker volumes, this storage data is preserved across container restarts. Kubernetes supports both local and cloud storage services, such as Azure Disks and Azure Files, through the Azure File CSI Driver.

Lastly, Kubernetes supports secret and configuration management. It allows you to securely store and manage the credentials, tokens, and SSH keys your applications use to connect to other services. This centralized secret management system helps you deploy and update secrets and configuration settings without rebuilding your container images or exposing sensitive data.

While Kubernetes offers numerous advantages, it does not solve all problems related to modern application development and deployment. It does not provide built-in continuous integration/continuous deployment (CI/CD) pipelines, monitoring, alerting, or logging tools. It also does not include storage services, caching mechanisms, or any specific programming runtimes or middleware. Importantly, Kubernetes does not impose any restrictions on programming languages, making it compatible with any technology that supports containerization.

Therefore, you still need other tools to build the application and deploy the resulting container images to a container registry, as well as separate solutions for monitoring and alerting.

Kubernetes architecture

As mentioned, the Kubernetes cluster comprises the control plane and nodes (Figure 6-1). The nodes can be physical or virtual machines. Internally, Kubernetes, like Docker, uses a client-server architecture. However, Kubernetes deploys more general objects called Pods. A *Pod* is a group of containers that share storage and network resources with nodes. Thus, a Pod can be thought of similarly to the multi-container application created with Docker Compose.

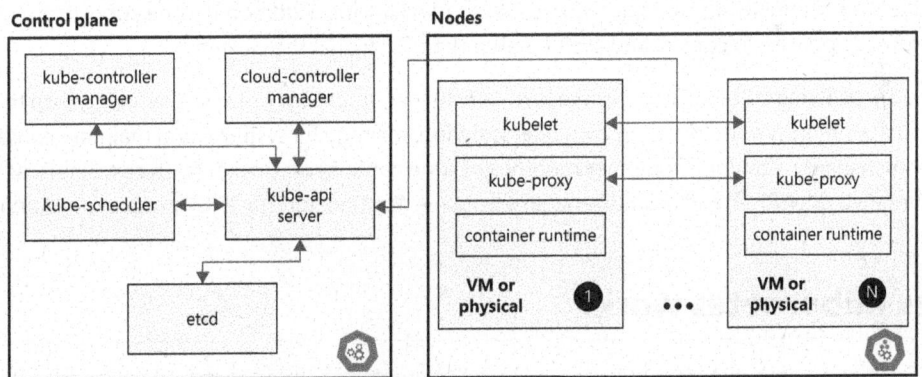

FIGURE 6-1 Architecture of the Kubernetes cluster.

To configure the cluster and deploy applications, you use the Kubernetes API, which is exposed by the kube-api server. This server interacts with other control plane components, including the kube-scheduler, kube-controller-manager, etcd, and cloud-controller-manager.

The kube-scheduler is responsible for assigning Pods to available nodes based on the hardware resources known to the scheduler.

The kube-controller-manager runs control loops that periodically check the state of the cluster against the desired state. If there is a discrepancy, the control loops update the cluster's state. Kubernetes implements several control loops, each responsible for a specific part of the cluster, all running under the same process for convenience.

A key-value store, the etcd holds the cluster data and is designed to support persistent, multi-version declarative configurations. It is optimized for infrequent updates and reliable queries that multiple control loops can concurrently access. When a new state is declared, the etcd does not modify the previous state but instead creates a new version, with all versions accessible to the control loops.

The cloud-controller-manager incorporates cloud-specific control logic. Its primary function is to link the Kubernetes cluster to the cloud provider's API, segregating the elements that interface with the cloud from those that interact solely with the cluster.

The cloud-controller-manager operates controllers specific to the cloud provider under a single process, similar to the kube-controller-manager. If you are running Kubernetes on your own on-premises infrastructure, a cloud-controller-manager is not necessary in your cluster.

Each node in the Kubernetes cluster contains the following components: a kubelet, a kube-proxy, and a container runtime.

The kubelet manages containers created by Kubernetes. It communicates with the control plane to obtain Pod specifications and report on the node's status, including its hardware resources. Given the Pod specifications, the kubelet pulls required container images, runs them, ensures they are healthy, and manages resources and volumes attached to the Pods.

The kube-proxy provides network connectivity to and between Pods and other services in the Kubernetes cluster. It manages service discovery by maintaining a list of Pods and their IP addresses and distributes incoming traffic among the Pods for load balancing. Additionally, the kube-proxy can enforce network policies to control and secure network traffic within the cluster.

Finally, the container runtime handles the low-level management of containers, working with the underlying operating system to ensure container isolation, manage filesystems, and maintain container network connectivity. Common container runtimes include containerd, Docker (with containerd as its default runtime), rkt, CRI-O, and any Kubernetes Container Runtime Interface (CRI) implementation.

How does Kubernetes work?

Figure 6-2 offers a single-picture explanation of how Kubernetes operates, sketched by Brendan Burns, one of the original creators of Kubernetes.

You start with the container image (the img square, top-left corner Figure 6-2), then use this image to create a Deployment. This Deployment is the declarative description of the desired state of your application, typically defined in the YAML format (the deploy.yaml file in the top-right corner).

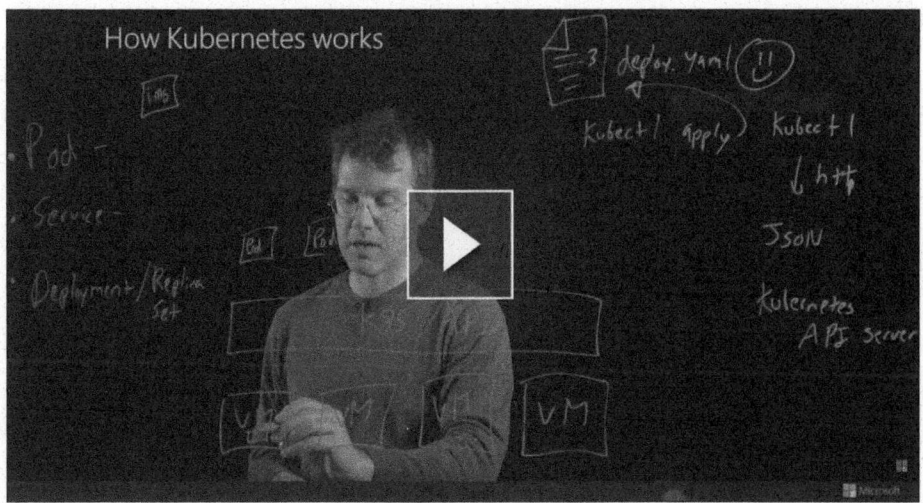

FIGURE 6-2 A single image explaining how Kubernetes works.

A Deployment provides the specification for the Pod and ReplicaSet. Kubernetes uses these declarations to create Pods (Pod specification) and ensures the desired number of Pods runs in the cluster (ReplicaSet). Therefore, the deployment declaration typically includes elements such as:

- The container image used to spin up containers,
- The number of container instances (container replicas),
- Ports on which containers will listen for incoming requests.

Once the Pods are deployed to the cluster, you create a Service. This Service is a network abstraction component that allows you to expose the Pod to other Pods, services, or external clients.

After creating the declaration file that describes the desired state of your workload, you send this information to the Kubernetes API Server (kube-api server). To simplify this process, Kubernetes provides kubectl, a command-line tool that enables you to interact with the kube-api server. For example, if your deploy.yaml file contains the declaration for the Deployment and a Service, you use a single command, **kubectl apply -f deploy.yaml**, to provide Kubernetes with the workload declaration. Then, the kube-api server communicates with other cluster components to deploy the workload and run the Pods on the available nodes, denoted as VM blocks in the bottom center of Figure 6-2.

Local Kubernetes cluster

Now that you are familiar with the Kubernetes architecture and understand how it works, you're ready to put this knowledge into practice by deploying an application to a local Kubernetes cluster. To start the local Kubernetes cluster, you will use Docker Desktop. Open it, and then click the Settings icon (top-right corner, next to the Sign In button). In the Settings menu, navigate to the Kubernetes tab. Select the Enable Kubernetes checkbox, and then click Apply & Restart (Figure 6-3).

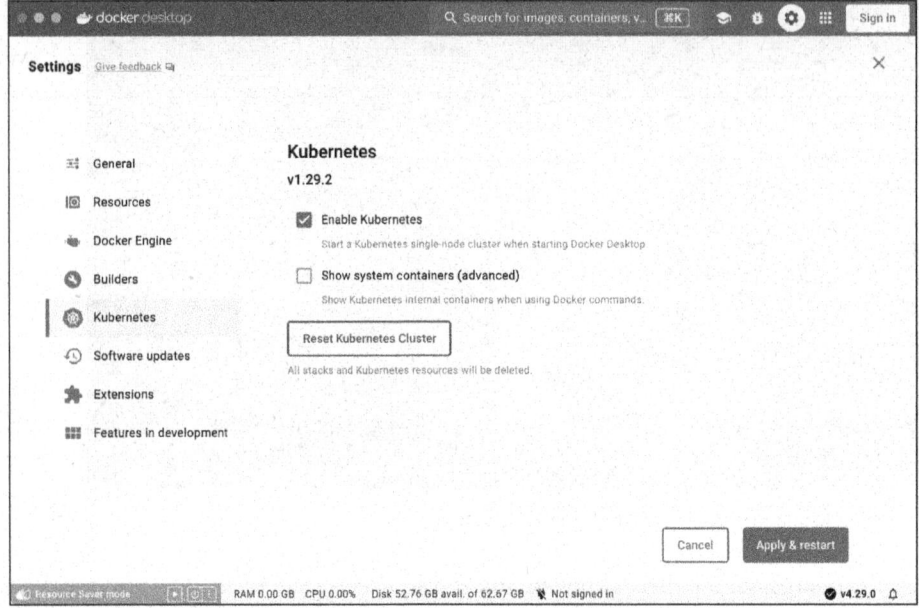

FIGURE 6-3 Setting up a local Kubernetes cluster in Docker Desktop.

In the Kubernetes Cluster Installation pop-up window that appears, confirm the installation by clicking Install (Figure 6-4).

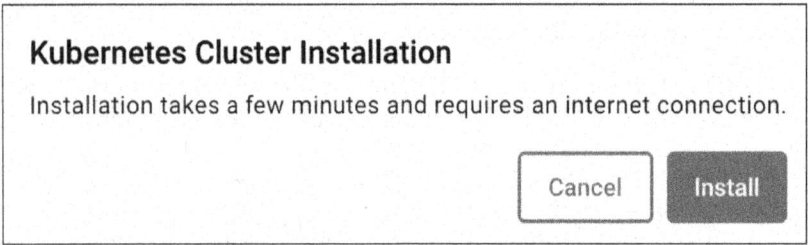

FIGURE 6-4 Installing the Kubernetes cluster in Docker Desktop.

Setting up the local Kubernetes cluster takes a few moments. When it's finished, Docker Desktop will display an additional status window for the Kubernetes cluster in the bottom-left corner. Docker Desktop uses several Docker images to create the Kubernetes cluster:

- registry.k8s.io/kube-apiserver
- registry.k8s.io/kube-scheduler
- registry.k8s.io/kube-controller-manager
- registry.k8s.io/kube-proxy
- registry.k8s.io/etcd

These images contain the Kubernetes components previously discussed. You will use kubectl to communicate with the cluster.

kubectl

The local Kubernetes cluster you created using Docker Desktop is now ready. Also, kubectl is configured to communicate with this cluster. Generally, you can use kubectl to interact with various clusters by configuring the connection using the **kubectl config** command. For example, to retrieve information about the current cluster, type:

kubectl config current-context

In response, you will see a message confirming your connection to the Kubernetes cluster created with Docker Desktop (see Figure 6-5).

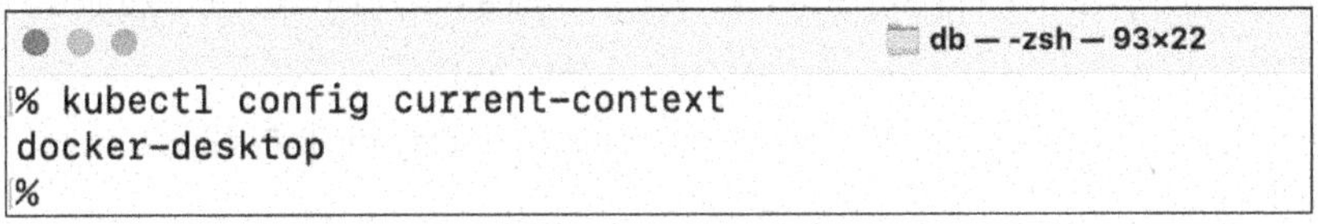

```
% kubectl config current-context
docker-desktop
%
```

FIGURE 6-5 Retrieving the current context with kubectl.

Next, display the list of nodes by typing:

kubectl get nodes

In Figure 6-6, the nodes list contains just a single element, indicating the example cluster has only one node named docker-desktop. This node is the host machine used to run Docker Desktop.

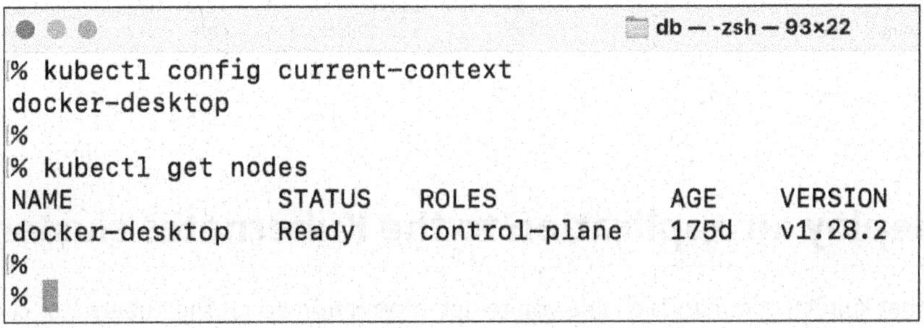

```
% kubectl config current-context
docker-desktop
%
% kubectl get nodes
NAME              STATUS    ROLES           AGE    VERSION
docker-desktop    Ready     control-plane   175d   v1.28.2
%
%
```

FIGURE 6-6 Displaying the list of nodes.

Now, try displaying a list of all Pods running in the cluster. To do so, use the following command:

kubectl get pods --all-namespaces

The **--all-namespaces** flag ensures that kubectl displays Pods from all namespaces. Kubernetes uses namespaces to logically group various workloads. Core Kubernetes components are deployed under the kube-system namespace (see Figure 6-7).

```
% kubectl config current-context
docker-desktop
%
% kubectl get nodes
NAME             STATUS   ROLES          AGE    VERSION
docker-desktop   Ready    control-plane  175d   v1.28.2
%
% kubectl get pods --all-namespaces
NAMESPACE     NAME                                     READY   STATUS    RESTARTS   AGE
kube-system   coredns-5dd5756b68-57v75                 1/1     Running   0          175d
kube-system   coredns-5dd5756b68-m6wqf                 1/1     Running   0          175d
kube-system   etcd-docker-desktop                      1/1     Running   0          175d
kube-system   kube-apiserver-docker-desktop            1/1     Running   0          175d
kube-system   kube-controller-manager-docker-desktop   1/1     Running   0          175d
kube-system   kube-proxy-4j98q                         1/1     Running   0          175d
kube-system   kube-scheduler-docker-desktop            1/1     Running   0          175d
kube-system   storage-provisioner                      1/1     Running   0          175d
kube-system   vpnkit-controller                        1/1     Running   0          175d
%
```

FIGURE 6-7 Retrieving a list of all Pods.

There is a default namespace used by Kubernetes if you deploy a workload without explicitly specifying the namespace.

To complement this discussion, use the following command to display the list of all services deployed in your cluster:

`kubectl get svc --all-namespaces`

You will see two services: kubernetes and kube-dns. The kubernetes service provides access to the kube-api-server for other workloads running inside the cluster, while kube-dns allows services to be accessed by their names (see Figure 6-8).

```
% kubectl get svc --all-namespaces
NAMESPACE     NAME         TYPE        CLUSTER-IP   EXTERNAL-IP   PORT(S)                  AGE
default       kubernetes   ClusterIP   10.96.0.1    <none>        443/TCP                  175d
kube-system   kube-dns     ClusterIP   10.96.0.10   <none>        53/UDP,53/TCP,9153/TCP   175d
%
```

FIGURE 6-8 A list of services in the cluster.

How do you deploy an application to the Kubernetes cluster?

You just learned that kubectl commands enable you to get information about the Kubernetes cluster and the workloads running inside it. Next, you will use kubectl to deploy the containerized People. WebApp application using the Docker image you prepared in Chapter 4 (people.webapp:v1).

To deploy the application, you will use two YAML declarations. First, you will use the Deployment, whose declaration is shown in Listing 6-1.

LISTING 6-1 A Declaration of the Deployment for the People.WebApp.

```yaml
apiVersion: apps/v1
kind: Deployment
metadata:  name: people-webapp-deployment
spec:
  replicas: 2
  selector:
      matchLabels:
          app: people-webapp
  template:
      metadata:
        labels:
            app: people-webapp
      spec:
        containers:
        - name: people-webapp
          image: people.webapp:v1
          ports:
          - containerPort: 5000
```

The above declaration will create a Deployment named `people-webapp-deployment` (`metadata.name` field). The Deployment will roll out a ReplicaSet, which ensures that two Pods are running (see `replicas` field under `spec`). To find the Pods to be managed and monitored, the ReplicaSet uses the `selector` field. Here, the Pods will be matched using the label `people-webapp`, defined under the `template` field. Moreover, the template contains the Pod specification. In this case, the Pod specification includes only one `people-webapp` container. This container will be spun up using the `people.webapp:v1` Docker image. Finally, the app inside the container will listen for requests on port 5000.

To create the Deployment, use the following command:

kubectl apply -f https://raw.githubusercontent.com/dawidborycki/↵

     People.WebApp.Declarations/main/Kubernetes/people_deployment.yml

The command outputs: "deployment.apps/people-webapp-deployment created." To see the list of Pods created by this Deployment, type:

kubectl get pods

The result is a list of two Pods, as shown in Figure 6-9.

```
% kubectl apply -f https://raw.githubusercontent.com/dawidborycki/People.WebApp.D
eclarations/main/Kubernetes/people_deployment.yml

deployment.apps/people-webapp-deployment created
%
% kubectl get pods
NAME                                          READY   STATUS    RESTARTS   AGE
people-webapp-deployment-755cc567db-jsnnk     1/1     Running   0          14s
people-webapp-deployment-755cc567db-rhc4m     1/1     Running   0          14s
%
```

FIGURE 6-9 Creating a Deployment and retrieving the list of Pods.

This confirms that the application is running inside the cluster. Each Pod has been assigned a local IP address within the cluster's network. Confirm this by typing:

```
kubectl describe pod <pod-name>
```

where you replace the **<pod-name>** with the actual Pod name assigned by the Kubernetes. In my case that is people-webapp-deployment-755cc567db-jsnnk or people-webapp-deployment-755cc567db-rhc4m (see Figure 6-9).

After invoking the **kubectl describe pod** command, you will see a detailed description of the Pod, as shown in Figure 6-10.

```
% kubectl describe pod people-webapp-deployment-755cc567db-rhc4m
Name:             people-webapp-deployment-755cc567db-rhc4m
Namespace:        default
Priority:         0
Service Account:  default
Node:             docker-desktop/192.168.65.3
Start Time:       Wed, 08 May 2024 09:15:25 +0200
Labels:           app=people-webapp
                  pod-template-hash=755cc567db
Annotations:      <none>
Status:           Running
IP:               10.1.0.63
IPs:
  IP:             10.1.0.63
Controlled By:    ReplicaSet/people-webapp-deployment-755cc567db
Containers:
  people-webapp:
    Container ID:   docker://f419bcf1e2babddc5507837631dac39c1ed24503a0b7bb1e362baab35b4f19c
    Image:          people.webapp:v1
    Image ID:       docker-pullable://people.azurecr.io/people.webapp@sha256:80b05b4518a639cdf2c94dd302fe789ae84aaa5439fdd3346ba50230789329e
```

FIGURE 6-10 A fragment of the Pod description.

The Pod description provides relevant information such as the namespace, the node on which the Pod is running, start time, labels, status, IP address, associated ReplicaSet, and detailed information about the containers. Though not shown in Figure 6-10, a Pod description includes information about volumes and a list of events, such as creating and starting a container. Typically, you use this information to diagnose the state of the applications running in the cluster.

By analyzing descriptions of each Pod, you will see that Pods have different local IP addresses. This works similarly to spinning up two containers using Docker. However, with Kubernetes, you can go further and expose Pods as a single unit. Listing 6-2 exposes the Pods using a NodePort service. This service will map all the requests sent to the Kubernetes node (the host machine) on port 30000 to the Pods listening on port 5000.

LISTING 6-2 A Declaration of the Service for the People.WebApp.

```
apiVersion: v1
kind: Service
metadata:
  name: people-webapp-service
spec:
  selector:
    app: people-webapp
  type: NodePort
  ports:
  - port: 5000
    nodePort: 30000
```

Like the Deployment declaration, the service declaration uses a selector field to find associated Pods. In Listing 6-2, the service will be used for all Pods labeled as people-webapp. Then, you specify the service type. Here, that is NodePort. It will expose the service on the node port 30000. All requests sent to the host machine on this port will be redirected to port 5000 of containers running inside each underlying Pod.

To deploy that service, type the following command:

kubectl apply -f https://raw.githubusercontent.com/dawidborycki/↵

    People.WebApp.Declarations/main/Kubernetes/people_service.yml

You can then check the status of the service with the following command (shown in Figure 6-11):

kubectl get svc

```
% kubectl apply -f https://raw.githubusercontent.com/dawidborycki/People.WebApp.Declarati
ons/main/Kubernetes/people_service.yml
service/people-webapp-service created
%
% kubectl get svc
NAME                    TYPE        CLUSTER-IP       EXTERNAL-IP   PORT(S)          AGE
kubernetes              ClusterIP   10.96.0.1        <none>        443/TCP          175d
people-webapp-service   NodePort    10.103.135.220   <none>        5000:30000/TCP   8s
%
```

FIGURE 6-11 Creating a service.

The application is now exposed using the Kubernetes service. To see the application running, open your web browser and go to localhost:30000. You will then see the People.WebApp application running in the local Kubernetes cluster (Figure 6-12).

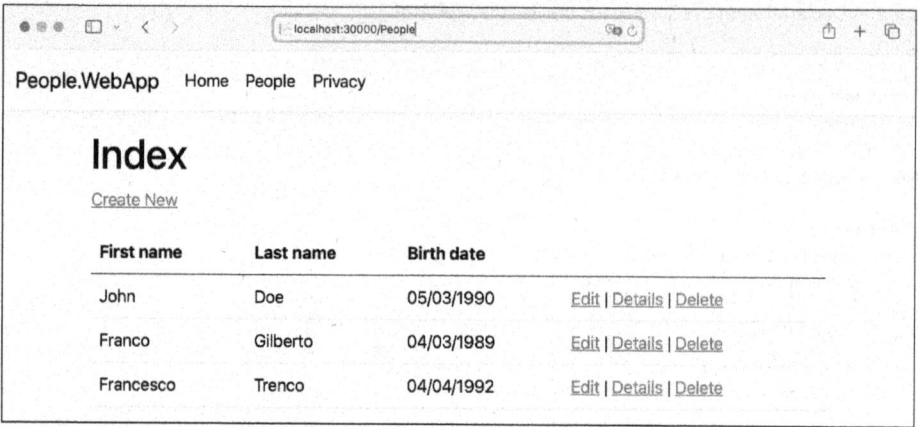

FIGURE 6-12 An application running in the Kubernetes cluster.

Summary

In this chapter, you learned how Kubernetes works and what the major components of a Kubernetes cluster are. Then, you put this theoretical knowledge in practice and deployed the People.WebApp to the cluster. Finally, you exposed the application using the NodePort service. Along the way, you learned how to use kubectl to manage the cluster's workloads. In the next chapter, you will see how to create a Kubernetes cluster in Microsoft Azure.

CHAPTER 7

Azure Kubernetes Service

In this chapter, you will learn how to create a Kubernetes cluster using Azure Kubernetes Service (AKS). You will then deploy People.WebApp to this cluster. Following the deployment, you will expose the application globally using the Kubernetes LoadBalancer service. This service integrates seamlessly with core Azure infrastructure resources, including the public Azure Load Balancer, ensuring the application receives a public IP and becomes accessible to anyone on the internet.

Throughout these operations, you will discover that you can manage the cluster created with Azure Kubernetes Service using the same kubectl tool employed for any other Kubernetes cluster.

How Azure Kubernetes Service can help you

Azure Kubernetes Service offers a fully managed Kubernetes environment. Azure handles the control plane, and the cluster nodes are provided as Azure Virtual Machines. This setup allows for quick and easy provisioning of clusters without the need for complex installation and management tasks.

With such architecture, you can easily scale your cluster by adding more virtual machines (VMs). The cluster size adjusts automatically based on current load. Azure Kubernetes Service communicates with the control plane through the cloud-controller-manager, which retrieves Pod scheduling information from the kube-scheduler. If more Pods need to be launched than the available hardware resources can support, the auto-scaler feature of Azure Kubernetes Service will add more nodes up to a specified limit and remove them when they are no longer needed. This makes managing containerized applications at scale effortless.

Azure Kubernetes Service is essentially a serverless offering, abstracting most administrative tasks. Additionally, it is integrated with continuous integration and continuous delivery (CI/CD) systems, allowing for modern application deployment pipelines where deployments can be initiated by committing new code versions to the repository.

Integration with other Azure services, such as Azure Virtual Network, enhances enterprise-grade security and governance through Microsoft Entra. Monitoring tools like Azure Monitor and Application Insights allow you to keep tabs on the health of your cluster and workloads.

Ultimately, Azure Kubernetes Service unifies development and operations teams on a single platform, enabling rapid building, delivery, and scaling of applications—thus embodying the workflows, patterns, and practices of modern application development and deployment.

What does it cost?

Azure Kubernetes Service offers several pricing tiers: free, standard, and premium. In the free tier, you are not charged for the control plane; you pay only for the nodes that run your applications. This tier is suitable for learning and running noncritical workloads. For production and mission-critical solutions, however, the standard or premium tiers are recommended, which include charges for every hour the cluster runs (ranging from $0.10 to $0.60 per hour, as of this writing).

What resources do you need?

When you create a cluster using Azure Kubernetes Service, the Azure platform provides a single-tenant control plane, including a dedicated kube-api server and other essential Kubernetes components. During cluster creation, you specify the number and size of the nodes, and Azure establishes secure communications between the control plane and the nodes. You then manage the cluster through the kubectl tool, just as you would with any Kubernetes cluster.

Azure equips the VMs used as cluster nodes with the kubelet, kube-proxy, and container runtime. These components consume hardware resources (memory and CPU), which means the total hardware resources of the VM differ from the resources allocatable for cluster tasks. This should be considered when selecting VM sizes for your nodes.

Azure Kubernetes Service utilizes node pools, which are groups of nodes sharing the same configuration, such as VM size. Each cluster must have at least one node pool, known as the default node pool, which should contain at least two Linux-based VMs. If you need to deploy workloads on Windows-based VMs, you must create an additional node pool.

Creating a cluster using Azure Kubernetes Service

Now that you are familiar with the essential features of Azure Kubernetes Service, you're ready to try creating a cluster in Azure. First, navigate to the Azure portal, and enter **Kubernetes** in the search box. From the list that appears, select Kubernetes Services from the Services group (Figure 7-1).

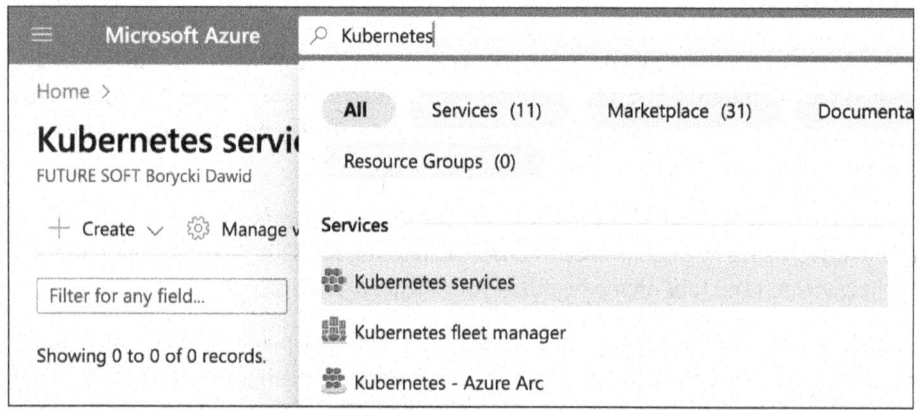

FIGURE 7-1 A search box in the Azure portal indicating the Kubernetes services.

In the Kubernetes Services dashboard that opens, click + Create, and then select Create A Kubernetes Cluster (see Figure 7-2).

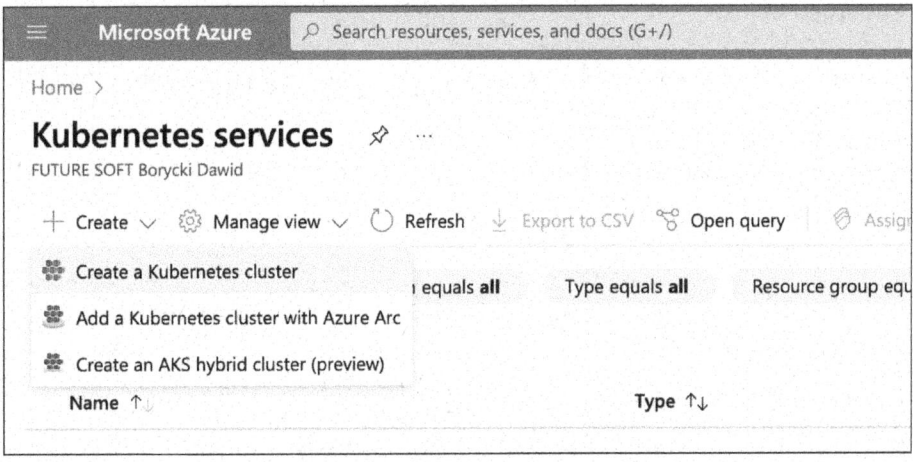

FIGURE 7-2 Kubernetes services in the Azure portal.

The Create Kubernetes Cluster wizard appears (shown in Figure 7-3). Use the Basics tab to configure the cluster as follows. These steps assume that you have already created an Azure Container Registry. (See Chapter 5, "Azure Container Registry," for details.)

1. Subscription: **Select your subscription**
2. Resource Group: **rg-aks-people**
3. Cluster Preset Configuration: **Dev/Test**
4. Kubernetes Cluster Name: **aks-people**
5. Region: **East US** (or any other region).
6. Availability Zones: **Select all** (Note that no selection can be available if you selected a different Azure region in step 5.)
7. AKS Pricing Tier: **Free**
8. Kubernetes Version: **Default** (At the time of this writing, the default version was 1.28.9.)
9. Automatic Upgrade: **Enabled with patch** (recommended)
10. Automatic Upgrade Scheduler: **Every week on Sunday** (recommended)
11. Node Security Channel Type: **Node Image**
12. Security Channel Scheduler: **Every week on Sunday** (recommended).
13. Authentication and Authorization: **Local accounts with Kubernetes RBAC**

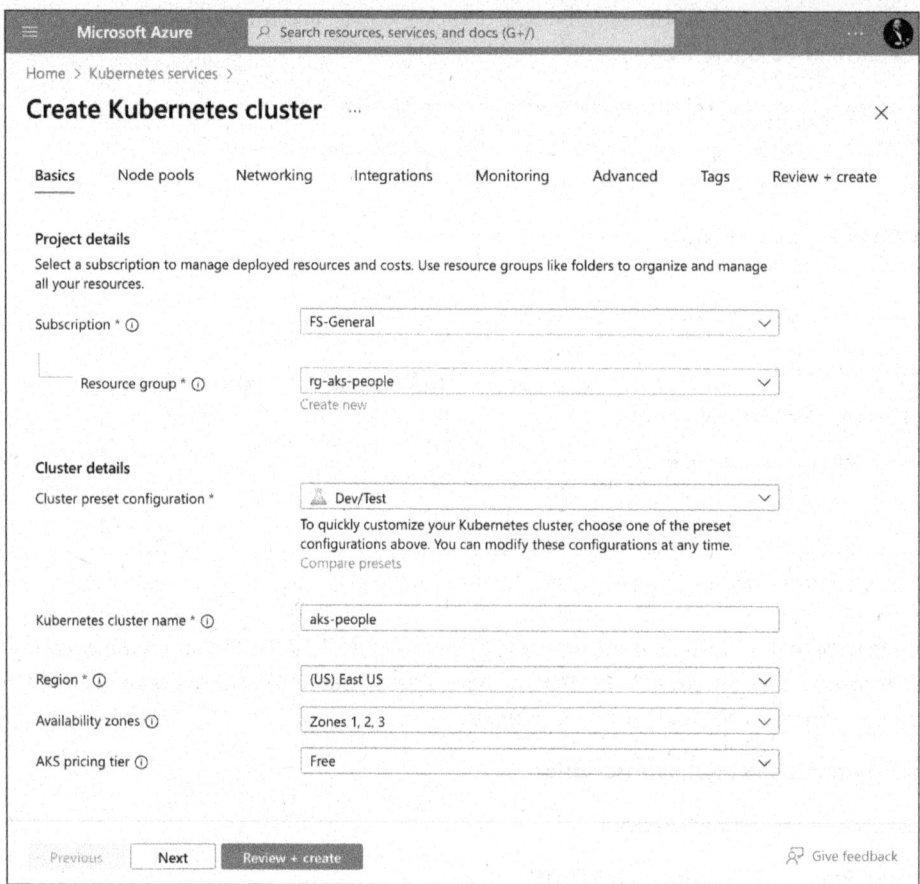

FIGURE 7-3 Creating the Kubernetes cluster.

Click Next to go to the Node Pools tab (see Figure 7-4).

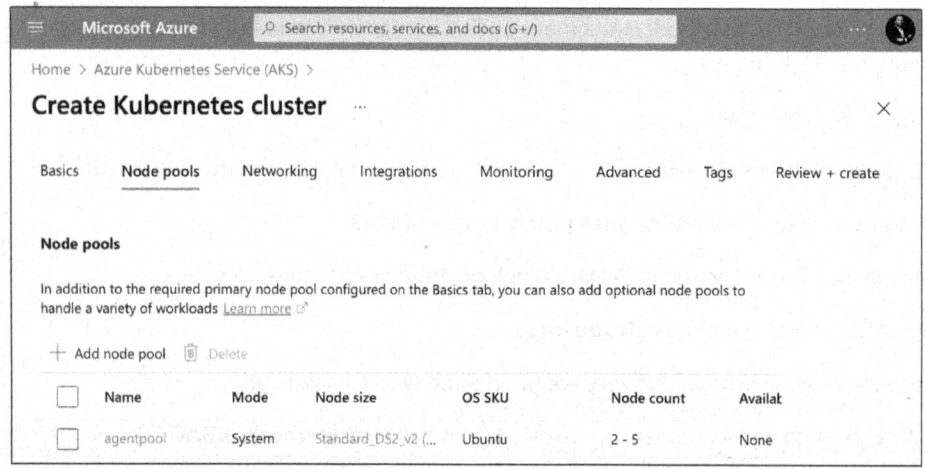

FIGURE 7-4 Configuring a Node pool.

Under Node Pools, select the agentpool link to open the Update Node Pool wizard, where you can select the size of VMs for the nodes, configure the scaling method, and specify the node count. Use this page to configure the node pool as follows:

1. Node Pool Name: **agentpool**
2. Mode: **System**
3. OS SKU: **Ubuntu Linux**
4. Availability Zones: **Select all available**
5. Node Size: **Standard DS2 v2**
6. Scale Method: **Autoscale**
7. Minimum Node Count: **1**
8. Maximum Node Count: **3**

Click Update to return to the Create Kubernetes Cluster wizard. Switch to the Integrations tab, and select People from the Container Registry dropdown (see Figure 7-5).

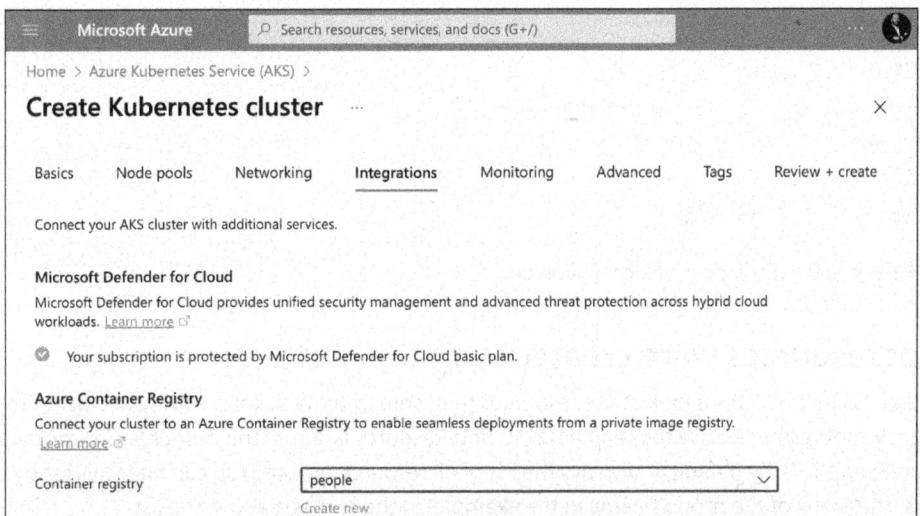

FIGURE 7-5 Integrating the cluster with Azure Container Registry.

Finally, click the Review + Create button. The Azure platform will now validate your configuration, and you will see a configuration summary similar to Figure 7-6.

Click the Create button to start provisioning the Kubernetes cluster in Azure. Wait a few moments for the cluster to be created. Once the deployment is complete, the Azure portal will display the Your Deployment Is Complete page.

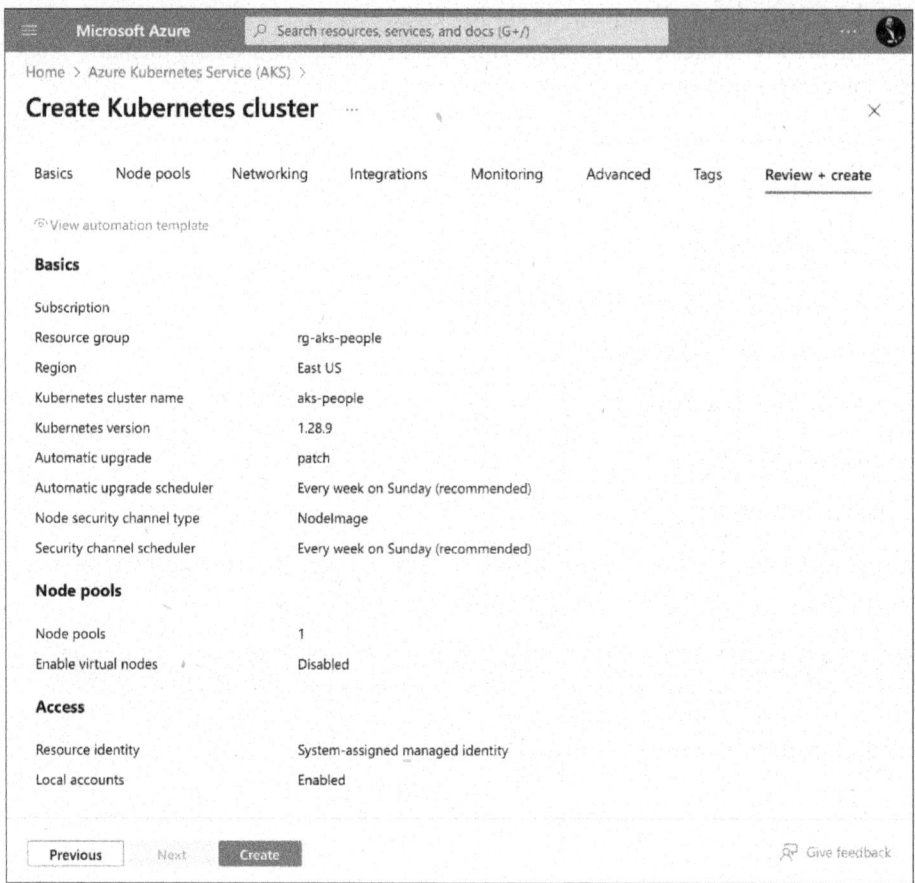

FIGURE 7-6 A summary of the cluster configuration.

What resources were created with the cluster?

Before going further, take a look at the resources that were deployed along with your cluster. To view all the relevant resources, use the search box to find Resource Groups. The Resource Groups page will appear (Figure 7-7). By default, it displays the list of all resource groups. You can filter this list by typing **rg-aks** (the prefix of the group's name in the example) in the text box above the list.

The resulting list of groups includes two elements: rg-aks-people and MC_rg-aks-people_aks-people_<REGION>.

The rg-aks-people group, which you created manually, contains the following resources:

- **aks-people** The Azure Kubernetes cluster
- **people** The container registry

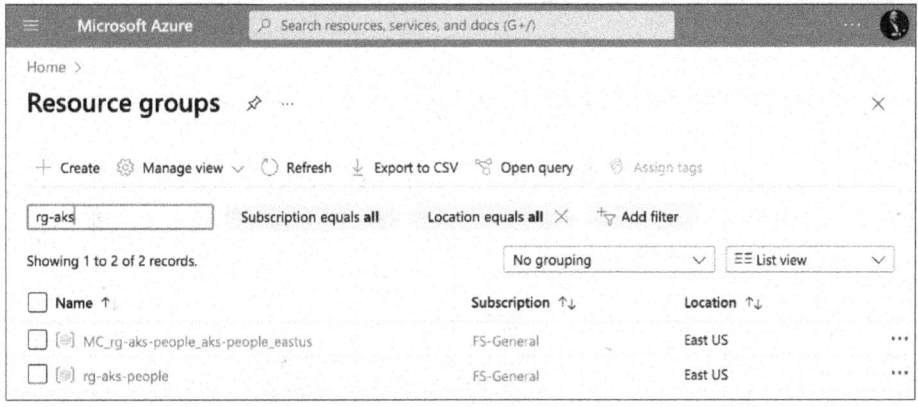

FIGURE 7-7 A list of resource groups.

- **RecommendedAlertRules-AG-1** An action, which will send you an email whenever the underlying metric is in the alert state

- **CPU Usage Percentage - aks-people** A metric alert rule that will trigger a notification (through RecommendedAlertRules-AG-1) when the CPU usage of the Kubernetes cluster crosses the threshold of 95 percent

- **Memory Working Set Percentage - aks-people** A metric alert rule that will be in the alert state when the memory utilization reaches 100 percent

The MC_rg-aks-people_aks-people_<REGION> group was created by Azure with the cluster and contains the following resources (see Figure 7-8):

- **kubernetes** A load balancer for the virtual machine scale set.

- **aks-vnet** The Azure Virtual Network, into which the nodes are connected, enabling the connectivity to the pods.

- **aks-people-agentpool** A managed identity associated with the node pool. You can use this identity to configure access for the applications running in the pool. For example, you can configure the Azure security rules, which will enable Pods running in this node to securely connect to the Azure SQL server.

- **aks-agentpool-nsg** A network security group (NSG) associated with the agent pool. You can use this NSG to configure network traffic filtering rules for the Pods running in the node pool.

- **aks-agentpool-vmss** A virtual machine scale set that defines the group of load-balanced virtual machines. This set is used by Azure Kubernetes Service to scale the cluster automatically,

- **Public IP address** A public IP address for the load balancer.

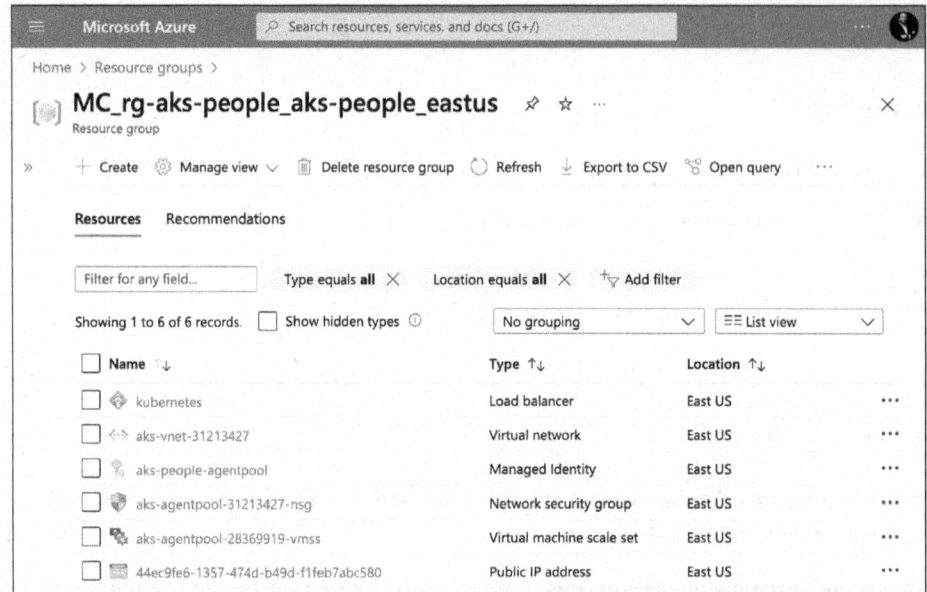

FIGURE 7-8 A list of Azure eesources deployed for the Kubernetes cluster.

> **Note** When selecting the node size for your Kubernetes cluster in Azure, consider that Azure VMs hosting Kubernetes nodes reserve some hardware resources for Kubernetes system components (such as kubelet and kube-proxy). This means the available CPU and memory for your workloads will be less than the total hardware resources of the VM. Always choose a VM size slightly larger than your estimated resource needs to accommodate these overheads.

Connecting to the cluster

You just created the Kubernetes cluster and investigated the Azure resources deployed with it. Now, you will take the next step and connect to the cluster. First, I will show you how to achieve this connection using the local Azure CLI and kubectl. Then, you will proceed to use Azure Cloud Shell.

Using the local machine

To connect to the cluster, open the command prompt or terminal and then type the following commands:

```
az login

az aks get-credentials -g rg-aks-people -n aks-people
```

Note that if you have multiple subscriptions, you must invoke the **az account set --subscription <subscription_id>** command before using **az aks get-credentials**. To find the subscription ID associated with your cluster, type **aks-people** (the name of your cluster) in the Azure portal search box. The subscription ID will appear in the overview as Figure 7-9 illustrates.

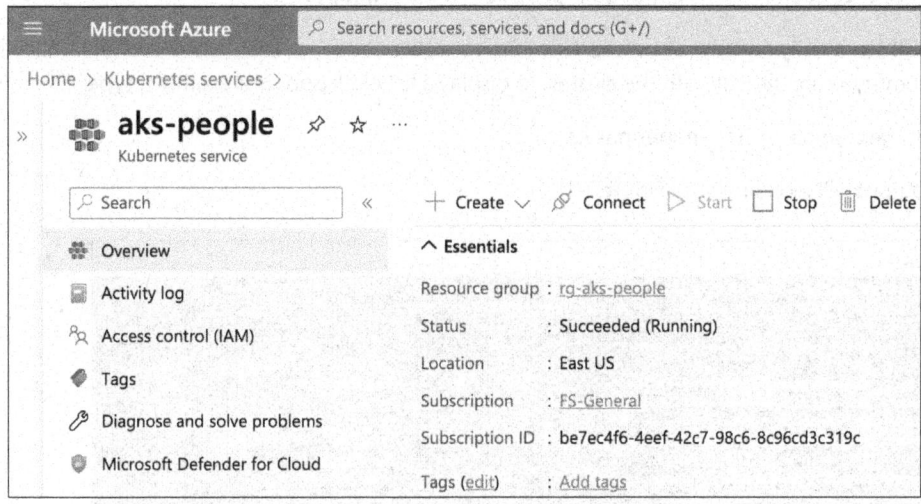

FIGURE 7-9 An overview of the Azure Kubernetes cluster.

The **az aks get-credentials** command configures your kubectl tool to communicate with the kube-api server of the selected Azure Kubernetes cluster. From now on, all kubectl commands will target that cluster. To verify this, use the following commands:

kubectl get nodes

kubectl get svc

The result is a list of nodes and services in the default namespace similar to Figure 7-10.

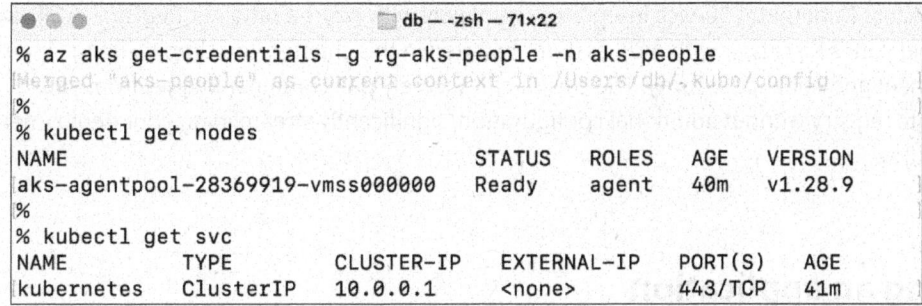

FIGURE 7-10 Using kubectl against the cluster deployed to Azure.

Currently, the cluster has one node because you set the minimum node count to 1. Similarly, like the local cluster, the Azure cluster includes the Kubernetes service, responsible for providing access to the kube-api-server for other workloads running inside the cluster.

Using the Azure Cloud Shell

Now, take a look at how to connect to the cluster using Azure Cloud Shell. To do this, open the Cloud Shell and then type:

```
az aks get-credentials -g rg-aks-people -n aks-people
```

You will see a similar output as before. Notably, kubectl is already available in Cloud Shell, allowing you to communicate directly with the cluster. To display a list of all pods, for example, type:

```
kubectl get pods --all-namespaces
```

The output will look similar to Figure 7-11.

```
Bash                                                                        -  □  ×
dawid [ ~ ]$ az aks get-credentials -g rg-aks-people -n aks-people
Merged "aks-people" as current context in /home/dawid/.kube/config
dawid [ ~ ]$
dawid [ ~ ]$ kubectl get pods --all-namespaces
NAMESPACE     NAME                                              READY   STATUS    RESTARTS       AGE
kube-system   ama-metrics-6c6cb9996f-6n14w                      2/2     Running   0              50m
kube-system   ama-metrics-ksm-d9c6f475b-bvpdm                   1/1     Running   0              50m
kube-system   ama-metrics-node-6rv7g                            2/2     Running   0              50m
kube-system   ama-metrics-operator-targets-7cc6bfb94-snktr      2/2     Running   2 (50m ago)    50m
kube-system   azure-ip-masq-agent-rnhs4                         1/1     Running   0              54m
kube-system   cloud-node-manager-d5pgb                          1/1     Running   0              54m
kube-system   coredns-767bfbd4fb-hdqmr                          1/1     Running   0              53m
kube-system   coredns-767bfbd4fb-zrstx                          1/1     Running   0              55m
kube-system   coredns-autoscaler-c6649b67c-86mv2                1/1     Running   0              55m
kube-system   csi-azuredisk-node-f87c5                          3/3     Running   0              54m
kube-system   csi-azurefile-node-smqhn                          3/3     Running   0              54m
kube-system   konnectivity-agent-5f76d6dc44-ds9vj               1/1     Running   0              49m
kube-system   konnectivity-agent-5f76d6dc44-tkdjd               1/1     Running   0              49m
kube-system   kube-proxy-55tvs                                  1/1     Running   0              54m
kube-system   metrics-server-5cd44496f4-ng2ng                   2/2     Running   0              50m
kube-system   metrics-server-5cd44496f4-v2pgv                   2/2     Running   0              50m
dawid [ ~ ]$
```

FIGURE 7-11 Connecting to the cluster in Azure Cloud Shell.

You now have all the tools needed to deploy the application to the Azure Kubernetes cluster.

> **Tip** Azure Kubernetes Service integrates seamlessly with Azure Container Registry (ACR). By linking your AKS cluster with ACR, as demonstrated in this chapter, you simplify image management and enhance security. The cluster can securely pull container images from your private registry without additional configuration, significantly streamlining your deployment workflow.

Deploying an application

To deploy the People.WebApp application to the Azure Kubernetes cluster, we need only the single YAML file in Listing 7-1.

LISTING 7-1 A Declaration of the Deployment for People.WebApp.

```yaml
apiVersion: apps/v1
kind: Deployment
metadata:
  name: people-webapp-deployment
spec:
  replicas: 2
  selector:
    matchLabels:
      app: people-webapp
  template:
    metadata:
      labels:
        app: people-webapp
    spec:
      containers:
      - name: people-webapp
        image: people.azurecr.io/people.webapp:v1
        imagePullPolicy: Always
        ports:
        - containerPort: 5000
---
apiVersion: v1
kind: Service
metadata:
  name: people-webapp-service
spec:
  selector:
    app: people-webapp
  type: LoadBalancer
  ports:
  - port: 80
    targetPort: 5000
```

The declaration contains two elements: `Deployment` and `Service`. Both are in a single file and are separated by `---`. The `Deployment` declaration is nearly the same as for the local deployment. There are only two differences. First, the container image will be pulled from Azure Container Registry (image: `people.azurecr.io/people.webapp:v1`). Second, I added the `imagePullPolicy: Always` to indicate that the container image should be pulled from the repository whenever the remote image has a different image digest (image identifier) than the local one.

The `Service` declaration looks similar to what you used previously. However, `type` is now set to `LoadBalancer`. This means that the pods associated with the service will be exposed to the public using an external load balancer. As Kubernetes itself does not provide the load balancer, the latter will be provided by Azure.

Note that if you are using an ARM-powered device, Docker will build your local image for that architecture. Therefore, the image you pushed to the Azure Container Registry will not be compatible with the cluster nodes since they use the x64 processor architecture. In such cases, you need to build the local image for linux/amd64:

```
docker build -t people.azurecr.io/people.webapp:v1 --platform linux/amd64 .
```

The **--platform linux/amd64** option specifies the target platform for which the image is built. Note that you are also tagging the image using the login server of the container registry.

Then, you need to re-push the image to the container registry using the following commands:

az acr login -n people

docker push people.azurecr.io/people.webapp:v1

You are now ready to deploy the application. Use either the local terminal or Azure Cloud Shell, in which you type the following command:

```
kubectl apply -f https://raw.githubusercontent.com/dawidborycki/↵
    People.WebApp.Declarations/main/Kubernetes/people_aks.yml
```

Then, verify that two pods are running by using the command:

kubectl get pods

Finally, retrieve the public IP of the application with:

kubectl get svc

Figure 7-12 summarizes these commands.

```
dawid [ ~ ]$ kubectl apply -f https://raw.githubusercontent.com/dawidborycki/People.WebApp.Declaration
s/main/Kubernetes/people_aks.yml
deployment.apps/people-webapp-deployment created
service/people-webapp-service created
dawid [ ~ ]$
dawid [ ~ ]$ kubectl get pods
NAME                                          READY   STATUS    RESTARTS   AGE
people-webapp-deployment-87864d9b4-kcr67      1/1     Running   0          76s
people-webapp-deployment-87864d9b4-nhwwk      1/1     Running   0          76s
dawid [ ~ ]$
dawid [ ~ ]$ kubectl get svc
NAME                   TYPE           CLUSTER-IP     EXTERNAL-IP     PORT(S)        AGE
kubernetes             ClusterIP      10.0.0.1       <none>          443/TCP        91m
people-webapp-service  LoadBalancer   10.0.125.228   4.157.180.226   80:30919/TCP   80s
dawid [ ~ ]$
```

FIGURE 7-12 Deploying the People.WebApp to Azure Kubernetes Service.

Note the IP address under the EXTERNAL-IP column for the people-webapp-service, which is 4.157.180.226. This address is where the application will listen for incoming requests. Therefore, by typing this IP into a web browser, you will be able to access the application as seen in Figure 7-13.

You've just deployed your first application to the Azure Kubernetes Service. After configuring the kubectl, deploying the application was as straightforward as using the local cluster.

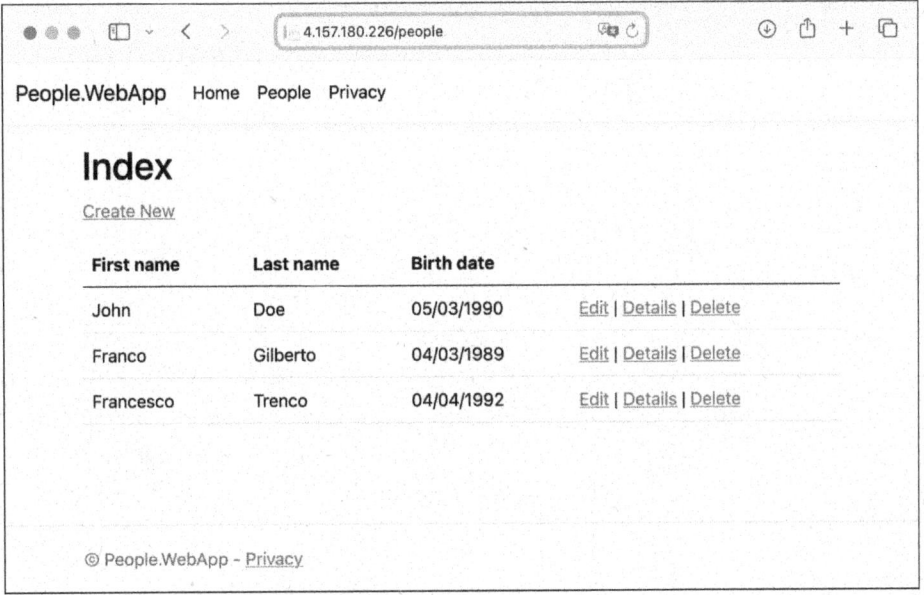

FIGURE 7-13 A People.WebApp running in Azure Kubernetes Service.

 Note If you're developing on an ARM-based device (such as Apple Silicon Macs), ensure that your container images are built for the correct architecture (linux/amd64) when deploying to Azure Kubernetes Service. Otherwise, your images will fail to run on AKS nodes, which typically use the x64 architecture. You can build compatible images using the **--platform linux/amd64 parameter** with Docker, as shown earlier in this chapter.

Summary

In this chapter, you created a Kubernetes cluster in Azure. You learned that you could manage this cluster in the same way as the local one, namely, by using the kubectl tool. You used kubectl to deploy People.WebApp to the cluster and subsequently exposed this application to the internet using Azure Load Balancer. In the next step, you will learn how to integrate other Azure services (such as Azure SQL Database and Azure Key Vault) with the application running in the cluster.

CHAPTER 8

Azure SQL Database and Azure Key Vault

In the previous chapter, you learned how to deploy applications to Azure Kubernetes Service. The application you used stored data in an in-memory database, meaning any data added would be lost upon restarting the application. To address this, this chapter will show you how to use a persistent SQL database provisioned using the Azure SQL Database service.

To connect the application to this database, you need a connection string. Similar to how you handled settings in Docker Compose, you will pass this connection string to the application using environment variables. This method allows you to update application settings without needing to rebuild the container image.

This approach has a downside, however: The connection string is stored in plain text. To minimize the risk of exposing the connection string, you will use Azure Key Vault. Specifically, you will securely store the connection string as a secret after creating the key vault. Then, you will modify the application to retrieve this secret directly from the key vault, eliminating the need to store the connection string in plain text.

Azure SQL Database

Azure SQL Database is a scalable, relational database service built for the cloud, designed to provide the highest availability. This service supports the increasing demand for large databases, accommodating sizes up to 100 TB. Azure SQL Database features autoscaling and can operate in serverless mode to adapt to unpredictable changes in your workloads.

Like any other SQL database, Azure SQL Database requires an underlying server that provides the computing and storage resources necessary for database operations. After creating the server and database, you can use a connection string to access the database, similar to how you would connect to a local SQL database.

Azure SQL database is available in several pricing options:

- **vCore** You choose the number of virtual cores for the server. The server computer performance and the price increase with the number of cores.

- **Database Transaction Unit (DTU)** A DTU measures the compute, storage, and I/O resources required to perform database operations. In this case, you need to predefine the performance up front.

- **Serverless** In this model, the computing performance is automatically scaled, depending on the demand. You are charged for the computing time.

You can establish a SQL Database elastic database pool, where all databases within the pool collectively share a common set of compute and storage resources. Each database can leverage resources according to its specific requirements while staying within the defined limits, which can be adjusted based on the current workload.

In the following section, you will create an instance of the Azure SQL Database to provide persistent storage for People.WebApp running in the Azure Kubernetes Service.

Creating the database

To create the database, go to the Azure portal and type **SQL** in the search box. Then, select SQL Databases (see Figure 8-1).

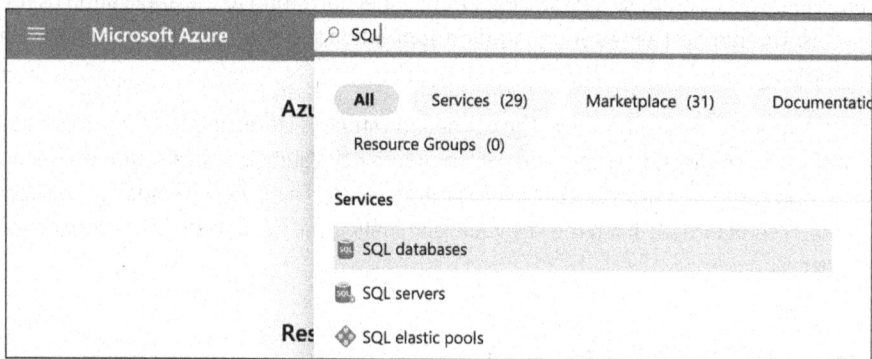

FIGURE 8-1 Looking for SQL databases.

You will then see the SQL Databases page shown in Figure 8-2.

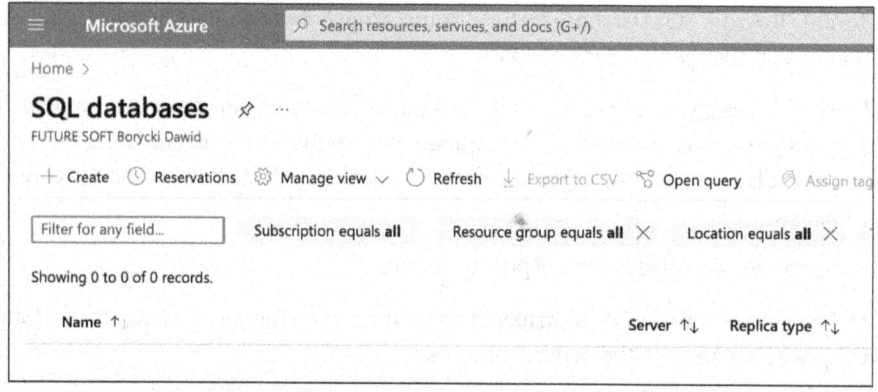

FIGURE 8-2 The SQL Databases dashboard.

In the SQL Databases dashboard, click the + Create button to open the Create SQL Database wizard. Use it to configure the database as follows (Figure 8-3):

1. Subscription: **Select your subscription**
2. Resource Group: **rg-aks-people**
3. Database Name: **people**

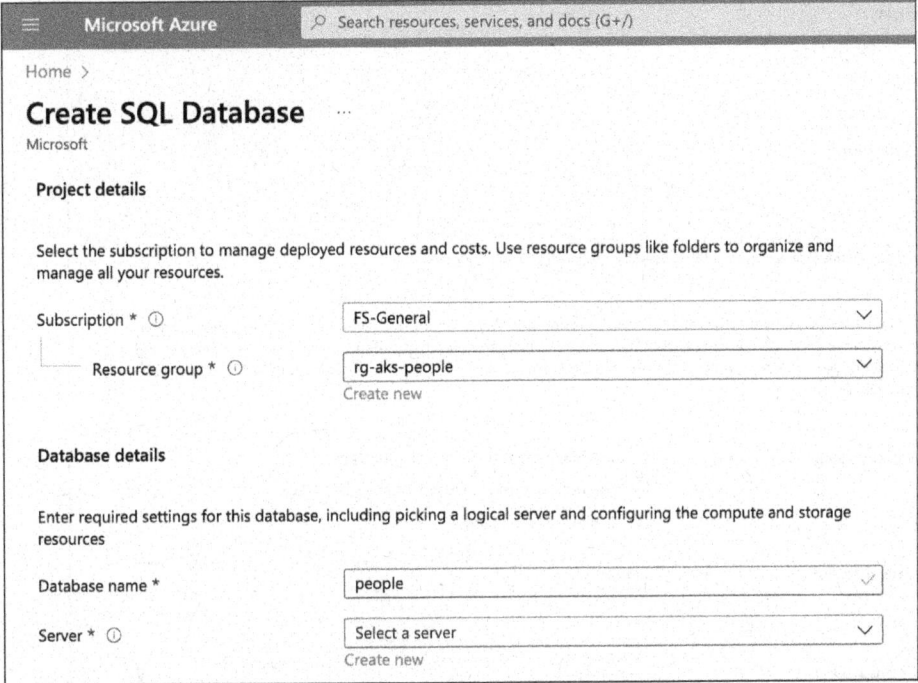

FIGURE 8-3 Configuring a database.

Now, you need to create the server for the database. To do so, click the Create New link (below the Server dropdown). You will see another wizard: Create SQL Database Server. Use it to configure the server as follows (Figure 8-4):

1. Server name: **aks-sql-people** (Note that server name must be globally unique. Use a different name if the one you choose is already taken.)
2. Location: **East US** (or any other)
3. Authentication: **Use SQL Authentication**
4. Server Admin Login: **azure**
5. Password: **<your_password>** (for example, P@ssw0rD)

FIGURE 8-4 Creating a SQL database server.

Click OK to create the server, and you will return to the Create SQL Database wizard. The server dropdown should now point to aks-sql-people (East US). Next, configure the remaining settings (Figure 8-5):

1. Want To Use SQL Elastic Pool: **No**

2. Workload Environment: **Development**

3. Compute + Storage: **Keep the default** (General purpose – Serverless)

4. Backup Storage Redundancy: **Locally-Redundant Backup Storage**

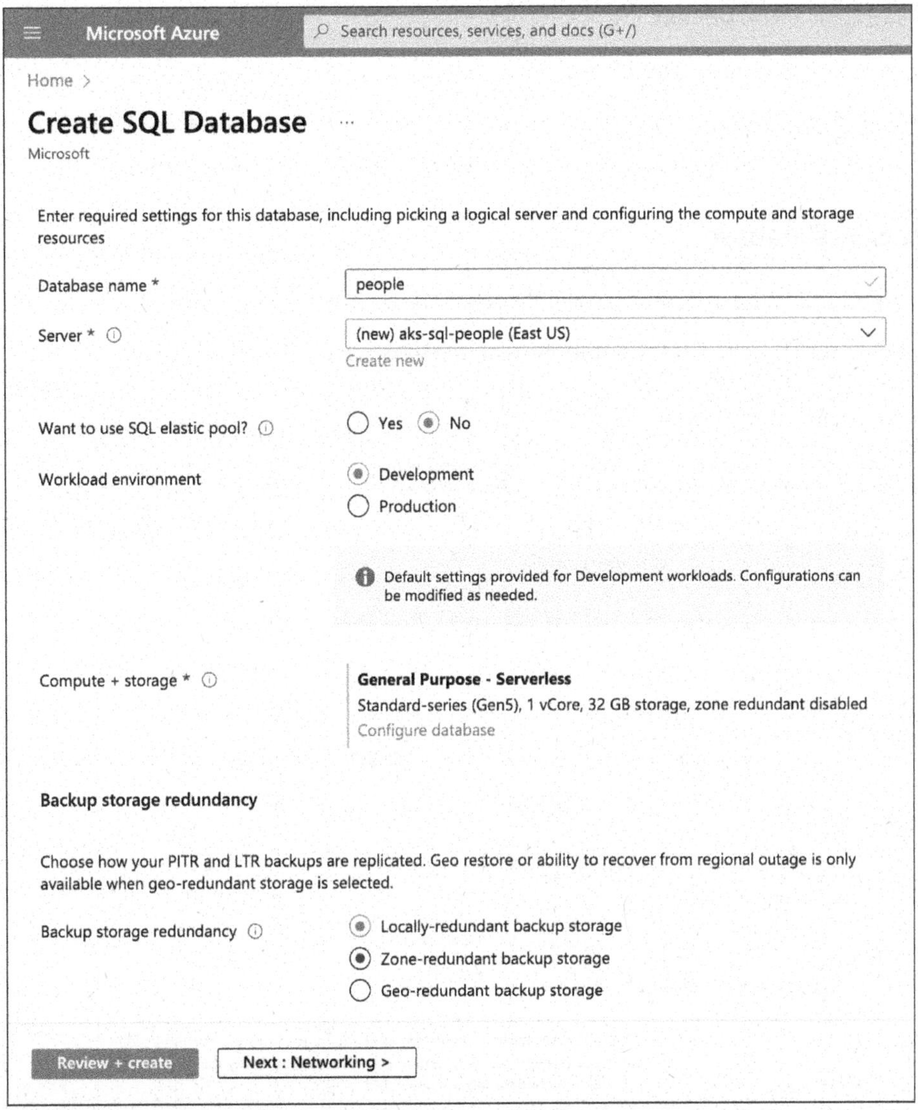

FIGURE 8-5 The final form of the Basics tab of the Creating SQL Database Server wizard.

With the Basics tab complete, click Next : Networking, then configure the Networking tab settings (Figure 8-6):

1. Connectivity Method: **Public Endpoint**

2. Firewall Rules:

    a. Allow Azure Services And Resources To Access This Server: **Yes**

    b. Add Current Client IP Address: **No**

3. Connection Policy: **Default**

4. Encrypted Connections: **TLS 1.2**

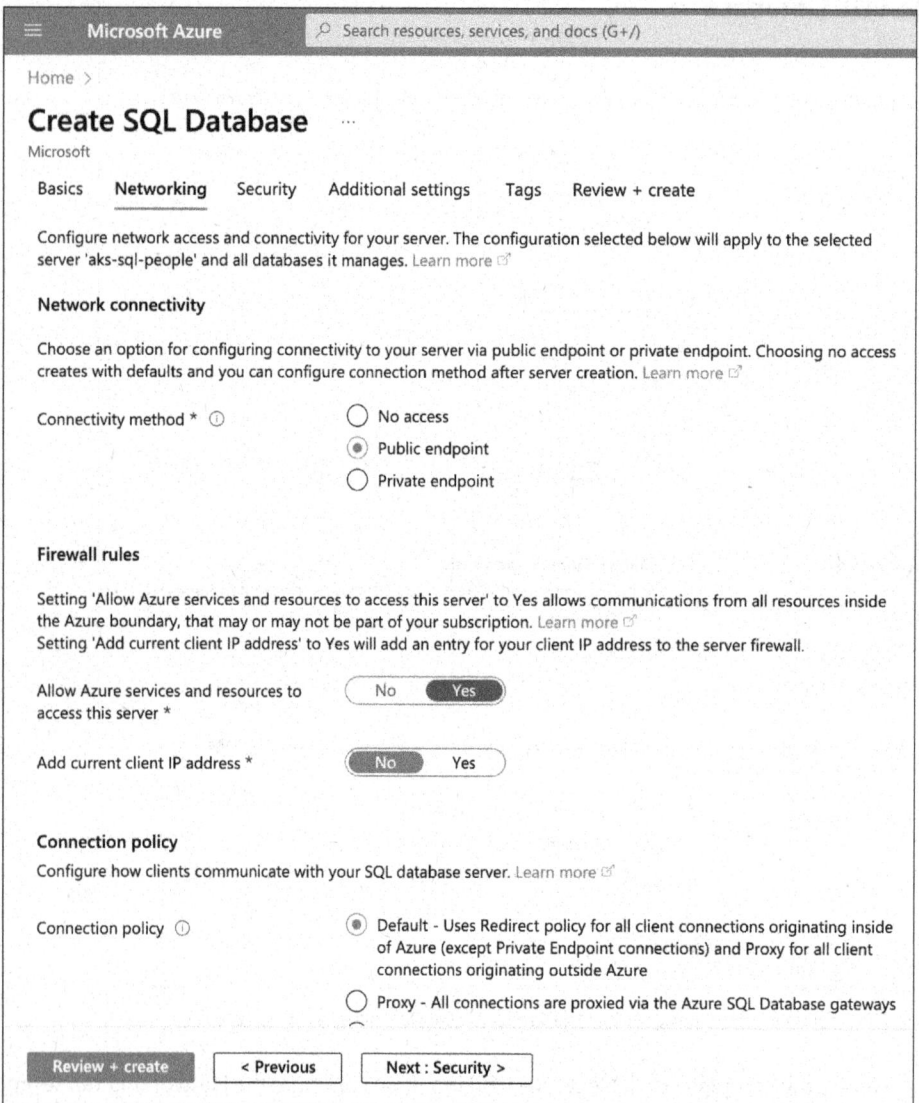

FIGURE 8-6 A fragment of the Networking tab of the SQL database configuration process.

Now, click Review + Create to go to the Review tab, and there click Create. Wait a few moments for the resources to be deployed. Once this is done, click the Go To Resource button. You will be redirected to the SQL database page shown in Figure 8-7.

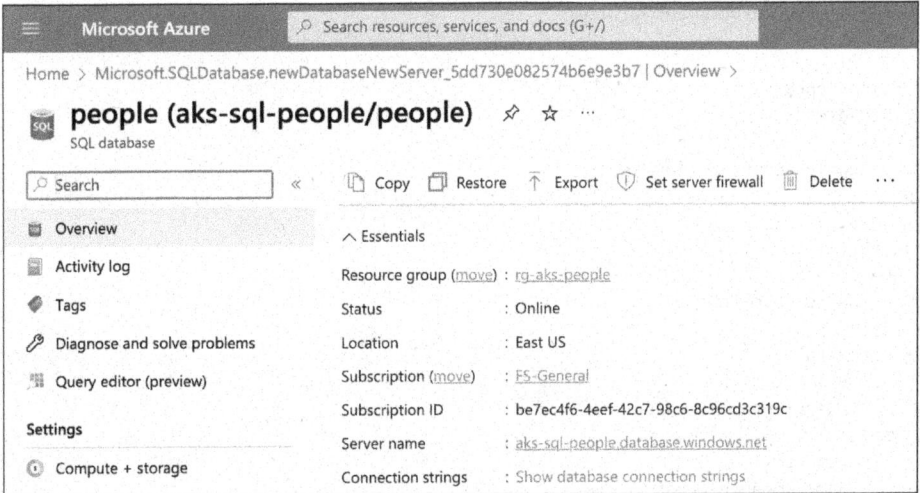

FIGURE 8-7 An overview of the SQL database.

Next to Connection Strings (bottom right), click the Show Database Connection Strings link. Copy the ADO.NET (SQL Authentication) connection string. It should look like the one in Listing 8-1.

LISTING 8-1 Azure SQL Database Connection String.

```
Server=tcp:aks-sql-people.database.windows.net,1433;Initial Catalog=people;Persist Security
Info=False;
User ID=azure;Password={your_password};MultipleActiveResultSets=False;
Encrypt=True;TrustServerCertificate=False;Connection Timeout=30;
```

Modify the string such that you replace {your_password} with the actual password you used when creating the SQL server. You will need the resulting connection string to update the Deployment of the People.WebApp.

> **Note** When configuring Azure SQL Database for development or testing, the serverless pricing model is highly recommended. This model automatically scales compute resources based on usage, making it both cost-effective and flexible for workloads with unpredictable usage patterns. However, remember to evaluate performance requirements before selecting this option for production workloads.

Configuring the connection

You've just created the SQL database. Now, you will configure People.WebApp to use the SQL database instead of the in-memory datastore. As with Docker Compose, you will modify the settings of People.WebApp using the environment variable of the container. More specifically, to define environment variables, you will use the declaration of the Deployment as indicated in Listing 8-2.

LISTING 8-2 Defining Environment Variables.

```yaml
apiVersion: apps/v1
kind: Deployment
metadata:
  name: people-webapp-deployment
spec:
  replicas: 2
  selector:
    matchLabels:
      app: people-webapp
  template:
    metadata:
      labels:
        app: people-webapp
    spec:
      containers:
      - name: people-webapp
        image: people.azurecr.io/people.webapp:v1
        imagePullPolicy: Always
        ports:
        - containerPort: 5000
        env:
        - name: ASPNETCORE_ENVIRONMENT
          value: Development
        - name: UseInMemoryDatabase
          value: "False"
              - name: ConnectionStrings__PeopleDbConnection
          value: "<paste_your_connection_string_here>"
```

In Listing 8-2, I added an env field containing a list of environment variables. Each variable is defined using a name-value pair. The following three environment variables will override the settings of the People.WebApp:

- **ASPNETCORE_ENVIRONMENT** Set to Development so that you can see any potential errors that might appear when configuring the database connection string.

- **UseInMemoryDatabase** Set to False to disable the in-memory database.

- **ConnectionStrings__PeopleDbConnection** Updates the PeopleDbConnection setting under the ConnectionStrings in the appsettings.json of the People.WebApp. Set this variable to the connection string you obtained in Listing 8-1.

To modify the Deployment, follow these steps:

1. Open Azure Cloud Shell, and type the following command:

   wget https://raw.githubusercontent.com/dawidborycki/People.WebApp. Declarations/↵

       main/Kubernetes/people_aks_sql.yml

   This command downloads the people_aks_sql.yml file to Azure Cloud Shell.

2. Open the `people_aks_sql.yml` file in the code editor with the following command:

   `code people_aks_sql.yml`

3. Paste your connection string on line 17 after `value:`, as illustrated in Figure 8-8.

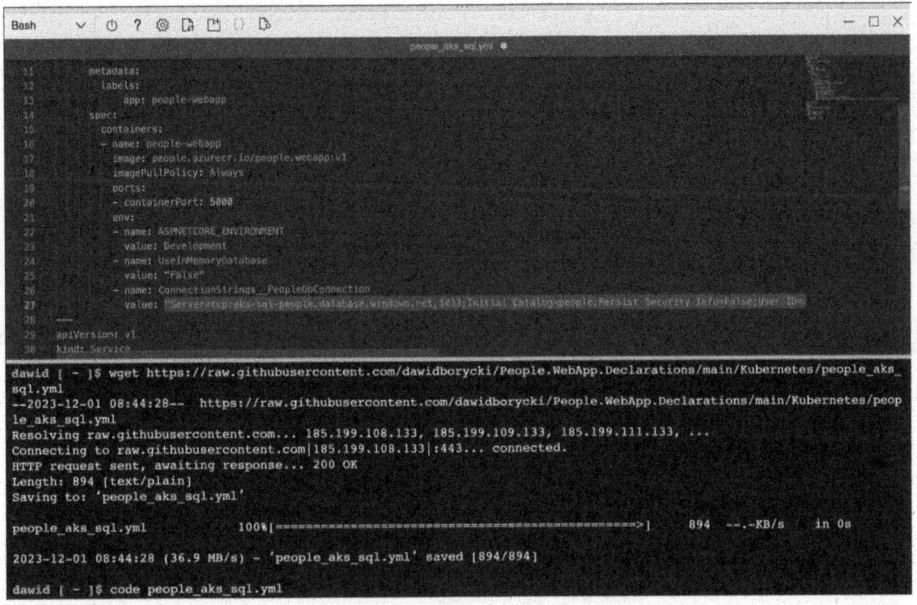

FIGURE 8-8 Updating the people_aks_sql.yml.

4. Save the `people_aks_sql.yml` file. To do so, click the ellipsis in the top-right corner of the code editor and select Save (CTRL+S) from the menu.

5. Close the file using the ellipsis menu, then select Close Editor.

6. Apply the changes to the Kubernetes cluster by typing:

   `kubectl apply -f people_aks_sql.yml`

   This command will update the Deployment configuration (see Figure 8-9). The Pods will be restarted, and People.WebApp will now connect to the Azure SQL database.

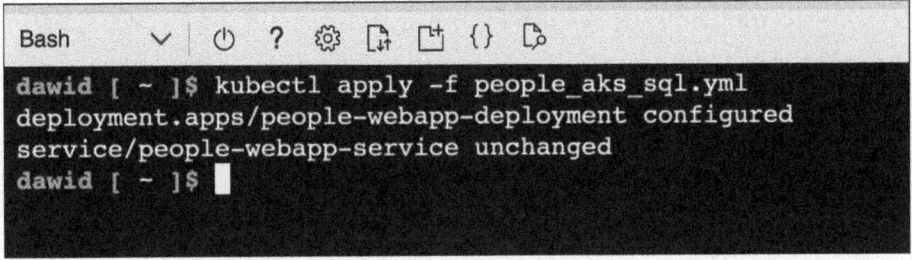

FIGURE 8-9 Updating the Deployment of the People.WebApp.

Previewing the Azure SQL Database

If you open the People.WebApp in your web browser and navigate to the People tab, you will see the now familiar interface. Notice that unlike in Figure 7-13, this time the data created by the application is stored in the Azure SQL Database.

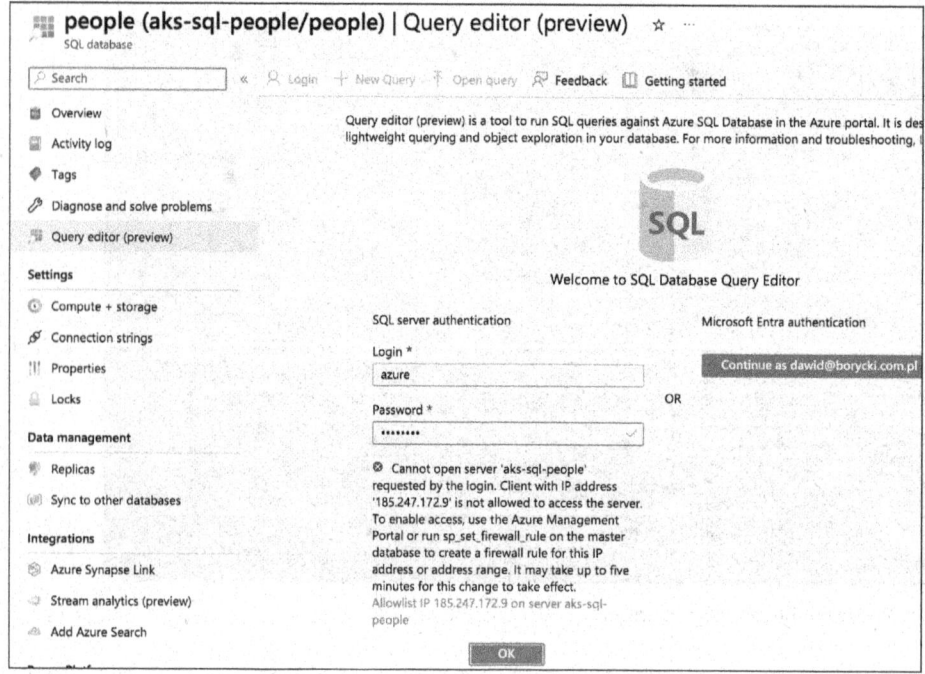

FIGURE 8-10 Connecting to the SQL Azure Database.

To see an overview of your database, type **people** in the Azure portal search box, then click the select People SQL Database. Next, click Query Editor (Preview) to open the login page. Here, enter your credentials, which are the same as those in the SQL connection string. Click OK. As in Figure 8-10, you may see the error message: "Cannot open server 'aks-sql-people' requested by the login. The client with IP address is not allowed to access the server." If this occurs, click the Allowlist IP On Server aks-sql-people link. This will set a firewall rule allowing you to connect to the SQL server. Click OK again, and open the Query Editor.

In the Query Editor, type the following SQL statement:

`SELECT * FROM [dbo].[People]`

Next, click Run to see the list of people in the database, as shown in Figure 8-11. Try to add new records using the People.WebApp, and rerun the SQL query to ensure the new data has been saved in the database.

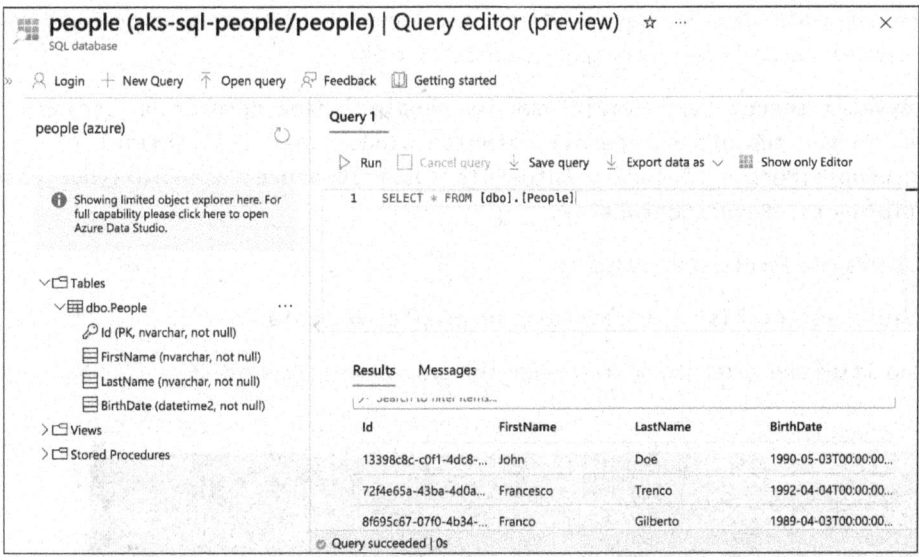

FIGURE 8-11 Querying data from the People database.

Azure Key Vault

Although you just connected the application to Azure SQL Database, the connection string is stored as open text in the YAML file that declares the Deployment. In real-world applications, you do not want to store sensitive information as open text in an easily accessible file like this. A repository is a better choice.

To solve this problem, you can use Azure Key Vault, which offers a secure storage space for efficiently managing your application secrets and ensuring proper data encryption, both in transit and at rest. Azure Key Vault enables you to securely store and rigorously manage access to tokens, passwords, certificates, API keys, and other secrets. This key management solution facilitates the effortless creation and control of encryption keys to secure corporate data. It also streamlines the enrollment, management, and deployment of both public and private Transport Layer Security/Secure Sockets Layer (TLS/SSL) certificates for seamless integration with Azure and internally connected resources.

In the following sections, you will learn how to create a secret under the Azure Key Vault and then how to programmatically retrieve this secret.

Creating the key vault

To create a key vault in Azure Key Vault, use Azure Cloud Shell and type:

```
az keyvault create -n kv-people -g rg-aks-people
```

This command creates a key vault named kv-people under the resource group rg-aks-people. Confirm the key vault was created with the command:

```
az keyvault list -o table
```

Once you have a key vault, you can create the secret. Remember to replace *{your_password}* with the actual password you used when creating the Azure SQL Server:

```
az keyvault secret set --vault-name kv-people --name connection-string
--value "Server=tcp:aks-sql-people.database.windows.net,1433;Initial
Catalog=people;Persist Security Info=False;User ID=azure;Password={your_passwor
d};MultipleActiveResultSets=False;"
```

Then, display the list of secrets by typing:

```
az keyvault secret list --vault-name kv-people -o table
```

You should see one secret named connection-string, as shown in Figure 8-12.

FIGURE 8-12 Retrieving the list of key vaults and secrets.

Retrieving the secret

The secret you created securely stores the connection string to the People database. I modified the application to use the Azure Key Vault Secrets configuration provider to retrieve it. This provider allows the application to access secrets from the Azure Key Vault as if they were defined in the appsettings.json.

To use the Azure Key Vault Secrets configuration provider in an ASP.NET Core app, install the `Azure.Extensions.AspNetCore.Configuration.Secrets` NuGet package. This package provides the `AddAzureKeyVault` extension method for the `Configuration` class. Modify the `Program.cs` file by adding the following lines:

```
builder.Configuration.AddAzureKeyVault(
    new Uri($"https://{builder.Configuration["KeyVaultName"]}.vault.azure.net/"),
    new DefaultAzureCredential(new DefaultAzureCredentialOptions()
    {
        ManagedIdentityClientId = builder.Configuration["ManagedIdentityClientId"]
    }));
```

These statements configure the Azure Key Vault Secrets configuration provider to connect to the specified key vault using default Azure credentials. When running the application locally, it uses credentials cached by the Azure CLI or a managed identity when running in the cloud.

For the application deployed to the Azure Kubernetes cluster, you use the managed identity associated with the node pool. This avoids the need to supply credentials to each pod individually. It is more practical to allow apps running in the node pool to automatically authenticate with the key vault to retrieve secrets, keys, or certificates.

To support the key vault configuration in the app, I added the following three entries to the `appsettings.json`:

```
"KeyVaultName": "kv-people",
"SecretName": "connection-string",
"ManagedIdentityClientId": ""
```

These entries allow you to specify the key vault and secret names and provide the client identifier for the managed identity. The Key Vault Secrets configuration provider uses this identifier to retrieve the secrets.

To see how the secret retrieval works, open the folder where you cloned the People.WebApp repository (**git clone https://github.com/dawidborycki/People.WebApp.git**). Switch to the required branch by entering the following command:

```
git checkout net8-keyvault
```

Then, run the application locally using:

```
dotnet run
```

The output from the above commands appears as shown in Figure 8-13.

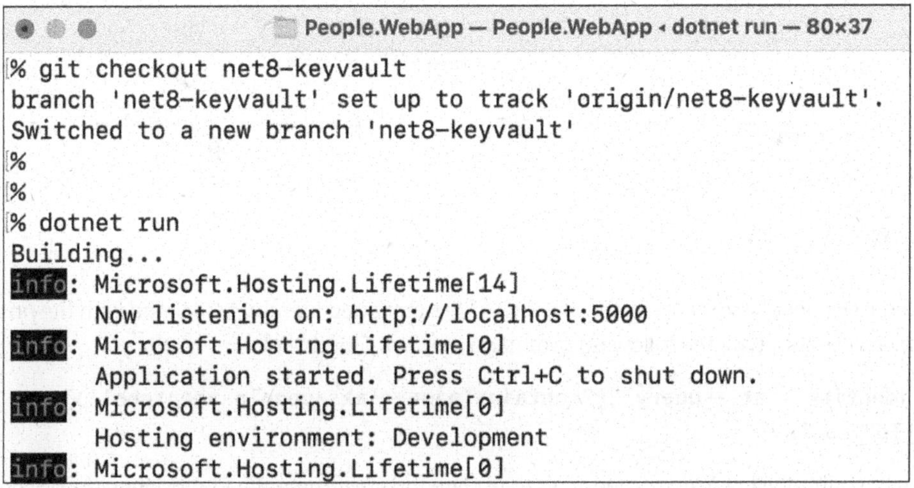
People.WebApp — People.WebApp ◂ dotnet run — 80×37
% git checkout net8-keyvault
branch 'net8-keyvault' set up to track 'origin/net8-keyvault'.
Switched to a new branch 'net8-keyvault'
%
%
% dotnet run
Building...
info: Microsoft.Hosting.Lifetime[14]
Now listening on: http://localhost:5000
info: Microsoft.Hosting.Lifetime[0]
Application started. Press Ctrl+C to shut down.
info: Microsoft.Hosting.Lifetime[0]
Hosting environment: Development
info: Microsoft.Hosting.Lifetime[0]

FIGURE 8-13 Running a modified People.WebApp locally.

Now, open the application in a web browser (localhost:5000), and you will see that the application functions as before. However, you no longer store the connection string as plain text. Instead, the connection string is securely retrieved from Azure Key Vault. Verify that the `appsettings.json` no longer contains the connection string.

Configuring the key vault permissions

Before deploying an updated People.WebApp to the Azure Kubernetes cluster, you need to configure the permissions to allow Pods running in the node pool to access the key vault you created. To do this, open Azure Cloud Shell and type the following commands:

```
AGENTPOOL_ID=$(az identity list --query "[?contains(name,
  'aks-people-agentpool')].principalId" -o tsv)

az keyvault set-policy -n kv-people --object-id $AGENTPOOL_ID --secret
-permissions get list
```

The first command retrieves the principal identifier of the managed identity named **'aks-people-agentpool'**, which was created with the cluster. The second command establishes an access policy for the **'kv-people'** resource. This policy allows Pods within the **'aks-people-agentpool'** to list and retrieve secrets.

You can view this policy in the Azure portal under the Access policies section of the kv-people resource, as illustrated in Figure 8-14.

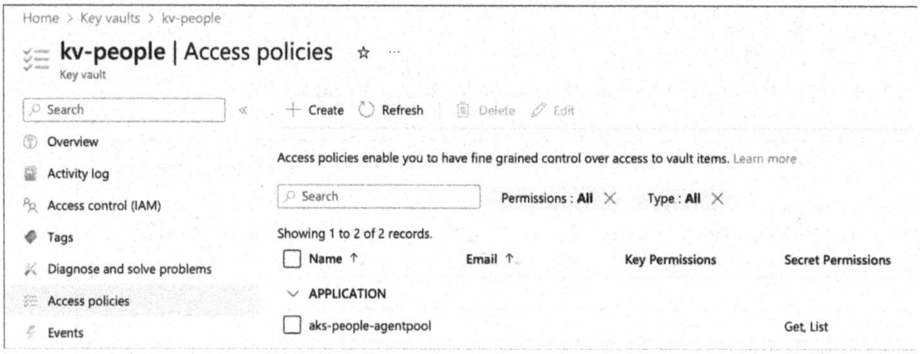

FIGURE 8-14 Access policies of Azure Key Vault.

The final step involves obtaining the client ID of the managed identity associated with the node pool. To retrieve this, type the following command in Azure Cloud Shell:

```
az identity list --query "[?contains(name, 'aks-people-agentpool')].
clientId" -o tsv
```

Store the output value. You will need this to update the environment variable when deploying the updated People.WebApp.

Updating the application

To update the application, you must build the Docker image locally, tag it, and push it to Azure Container Registry. Proceed as follows:

1. Open the local terminal or command prompt, and, under the People.WebApp folder, type the following command (ensure Docker Desktop is running first):

   ```
   docker build -t people.azurecr.io/people.webapp:v2 --platform=linux/amd64 .
   ```

2. Wait for the build to complete. Then, log in to Azure Container Registry:

   ```
   az acr login -n people
   ```

3. Push the image:

   ```
   docker push people.azurecr.io/people.webapp:v2
   ```

You now have the container image with an updated People.WebApp in Azure Container Registry. In the next step, you will use this container to update the application in the Azure Kubernetes Service. To do so, in Azure Cloud Shell, type:

```
wget https://raw.githubusercontent.com/dawidborycki/People.WebApp.Declarations/↵
      main/Kubernetes/people_aks_key_vault.yml
```

This downloads the people_aks_key_vault.yml file, which is detailed in Listing 8-3.

LISTING 8-3 A Deployment of an Updated People.WebApp.

```yaml
apiVersion: apps/v1
kind: Deployment
metadata:
  name: people-webapp-deployment
spec:
  replicas: 2
  selector:
    matchLabels:
      app: people-webapp
  template:
    metadata:
      labels:
        app: people-webapp
    spec:
      containers:
      - name: people-webapp
        image: people.azurecr.io/people.webapp:v2
        imagePullPolicy: Always
        ports:
        - containerPort: 5000
        env:
        - name: UseInMemoryDatabase
          value: "False"
        - name: KeyVaultName
          value: kv-people
        - name: ManagedIdentityClientId
          value: "<paste_your_client_id_here>"
```

Note that the image field is set to the new version of the container image. We now also have three environment variables:

1. `UseInMemoryDatabase` Is set to `False` to use the actual, persistent database.

2. `KeyVaultName` Is set to `kv-people`. Update this if you used a different name for the key vault.

3. `ManagedIdentityClientId` Paste here the client ID of the managed identity associated with the `aks-people-agentpool`. You can retrieve the client ID using the following command:

   `az identity list --query "[?contains(name, 'aks-people-agentpool')].clientId" -o tsv`

Note that the connection string is no longer stored as open text, which makes the solution much more secure. After updating the people_aks_key_vault.yml, deploy the application to the Azure Kubernetes Service by typing:

`kubectl apply -f people_aks_key_vault.yml`

The application will function as before. However, it now securely retrieves the connection string from Azure Key Vault.

> **Tip** To protect sensitive information such as database connection strings or passwords, always store these details securely in Azure Key Vault. By integrating Key Vault directly with your applications, you eliminate the risks associated with storing secrets in configuration files or environment variables, significantly enhancing your application's security posture.

> **Note** When deploying applications to Azure Kubernetes Service (AKS), leverage managed identities to authenticate securely with Azure resources. Managed identities remove the need for explicit credential management in your application code, simplifying authentication and ensuring that access to resources like Azure Key Vault and Azure SQL Database is secure, automated, and manageable.

Summary

In this chapter, you learned how applications deployed to Azure Kubernetes Service can utilize other Azure services. You created the Azure SQL Database to provide persistent storage for the People. WebApp, ensuring that data remains available to application pods after restarts. You also securely stored the database connection string as a secret in the Azure Key Vault.

Additionally, you learned how to programmatically retrieve this secret. For the ASP.NET Core application, the secret was accessed using the Azure Key Vault Secrets configuration provider, allowing the application to treat this secret as if it were stored in the application settings. Throughout the process, you used managed identities to define access policies, enabling pods running in the Azure Kubernetes node pool to retrieve secrets from Azure Key Vault.

This information equips you to rapidly develop comprehensive cloud solutions that leverage containerization, Kubernetes, and the Azure ecosystem.

In the next chapter, you will learn how to use Azure services to diagnose and monitor your solution.

CHAPTER 9

Diagnosing and Monitoring the Cluster

You have learned how to use various Azure services and the Kubernetes cluster, enabling you to deploy a multi-tier solution to Azure. As the number of deployed resources can quickly grow, you will also need approaches to diagnose and monitor your cluster. In this chapter, you will learn how to use the Azure portal to retrieve information about the cluster and workloads. This knowledge can be practically applied to quickly diagnose your cluster's deployments, services, and configurations. Then, you will see how to use monitoring tools, including metrics, alerts, and logs, to gain insights into both the hardware and software aspects of the cluster.

Kubernetes resources

In Chapter 7, "Azure Kubernetes Service," you used kubectl to list and manage Kubernetes, using either the terminal or Azure Cloud Shell. However, if you prefer visual tools, Azure has you covered. The Azure portal offers several tools that enable you to list and manage Kubernetes services, as you'll learn in the sections that follow.

Namespaces, workloads, and services

We'll start with namespaces. To access them, open the Azure Portal and navigate to the Azure Kubernetes cluster you created earlier. You can do this by typing the cluster name (**aks-people**) in the search box, which will take you to the cluster overview. Then, click Namespaces under Kubernetes Resources. You will see the list of namespaces as shown in Figure 9-1. This list contains the same elements as those generated by the **kubectl get ns** or **kubectl get namespaces** commands.

In the Namespaces tab, you can manage namespaces effectively. To create a new namespace, click the + Create button and select Namespace from the dropdown. A new pane will appear, allowing you to configure the namespace.

Similarly, you can remove selected namespaces using the Delete button. There is also a Show Labels toggle that lets you display or hide the Kubernetes labels associated with namespaces. Command-line users can view these labels using the **kubectl describe ns** command.

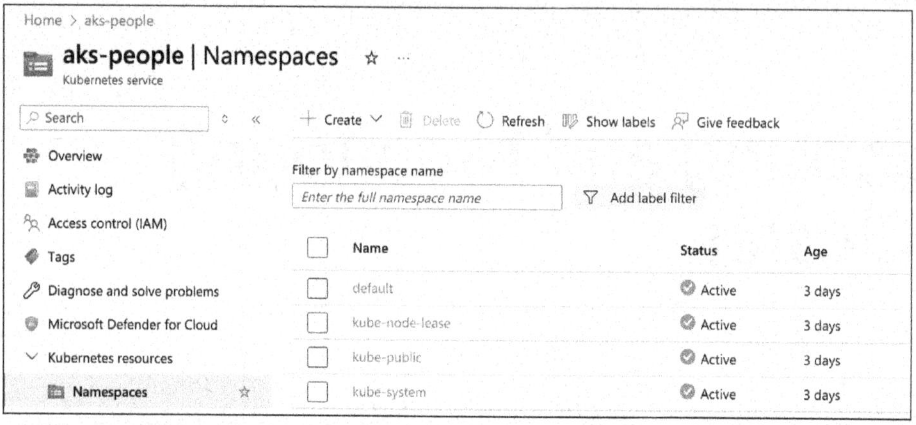

FIGURE 9-1 The list of namespaces in the cluster.

To quickly check the list of Deployments and Pods, navigate to the Workloads tab under Kubernetes resources (see Figure 9-2). This tab displays a list of replicas, stateful sets, and daemon sets, as well as allows you to manage Cron jobs. You can filter each workload by name, namespace, and labels, plus create new workloads by clicking the + Create button. Navigating between various objects is often much faster here than using kubectl, especially if you prefer a graphical interface.

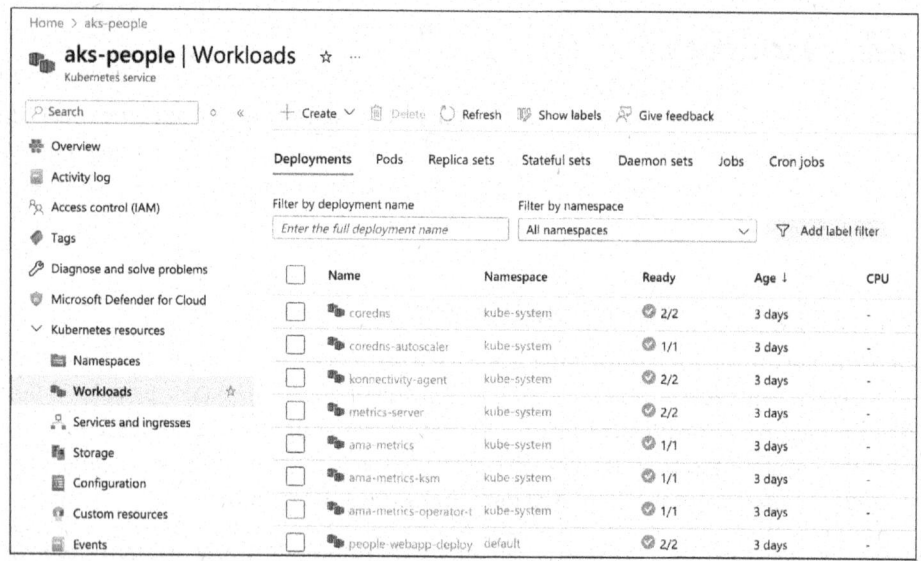

FIGURE 9-2 Managing Kubernetes workloads in the Azure portal.

Azure Portal also provides a quick overview of the services running in the cluster. To view these services, click the Services And Ingresses link under the Kubernetes resources (see Figure 9-3). This will display a list of all services, similar to what you would see with the `kubectl get svc --all-namespaces` command.

The list includes the service type, its associated cluster, and its external IP. For example, for the people-webapp-service, the displayed external IP is a hyperlink. Clicking this link will redirect you to People.WebApp running in the cluster.

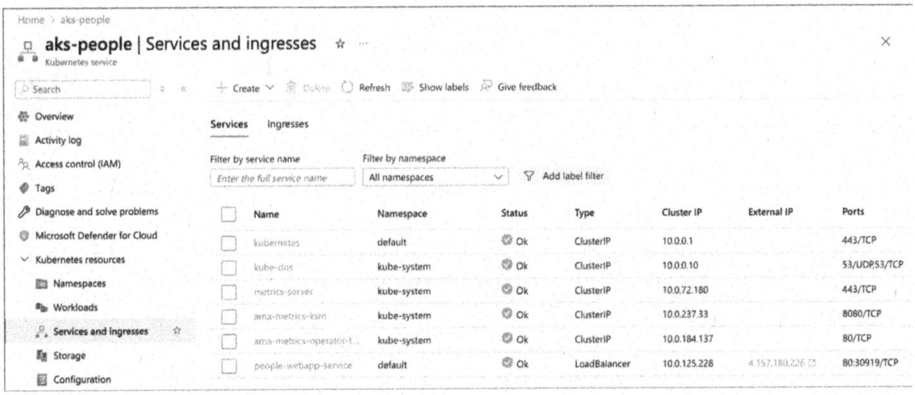

FIGURE 9-3 A list of services and ingresses in the Azure Kubernetes Cluster.

Storage and configuration

There are additional tabs you can use to manage the cluster. First, the Storage tab enables you to manage volumes and storage classes. Volumes can be attached to Pods, with the underlying service being either Azure Files or Azure Disks. These services offer different tiers that define the hardware and performance characteristics, such as HDD or SSD drives. To associate the storage service performance with the volumes, storage classes are used. As shown in Figure 9-4, several default storage classes are available for configuring volumes.

In Azure, you can create volumes for Pods in two ways. First, you can statically create a persistent volume, which is then attached to the cluster and running Pods. Alternatively, you can create a persistent volume claim, which dynamically uses the associated storage class to create the volume when needed.

Kubernetes allows you to store configuration data using ConfigMaps, which are designed to store non-confidential data in key-value pairs. ConfigMaps can be consumed by Pods in various ways, such as through environment variables, command-line arguments, or as configuration files within a volume. By utilizing ConfigMaps, you can effectively separate environment-specific configurations from your container images, enhancing the portability of your applications. This decoupling ensures that your applications can adapt to different environments without necessitating changes to the underlying container images.

For storing sensitive data such as passwords, tokens, or keys, Kubernetes natively provides Secrets. This feature safeguards sensitive information, eliminating the need to include confidential data directly within your application code, thus enhancing security by keeping sensitive information separate from the application logic. Additionally, you can configure Azure Key Vault to store these secrets, further strengthening security.

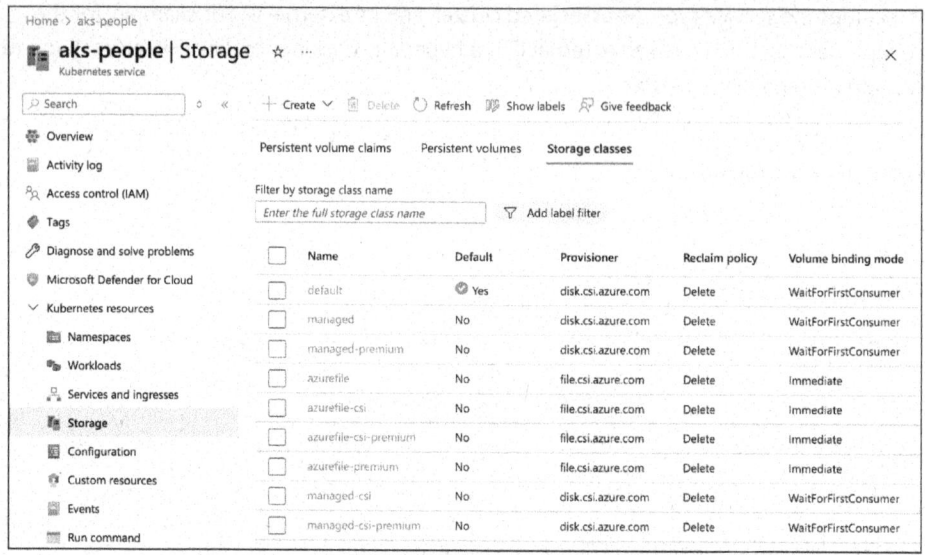

FIGURE 9-4 Storage classes.

You can manage ConfigMaps and Secrets for your Azure Kubernetes cluster from the Configuration tab under Kubernetes resources (see Figure 9-5). As with other resources, you can list, filter, and preview all ConfigMaps and Secrets. Also, you can create new ConfigMaps or Secrets using the + Create button.

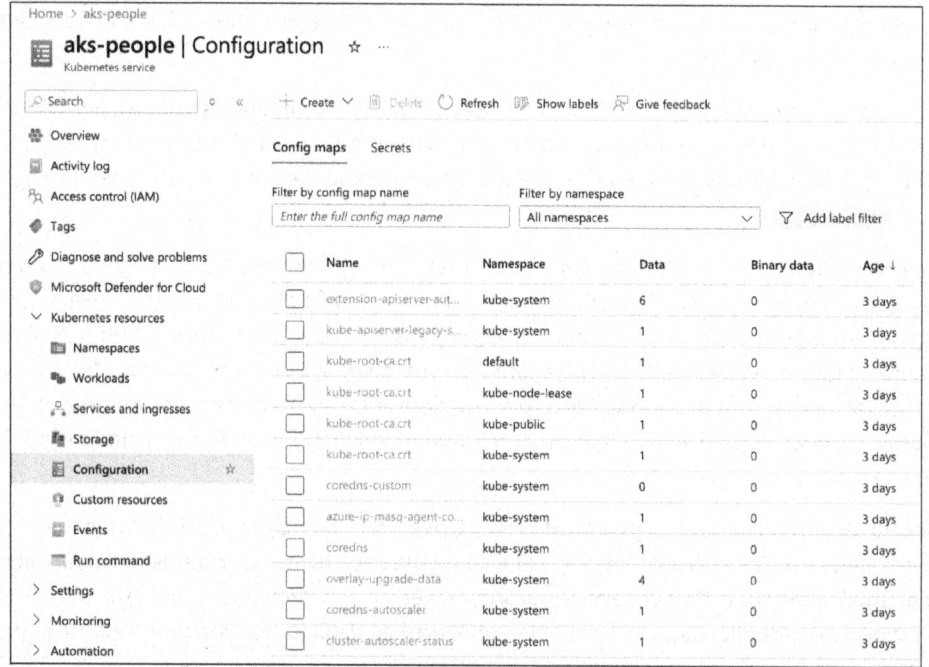

FIGURE 9-5 The Configuration tab of the Azure Kubernetes cluster.

Running commands

Finally, you can run kubectl and Helm commands directly from the Azure portal. To do this, use the Run Command tab under Kubernetes Resources. There, you can enter any command in the text box at the bottom of the screen, such as **kubectl get deployments**. After typing your command, click Run to execute the command against the cluster as seen in Figure 9-6. In the Run Command tab, you can also attach YAML files to execute more complex operations.

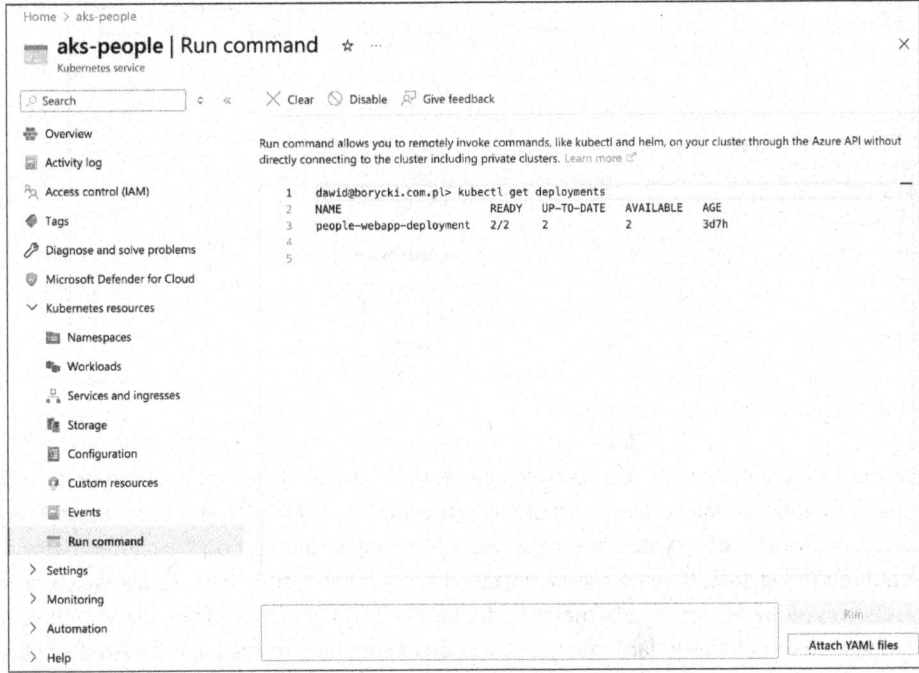

FIGURE 9-6 Running a command.

Monitoring

You have just seen that the Azure portal enables you to diagnose and manage Kubernetes resources without using the kubectl command-line tool. Now, it's time to explore the services available for monitoring your cluster and running Pods, accessible under the Monitoring tab of your cluster.

Alerts and metrics

Take a look at the Alerts tab, which allows you to manage and view alerts (see Figure 9-7). You can use alerts to proactively identify and resolve issues before they affect users. Alerts are designed to notify you of potential problems with cluster infrastructure or applications. They can be configured for various signal types, including metrics, logs, and the activity log. By default, two alert rules are created with the cluster (see Figure 9-8). You can view these alerts or create additional ones by clicking the Alert Rules link at the top of the Alerts tab.

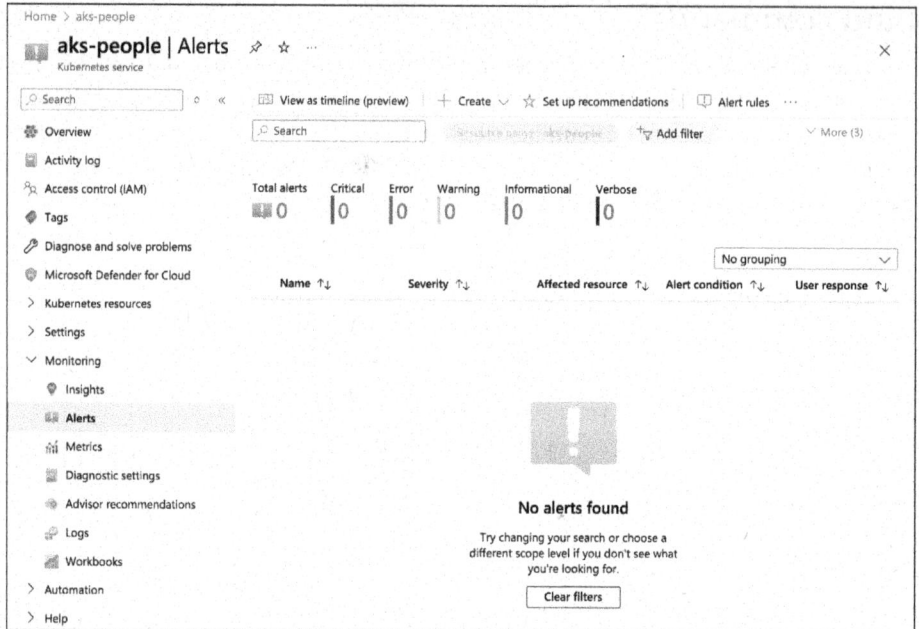

FIGURE 9-7 The Alerts tab for monitoring events.

Once you have defined alert rules, you will receive notifications when they are triggered. To diagnose issues and optimize the performance of the Azure Kubernetes cluster, you use metrics. Metrics, which are numeric data represented as time series, are crucial for monitoring the cluster. These are collected through the default metrics server installed in the kube-system namespace, which systematically retrieves metrics from all Kubernetes nodes serviced by kubelet. Additionally, you can enable Azure Managed Prometheus to facilitate the collection of container metrics and Kubernetes object metrics, including the state of Deployments.

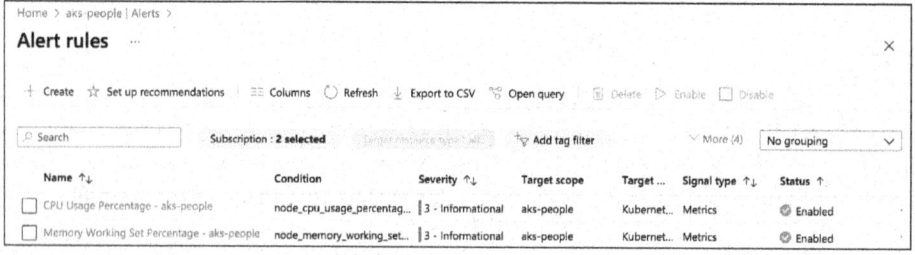

FIGURE 9-8 A list of alert rules.

Importantly, you can combine metrics with alerts. Specifically, you can first create charts that display the time courses of the metrics. Once you have a visual representation of the metric over time, you can identify trends. Based on these, you can set alerts to detect anomalies in the metric trends.

To see how to use metrics, click the Metrics tab. You will see an empty chart like the one shown in Figure 9-9. From the Metric dropdown (at right), select Number Of Pods By Phase, and change the

Aggregation setting to Sum to observe how the number of Pods varies over time. You can use this plot to investigate potential issues with Pod scheduling.

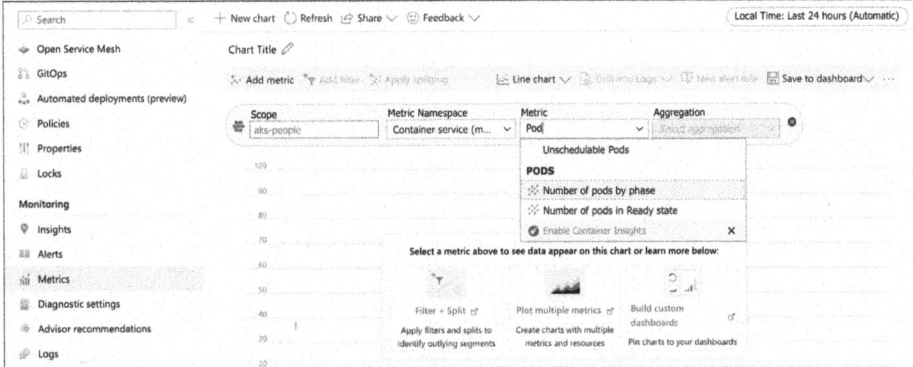

FIGURE 9-9 Using metrics to monitor time courses of various signals.

> **Note** When creating Kubernetes alerts in Azure, it's beneficial to combine them with metrics. Start by visualizing important metrics, such as CPU or memory usage, over time to detect trends or anomalies. Once you've identified a critical pattern, you can configure targeted alerts to proactively notify you before issues escalate.

Container Insights

Container Insights are provided to oversee the performance and well-being of container workloads deployed to the Azure Kubernetes cluster. Insights gather memory and processor metrics from controllers, nodes, and containers. Additionally, this feature enables access to container logs.

To see how Container Insights work, click Insights under the Monitoring group of your cluster. On the default page that opens, click the Configure Monitoring button to open the pane shown in Figure 9-10. Use this pane to enable Container Insights. Managed Prometheus is enabled by default when the cluster is created. Alternatively, you can install Grafana if you prefer to use it for visualizing metrics acquired by Prometheus. When you're done, click Configure at the bottom of the Configure Container Insights pane.

It will take a few minutes to deploy all the necessary resources. All resources will be deployed to the same resource group as the cluster (here, that is rg-aks-people). Once Deployment is completed, the Insights tab of the cluster will be available. At the top part of the screen, several controls allow you to configure what is displayed. First, change Time Range to 30 minutes, and then, turn on the Live option. After a few moments, you will see various metrics, such as node CPU and memory utilization, node count, and active Pod count (as shown in Figure 9-11).

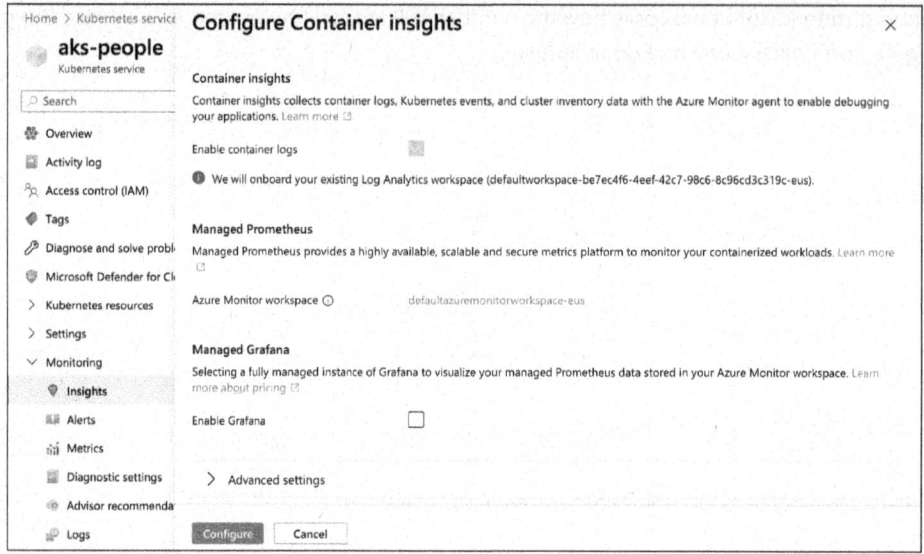

FIGURE 9-10 Configuring Container Insights.

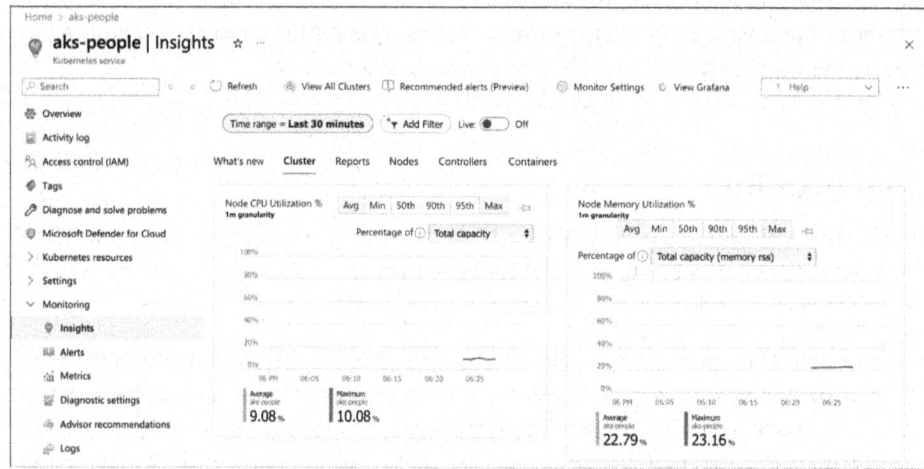

FIGURE 9-11 Container Insights showing the cluster metrics.

The metrics from Figure 9-11 provide high-level information about your cluster's nodes. However, you can obtain more granular details down to the Pod level. To do this, select the Nodes tab (located below the Add Filter button). You will then see a screen similar to Figure 9-12, which displays an element representing the cluster node, aks-agentpool. Upon expanding this element, you will see a list of Pods running on that node. By default, the list displays CPU usage, but you can also view information about memory utilization.

You can delve deeper and analyze each Pod's container CPU and memory usage. To do this, expand the container's node and select the container of interest.

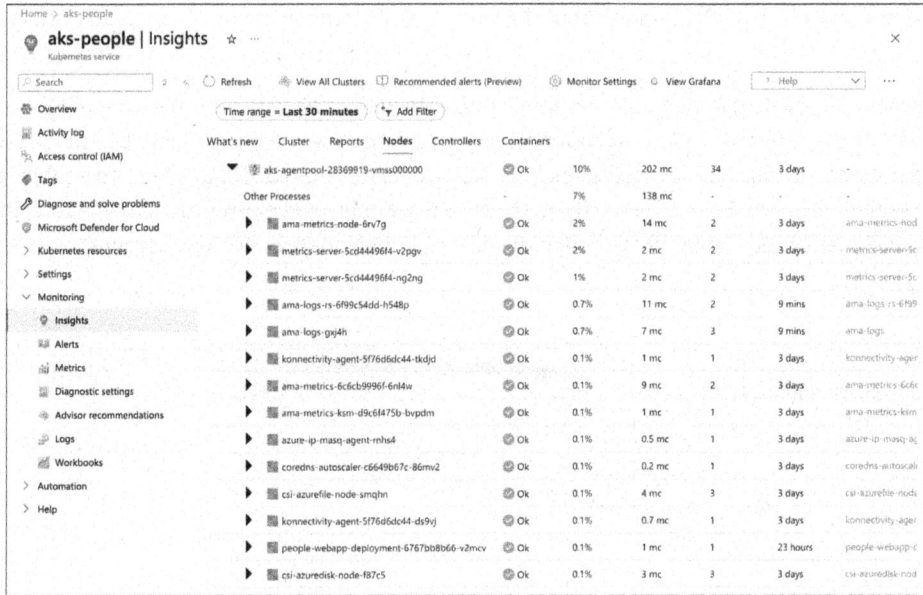

FIGURE 9-12 Cluster monitoring.

You can also access information about the container from the Containers tab, which displays a list of all containers running in the cluster. This list is particularly useful if you need to find a container by its name. For example, to locate the containers associated with People.WebApp, you can type **people** in the search box (see Figure 9-13).

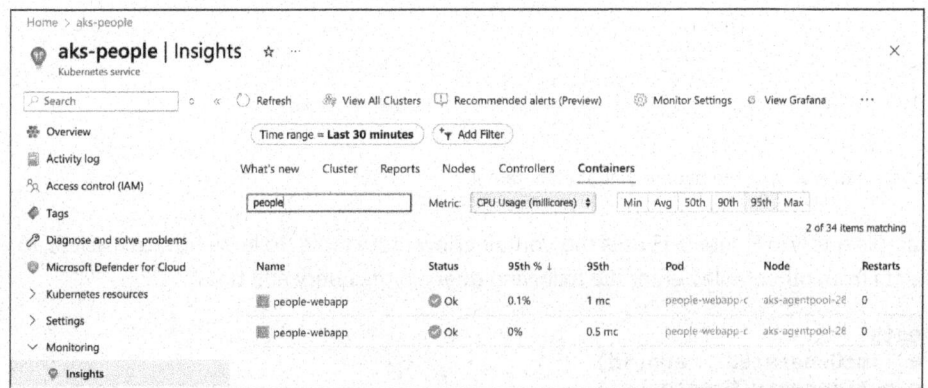

FIGURE 9-13 A list of containers running in the cluster.

After selecting one of the people-webapp containers, an overview pane of the container appears on the right. This pane, as shown in Figure 9-14, includes the container name, status, start time, and the image, as well as the Kubernetes namespace.

Click the View In Log Analytics link at the top of the overview to open a workbook containing a default query that displays logs generated by the container (see Figure 9-15). For the people-webapp container, the logs display information about the hosting environment, content root path, port, and more.

In practice, you use Log Analytics to monitor issues with your application by analyzing diagnostic logs to track the order of operations and identify any errors. You use the Kusto Query Language (KQL) to create solution-specific queries for log analysis. KQL works similarly to SQL queries and enables you to query entities organized into a hierarchy. In the case of a Kubernetes cluster running in Azure, this hierarchy includes various tables like ContainerInventory, KubeNodeInventory, KubeEvents, and Perf.

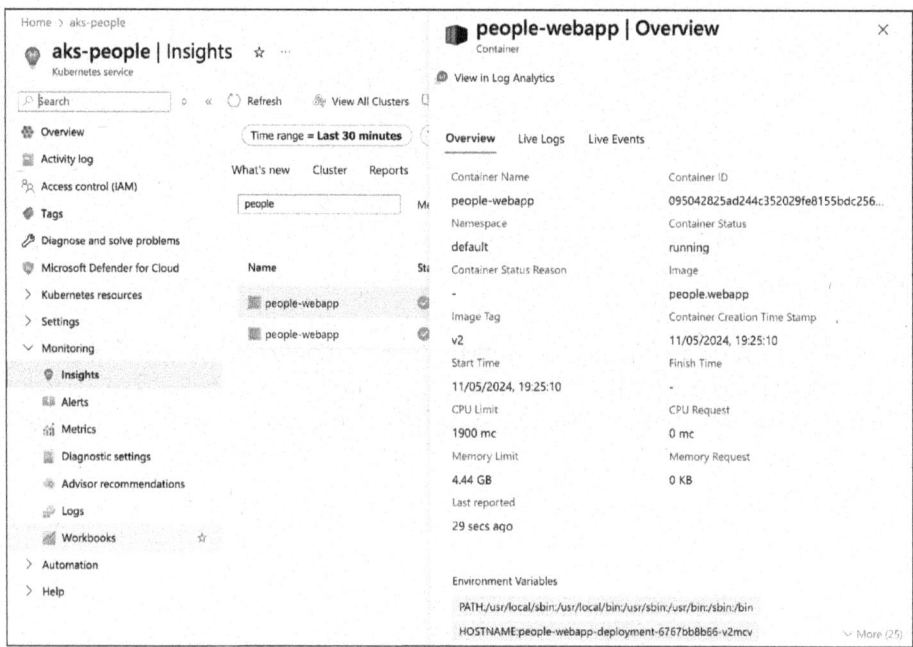

FIGURE 9-14 An overview of the people-webapp container.

The sample query in Figure 9-15 uses the ContainerInventory table. To learn how to use KQL to retrieve data from other tables, enter the following query in the query edit box:

```
KubeEvents
| where TimeGenerated > ago(5d)
| where not(isempty(Namespace))
| top 200 by TimeGenerated desc
```

After clicking the Run button, you will see a list of Kubernetes events from the last five days, including event descriptions, object kinds (like Pod or service), namespaces, and messages. When running complex applications composed of many Pods, you can use KQL to retrieve only the essential information needed to diagnose problems.

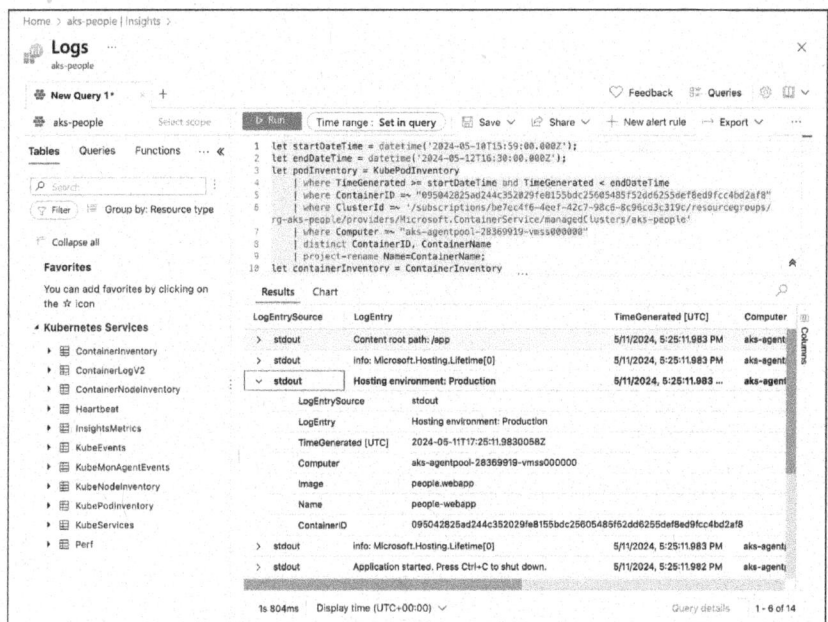

FIGURE 9-15 Logs of the people-webapp container.

Tip Although kubectl is widely used for Kubernetes management, the Azure portal provides a convenient graphical interface for quickly inspecting resources like namespaces, workloads, and services. This visual approach can significantly simplify troubleshooting, especially when you're navigating complex cluster environments or verifying configurations at a glance.

Tip Use Container Insights to efficiently monitor both high-level cluster health and detailed container-level metrics. It integrates seamlessly with Azure Managed Prometheus and optionally Grafana, providing comprehensive visibility into performance, resource utilization, and application logs—all within a centralized, easy-to-use dashboard.

Summary

This chapter aimed to demonstrate how to use the Azure portal to diagnose and monitor an Azure Kubernetes cluster. You learned how to quickly retrieve an overview of deployed Kubernetes workloads, services, storage, and configuration settings. Additionally, you explored how to use Azure's monitoring tools to gain insights into the cluster. In Part III, you will further use these tools to monitor cluster performance and manage autoscaling under various load conditions.

CHAPTER 10

Application Rollouts and Rollbacks

In the present era, technology evolves at an unprecedented rate, and user expectations continue to soar. As a result, software applications must continually adapt and improve to remain relevant, competitive, and secure. Continuous updates are pivotal in ensuring that applications stay bug-free and perform optimally. Additionally, they enable developers to address emerging security threats and integrate new features that enhance user experiences. In this dynamic environment, the concept of "set it and forget it" is no longer viable; instead, organizations must embrace a culture of ongoing development and refinement to meet the ever-evolving demands of their user base.

The need for continuous application updates is closely tied to application scaling. Because web traffic can fluctuate, applications must seamlessly scale to accommodate increased loads and ensure consistent performance. Constant application updates enable organizations to tackle scalability concerns, optimize resource allocation, and maintain the agility required to meet the demands of a growing and diverse user ecosystem.

This chapter will delve into the practical aspects of performing application updates, rollbacks, and manual scaling. You will begin by modifying the People.WebApp application to provide information about the Pod name responsible for processing incoming requests. Subsequently, you will learn how to execute a rollout of this new application version, access the rollout history, and perform rollbacks to specific versions when needed. Finally, you manually scale containerized applications in Kubernetes.

How to retrieve the Pod name

The Deployment of People.WebApp spins up two Pods. Each Pod runs a different container, but both containers connect to the same database. Therefore, it's not immediately clear which Pod processed a given request. To resolve this, you can modify People.WebApp to retrieve the Pod name using the `MachineName` property of the `Environment` class. The `MachineName` property returns the NetBIOS name of the computer. Thus, when running the ASP.NET Core app on a local computer, MachineName returns the computer's name. However, when the application runs in a Pod within the Kubernetes cluster, `MachineName` returns the Pod name.

You can incorporate this modification into People.WebApp by adding the `Environment.MachineName` property to the `Index.cshtml` file of the `HomeController`. This change allows the machine's name, in this context, the Pod name, to be displayed below the People.WebApp welcome message (see Listing 10-1).

LISTING 10-1 Retrieving the Machine Name.

```
@{
    ViewData["Title"] = "Home Page";
}

<div class="text-center">
    <h1 class="display-4">Welcome</h1>
    <p>The request was processed by: @Environment.MachineName</p>
</div>
```

Next, you can add another controller, `InfoApiController`. Listing 10-2 shows that the controller returns the machine name through a GET request.

LISTING 10-2 A Definition of the InfoApiController.

```
using Microsoft.AspNetCore.Mvc;

namespace People.WebApp.Controllers
{
    [Route("api/info")]
    [ApiController]
    public class InfoApiController : ControllerBase
    {
        [HttpGet]
        public string GetMachineName()
        {
            return $"The request was processed by: {Environment.MachineName}";
        }
    }
}
```

You can now retrieve the machine name in two ways: either from the People.WebApp main view or from the API controller. To see how this works, try running People.WebApp locally. First, ensure you are in the People.WebApp directory, then change the git branch to net8-podname:

git checkout net8-podname

Then, run the app using the following command:

dotnet run

After the application launches, open it in a web browser (localhost:5000). You will see the name of your local computer, as shown in Figure 10-1.

FIGURE 10-1 A modified People.WebApp displays the name of the machine that processed the request.

You can also retrieve the machine name by sending a GET request to localhost:5000/api/info. This can be done using a web browser, Swagger, or command-line tools like curl. Using curl you would type:

```
curl localhost:5000/api/info; echo
```

The result of this command should appear as shown in Figure 10-2. Note that the version of People.WebApp from the net8-podname branch also uses Azure Key Vault. Hence, if you encounter any errors when launching People.WebApp, ensure you execute **az login** before starting the app.

```
% curl localhost:5000/api/info; echo
The request was processed by: MBP-Dawid
%
%
```

FIGURE 10-2 Retrieving the machine name using the InfoApiController.

After confirming that the application functions locally, you can build the Docker image:

```
docker build -t people.azurecr.io/people.webapp:v3 --platform=linux/amd64.
```

This command tags the image with the name of the container registry. Replace **people** with the name of your container registry.

Next, push the image to the Azure Container Registry:

```
az acr login -n people
```

```
docker push people.azurecr.io/people.webapp:v3
```

You should now have three Docker images in the remote repository. Verify this using the following command:

```
az acr repository show-tags -n people --repository people.webapp -o table
```

This command displays the list of tags in the people.webapp repository as depicted in Figure 10-3.

```
% az acr repository show-tags -n people --repository people.webapp -o table
Result
--------
v1
v2
v3
%
%
```

FIGURE 10-3 A list of tags in the people.webapp repository.

Rollout

After preparing the Docker image of the updated People.WebApp, you can now roll it out to the Azure Kubernetes cluster. Start by listing the deployments in the default namespace:

kubectl get deployments

Then, update the Docker image of the people-webapp container under the people-webapp-Deployment:

kubectl set image deployments/people-webapp-deployment people-webapp=↵
      people.azurecr.io/people.webapp:v3

This command will output the following message: "deployment.apps/people-webapp-deployment image updated." See Figure 10-4 for details.

```
dawid [ ~ ]$ kubectl get deployments
NAME                      READY   UP-TO-DATE   AVAILABLE   AGE
people-webapp-deployment  2/2     2            2           4d1h
dawid [ ~ ]$ kubectl set image deployments/people-webapp-deployment people-webapp=people.azurecr.io/
people.webapp:v3

deployment.apps/people-webapp-deployment image updated
dawid [ ~ ]$
dawid [ ~ ]$ kubectl rollout status deployment/people-webapp-deployment
deployment "people-webapp-deployment" successfully rolled out
dawid [ ~ ]$
```

FIGURE 10-4 Rolling out the new version of People.WebApp.

To check the status of the rollout, use the **kubectl rollout status** command as follows:

kubectl rollout status deployment/people-webapp-deployment

The command's output will depend on the time elapsed between invoking the **kubectl set image** command and the **kubectl rollout status** command. After updating the container image in the Deployment declaration, Kubernetes will initiate the creation of two new containers using the new Docker image (people.webapp:v3). If the new containers start successfully, Kubernetes will terminate Pods created using previous versions of People.WebApp.

By updating the Deployment, you changed the desired state of the application. The new Pods are created using the Pod template defined under the Deployment. Pods are created and removed by the ReplicaSet. To get the list of ReplicaSets, type the following command:

kubectl get rs

As shown in Figure 10-5, the command will list several items, each of which corresponds to a version of People.WebApp that you deployed using various Docker images. However, only the most recent version has two Pods up and running. Previous ReplicaSets show a desired number of replicas of 0.

To check the status of Pods created by the ReplicaSet, you can type the following:

kubectl get pods

You will then see a list of two Pods. Their names include the deployment name and an identifier of the ReplicaSet.

```
dawid [ ~ ]$ kubectl get rs
NAME                                       DESIRED   CURRENT   READY   AGE
people-webapp-deployment-55cd5697fc        2         2         2       3m3s
people-webapp-deployment-6767bb8b66        0         0         0       40h
people-webapp-deployment-684db7756d        0         0         0       41h
people-webapp-deployment-87864d9b4         0         0         0       4d1h
dawid [ ~ ]$
dawid [ ~ ]$ kubectl get pods
NAME                                          READY   STATUS    RESTARTS   AGE
people-webapp-deployment-55cd5697fc-7hjdf     1/1     Running   0          3m23s
people-webapp-deployment-55cd5697fc-pc9j6     1/1     Running   0          3m19s
dawid [ ~ ]$
```

FIGURE 10-5 A list of ReplicaSets and Pods associated with the people-webapp-deployment.

Now, go to the public IP of the people-webapp-service. Use the **kubectl get svc** command to retrieve the external IP of that service (here, that is 4.157.180.226). You will see People.WebApp. Its welcome screen will display the Pod's name that processed the request (Figure 10-6). This name should be one of the two available Pods. Try to refresh the page several times to see that the Pod's name will eventually change.

FIGURE 10-6 The name of the Pod that processed the request.

Additionally, you can send multiple GET requests to the InfoApiController to see how Kubernetes balances the load. Here is a script that sends 10 requests to that controller (replace ***http://4.157.180.226/api/info*** with the IP address of your people-webapp-service):

```
for i in {1..10}; do curl 'http://4.157.180.226/api/info'; echo; done
```

The results should show that both Pods handle consecutive requests, confirming that Kubernetes effectively balances incoming traffic across available Pods (see Figure 10-7).

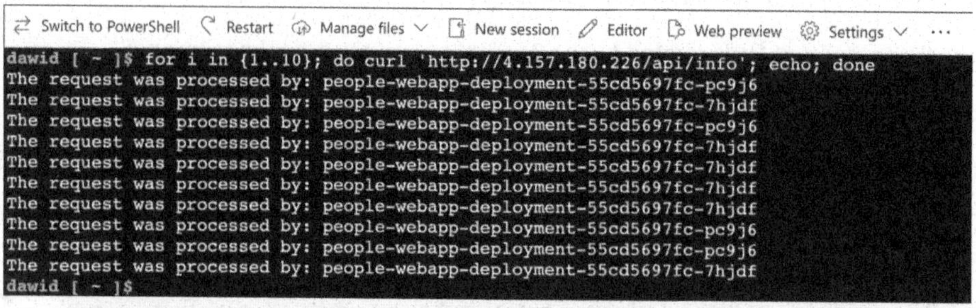

FIGURE 10-7 Kubernetes balances the load across available Pods.

> **Tip** When performing application rollouts in Kubernetes, always check the rollout status (**kubectl rollout status**) after initiating an update. This practice helps you quickly verify whether the new Pods are running correctly, ensuring that potential issues are detected and addressed promptly before impacting users.

> **Note** It's crucial to annotate your Kubernetes deployments using clear and descriptive change-cause messages (via **kubectl annotate**). Doing so makes your rollout history much easier to interpret, enabling swift rollbacks to specific versions when troubleshooting or addressing unexpected issues.

Rollout strategies

In all the previous examples, you used the default RollingUpdate rollout strategy, which incrementally replaces old Pods with new ones. However, you can customize how many additional Pods can be created above the desired count and the maximum number of Pods that can be unavailable during the update. These settings are controlled by the `maxSurge` and `maxUnavailable` parameters within the strategy field of the Deployment declaration file, as shown in Listing 10-3.

LISTING 10-3 Deployment Declaration with Rollout Configuration.

```
apiVersion: apps/v1
kind: Deployment
metadata:
  name: people-webapp-deployment
spec:
  replicas: 2
  selector:
    matchLabels:
      app: people-webapp   template:
    metadata:
      labels:
        app: people-webapp
    spec:
      containers:
      - name: people-webapp
        image: people.azurecr.io/people.webapp:v3
        imagePullPolicy: Always
        ports:
        - containerPort: 5000
        env:
               - name: UseInMemoryDatabase
          value: "False"
        - name: KeyVaultName
          value: kv-people
        - name: ManagedIdentityClientId
          value: "<paste_your_client_id_here>"
  strategy:
    type: RollingUpdate
    rollingUpdate:
      maxSurge: 50%
      maxUnavailable: 50%
```

The `RollingUpdate` strategy ensures updates occur with minimal downtime but requires additional hardware resources to perform the update.

Alternatively, if resources are limited and a brief downtime is acceptable, you might opt for the Recreate strategy. This method involves terminating all existing old-version Pods before creating new-version Pods.

Another method is the Blue-Green Deployment, which maintains two separate environments throughout the application lifecycle. The "blue" environment is the current production, and the "green" environment is for the new version. After the green environment is fully tested and validated, traffic is switched from blue to green, promoting the new version to production.

Canary Deployments gradually introduce a new version to a subset of users or traffic. Initially, only a small fraction of traffic is directed to the new version (the canary) to monitor its behavior and performance. If the canary proves stable, traffic is increasingly shifted to it. Conversely, if issues arise, the rollout can be halted or reversed. Implementing a canary deployment requires an additional Deployment and service for the canary, plus rules for redirecting a portion of traffic to this service.

Finally, A/B testing is similar to canary deployments but is used to test different variations or features of an application. It directs a specific percentage of users to different versions or configurations of your application, allowing data collection on user behavior to inform further decisions.

Rollout history and rollbacks

To demonstrate the versatility of Kubernetes, take a closer look how to use the **kubectl rollout history** command to rollback an application to a previous or a specific version. This capability is crucial when a new version fails to perform as expected.

First, view the rollout history of the people-webapp-deployment. Execute the following command:

```
kubectl rollout history deployment/people-webapp-deployment
```

The command shows the list of revisions (see Figure 10-8).

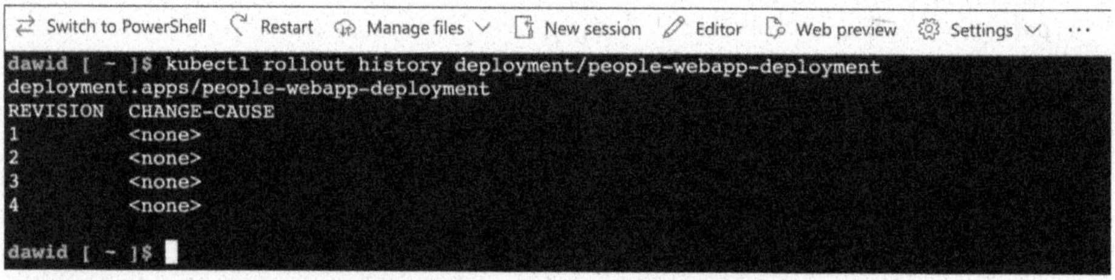

FIGURE 10-8 A list of revisions of the people-webapp-deployment.

There are four revisions, each corresponding to a version of People.WebApp:

- **Revision 1:** The original version of the application, prepared in Part I (people.webapp:v1)
- **Revision 2:** A modified Deployment including access to Azure SQL Database
- **Revision 3:** A modified version from Chapter 8, integrating access to Azure Key Vault (people.webapp:v2)
- **Revision 4:** A version displaying the Pod name (people.webapp:v3)

Currently, the `change-cause` for all Deployments is listed as `<none>`. To update this, you can use the `change-cause` annotation. For annotating the latest deployment, use the following command:

```
kubectl annotate deployments.apps people-webapp-deployment ↵
    kubernetes.io/change-cause="Pod name"
```

After executing this, rerun the kubectl rollout history for the people-webapp-deployment, and you will see the updated `change-cause`, as illustrated in Figure 10-9.

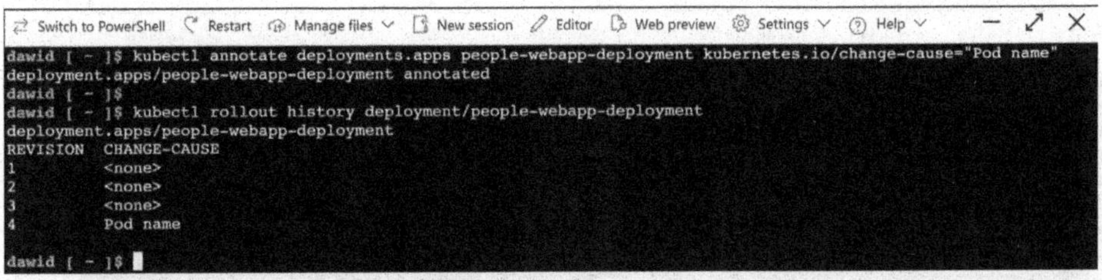

```
dawid [ ~ ]$ kubectl annotate deployments.apps people-webapp-deployment kubernetes.io/change-cause="Pod name"
deployment.apps/people-webapp-deployment annotated
dawid [ ~ ]$
dawid [ ~ ]$ kubectl rollout history deployment/people-webapp-deployment
deployment.apps/people-webapp-deployment
REVISION    CHANGE-CAUSE
1           <none>
2           <none>
3           <none>
4           Pod name

dawid [ ~ ]$
```

FIGURE 10-9 Annotating the Deployment.

In practice, you can add the `change-cause` annotation to the Deployment declaration, as shown in Listing 10-4.

LISTING 10-4 A Declaration of the Deployment with the change-cause.

```
apiVersion: apps/v1
kind: Deployment
metadata:
  name: people-webapp-deployment
  annotations:
      kubernetes.io/change-cause: Pod namespec:
  replicas: 2
  selector:
    matchLabels:
      app: people-webapp
  template:
    metadata:
      labels:
        app: people-webapp
    spec:
      containers:
      - name: people-webapp
        image: people.azurecr.io/people.webapp:v3
        imagePullPolicy: Always
        ports:
        - containerPort: 5000
        env:
        - name: UseInMemoryDatabase
          value: "False"
        - name: KeyVaultName
          value: kv-people
        - name: ManagedIdentityClientId
          value: "<paste_your_client_id_here>"
```

Given the list of deployments, to roll back the application to the previous version, type the following command:

`kubectl rollout undo deployment/people-webapp-deployment`

This command will revert the deployment to the previous version. If you open People.WebApp in the web browser, the Pod name will no longer be displayed on the welcome screen.

```
dawid [ ~ ]$ kubectl rollout undo deployment/people-webapp-deployment
deployment.apps/people-webapp-deployment rolled back
dawid [ ~ ]$
dawid [ ~ ]$ kubectl rollout history deployment/people-webapp-deployment
deployment.apps/people-webapp-deployment
REVISION  CHANGE-CAUSE
1         <none>
2         <none>
4         Pod name
5         <none>

dawid [ ~ ]$
```

FIGURE 10-10 Rolling back the Deployment.

You can now display the history of the people-webapp-deployment rollout to see that what was previously revision 3 has now become revision number 5 (see Figure 10-10).

When rolling back the deployment, you can also specify the revision. For example, to return to the first version of the application (people.webapp:v1), type:

`kubectl rollout undo deployment/people-webapp-deployment --to-revision=1`

Kubernetes will create a new revision number 6, as shown in Figure 10-11.

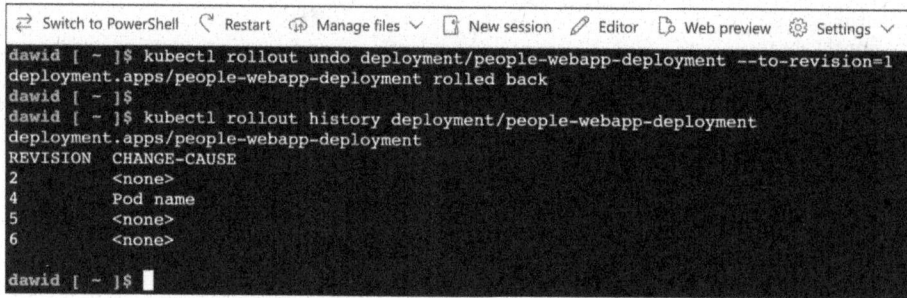

```
dawid [ ~ ]$ kubectl rollout undo deployment/people-webapp-deployment --to-revision=1
deployment.apps/people-webapp-deployment rolled back
dawid [ ~ ]$
dawid [ ~ ]$ kubectl rollout history deployment/people-webapp-deployment
deployment.apps/people-webapp-deployment
REVISION  CHANGE-CAUSE
2         <none>
4         Pod name
5         <none>
6         <none>

dawid [ ~ ]$
```

FIGURE 10-11 Rolling back to the specific revision.

To make revision 4 the current one again, execute:

`kubectl rollout undo deployment/people-webapp-deployment --to-revision=4`

To conclude this section, I'll show you how to restart the entire deployment:

`kubectl rollout restart deployment/people-webapp-deployment`

Use the last command to restart the entire Deployment when the application is in an error state from which it cannot recover on its own.

Manual scaling

In this final example, you will see how to manually scale the number of Pods for the Deployment. In previous examples, you used a fixed number of replicas, set to 2, which you defined in the Deployment declaration. To adjust the number of Pods for your Deployment, you use the **kubectl scale** command. For example, to set the number of Pods for People.WebApp to 8, type the following:

`kubectl scale deployment/people-webapp-deployment --replicas=8`

Then, check the number of Pods by typing:

`kubectl get pods`

The output of the above commands should look like in Figure 10-12.

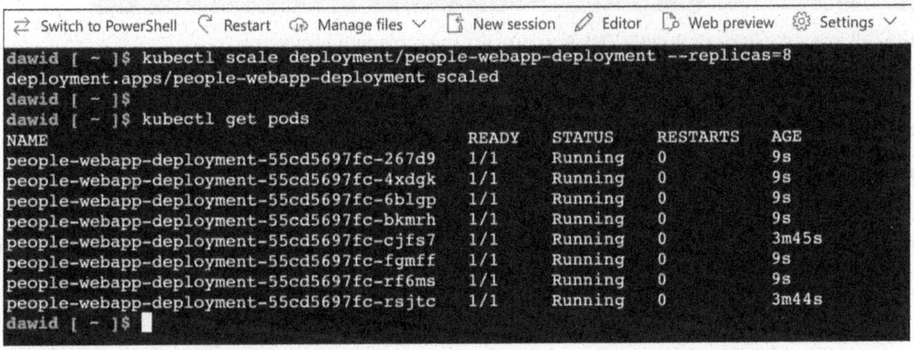

FIGURE 10-12 Manual Deployment scaling.

To confirm that all the Pods can handle incoming requests, send 20 requests to the `InfoApi Controller` of People.WebApp:

`for i in {1..20}; do curl 'http://4.157.180.226/api/info'; echo; done`

You should see output similar to that shown in Figure 10-13. Specifically, you will observe that different Pods handle incoming requests.

Manual scaling has the disadvantage of potentially using more resources than needed—currently, People.WebApp does not experience a high load, so you are maintaining many more Pods than necessary. To solve this problem, Kubernetes offers the Horizontal Pod Autoscaler (HPA), which adjusts the number of Pods based on CPU utilization. You will learn more about this feature in Part III.

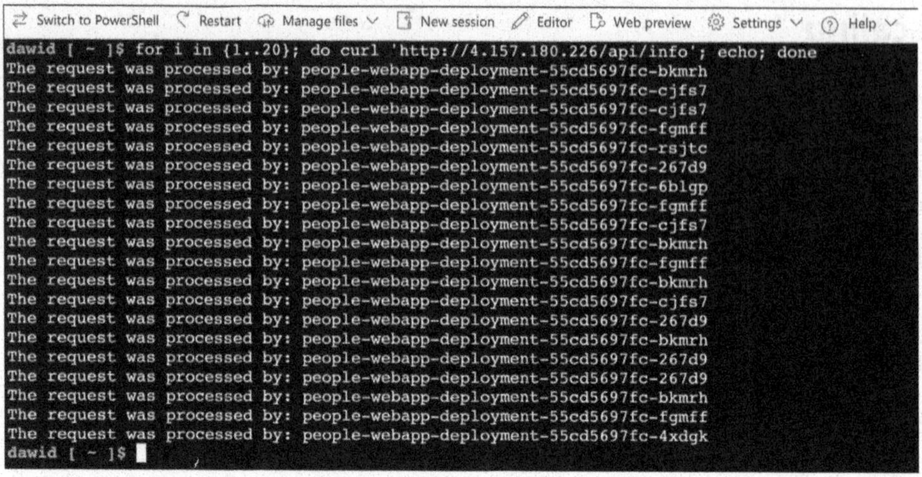

FIGURE 10-13 All available Pods of People.WebApp process the incoming requests.

> **Tip** While manual scaling (**kubectl scale**) offers immediate control over the number of running Pods, it can lead to inefficient resource utilization if not closely managed. For production environments, consider leveraging Kubernetes' built-in Horizontal Pod Autoscaler (HPA), which dynamically adjusts Pod counts based on actual resource usage, ensuring optimal performance and cost-effectiveness.

Summary

This chapter demonstrated how to perform application rollouts and rollbacks in a Kubernetes cluster. You explored how Kubernetes uses ReplicaSets to manage application rollouts and learned how to use rollout history to revert an application to a specific version. Additionally, you gained insights into manually scaling the application and retrieving information about the Pod responsible for processing incoming requests.

PART III

Automation

CHAPTER 11	Automating Image Builds and Deployment Using CI/CD Pipelines	141
CHAPTER 12	Load Testing, Horizontal Pod Autoscaling, and Cluster Autoscaling	161
CHAPTER 13	Deploying and Managing Kubernetes Applications with Helm	181
CHAPTER 14	Infrastructure as Code	205

Part II explored how to use Kubernetes for deploying containerized applications. Specifically, you created a managed cluster in Azure where you deployed People.WebApp and connected it to various Azure services, including SQL Database and Key Vault. Additionally, you learned how to use monitoring tools and perform application rollouts and rollbacks.

However, you performed all these tasks manually. After every change in the application, you manually built the new Docker image, pushed it to the Azure Container Registry, and updated the Kubernetes deployment, as outlined in step 1, 2, and 4-7 of Figure 5-1 (in Chapter 5, "Azure Container Registry"). Over the course of the application's lifetime, these processes needed to be continuously repeated, making it difficult to track changes and posing a risk of errors.

Therefore, this part delves into automating application deployment. You will learn how to incorporate continuous integration/continuous delivery (CI/CD) pipelines (step 3) to gain full control over the application and underlying resource deployment.

In Chapter 11, you will use GitHub Actions to create the CI pipeline, which will automate the building and pushing of Docker images to Azure Container Registry. This pipeline will be triggered whenever the source code is updated, and a pull request is accepted.

Then, in Chapter 12, you will explore how to automatically adjust the application's size (the number of Pods) using the Horizontal Pod Autoscaler discusses deploying applications using Helm charts, which will enable you to manage multiple declarations of deployments, services, and accompanying Kubernetes objects, such as HPA. Finally, in Chapter 14, you will learn how to use Infrastructure as Code (IaC) to deploy and update cloud resources in a declarative way, enabling you to achieve a complete continuous deployment pipeline triggered by changes in the source code.

CHAPTER 11

Automating Image Builds and Deployment Using CI/CD Pipelines

Automating image builds with a continuous integration (CI) pipeline is a crucial aspect of modern software development, streamlining the process of creating, testing, and deploying container images. This automation not only enhances efficiency, but also ensures consistency and reliability in your software delivery pipeline. Once a container image is prepared through the CI pipeline, it can seamlessly be deployed to the target cluster using the continuous deployment (CD) pipeline, further accelerating the deployment process. In this guide, you will practice the steps necessary to create such pipelines for People.WebApp.

Specifically, you will first import the People.WebApp repository into your GitHub account. Then, you will create a workflow declaration and a repository Secret. This Secret will store Azure credentials that enable the workflow to access your Azure resources, allowing it to push the Docker image to your Azure container registry and update the Deployment in Azure Kubernetes Service.

Setting up the workflow

Start by importing the repository:

1. Sign in to github.com.

2. Import the People.WebApp repository by clicking the + dropdown (top-right corner) and selecting Import Repository.

3. In the Import Your Project to GitHub section, do the following:

    a. Paste the clone address of your old repository: *github.com/dawidborycki/People.WebApp.git*.

    b. Enter your new repository details. Select your GitHub identifier from the Owner dropdown, and type **People.WebApp** under Repository Name.

    c. Click Begin Import.

When the import is complete, click the Code button to see and copy the clone URL, which should look like this: *https://github.com/<YOUR_GITHUB_ID>/People.WebApp.git*. Then, open the terminal or command prompt and execute the following commands:

`git clone https://github.com/<YOUR_GITHUB_ID>/People.WebApp.git`

`cd People.WebApp`

`git checkout net8-podname`

`git checkout ci-cd`

The first command clones the source code. The third command changes to the net8-podname branch, which contains the latest version of the application's source code. The last command creates a new ci-cd branch. The output of these commands will resemble Figure 11-1.

```
People.WebApp-TechReview — -zsh — 80×24
% git checkout net8-podname
branch 'net8-podname' set up to track 'origin/net8-podname'.
Switched to a new branch 'net8-podname'
%
% git checkout ci-cd
branch 'ci-cd' set up to track 'origin/ci-cd'.
Switched to a new branch 'ci-cd'
%
%
```

FIGURE 11-1 Creating a new ci-cd branch from net8-podname.

In the next step, you will create the workflow declaration. GitHub Actions expects workflow declarations to be located under the .github/workflows directory. To create this directory structure, use the following commands:

`mkdir -p .github/workflows`

`touch .github/workflows/people-webapp-ci-cd.yml`

If you are using Windows, you can use these commands instead:

`mkdir .github && mkdir .github\workflows`

`type nul > .github\workflows\people-webapp-ci-cd.yml`

Next, open the workflow declaration file (people-webapp-ci-cd.yml) in Visual Studio Code. Visual Studio Code might automatically prompt you to install the GitHub Actions extension. If so, install it. If the prompt does not appear, manually open the Visual Studio Extensions (click View/Extensions) and search for GitHub Actions. This extension will assist you in editing and running the workflow declaration.

In the people-webapp-ci-cd.yml file, add the following statements (Listing 11-1):

LISTING 11-1 GitHub Actions YAML for Automated Docker Image Deployment.

```
name: CI/CD Pipeline

on:
  push:
    branches:
      - ci-cd

env:
  IMAGE_NAME: people.webapp
  ACR_NAME: <REPLACE_THIS_WITH_YOUR_ACR_NAME>
  ACR_LOGIN_SERVER: <REPLACE_THIS_WITH_YOUR_ACR_LOGIN_SERVER>

jobs:
  build-and-push-docker-image:
    runs-on: ubuntu-latest
```

This declaration sets the name of the workflow to CI/CD Pipeline and specifies that the workflow should execute whenever new source code is pushed to the ci-cd branch. It then defines three environment variables accessible throughout the entire workflow:

- **IMAGE_NAME** Stores the name of the Docker image (here, it is people.webapp),
- **ACR_NAME** Defines the name of your Azure container registry (people),
- **ACR_LOGIN_SERVER** Stores the login server of your ACR (people.azurecr.io).

The declaration contains a jobs section. Currently, you have one job named build-and-push-docker-image, which will run on an Ubuntu-based virtual machine hosted by GitHub.

In the next step, you will extend the declaration of the pipeline to include tasks that will build the Docker image and then push it to your container registry.

Automatically building and pushing a Docker image

To automate the building and pushing of the Docker image, you will follow a process similar to the earlier manual one. Specifically, you'll replicate the same commands previously used to log in to Azure (**az login**) and Azure Container Registry (**az acr login**), build and tag the Docker image from the command line (**docker build -t**), and then push the resulting image to Azure Container Registry (**docker push**).

Because the job will be executed within a virtual machine provisioned by GitHub Actions, however, you need to check out the source code repository on that machine and execute all commands there. Note that in this context, there is no option to log in to Azure using the UI. Instead, you will log in using credentials stored as a workflow Secret named AZURE_CREDENTIALS. This Secret's setup will be covered in the next section.

Start by adding a steps section under the build-and-push-docker-image job declared in the people-webapp-ci-cd.yml file (Listing 11-2):

LISTING 11-2 Azure Login and Repository Checkout Steps.

```yaml
jobs:
  build-and-push-docker-image:
    runs-on: ubuntu-latest
    steps:
      - name: Checkout code
        uses: actions/checkout@v4

      - name: Login to Azure
        uses: azure/login@v1
        with:
          creds: ${{ secrets.AZURE_CREDENTIALS }}
```

There are two steps involved. The first step, `Checkout code`, retrieves the source code from the ci-workflow-docker branch. In the next step, you log in to Azure using the credentials stored under the AZURE_CREDENTIALS Secret. Both steps use preconfigured actions (`actions/checkout@v4` and `azure/login@v1`).

Next, add another step that will execute the `az acr login` command (Listing 11-3):

LISTING 11-3 Azure Authentication and ACR Login in Workflow.

```yaml
steps:
  - name: Checkout code
    uses: actions/checkout@v4

- name: Login to Azure
    uses: azure/login@v1
    with:
      creds: ${{ secrets.AZURE_CREDENTIALS }}

- name: Login to Azure Container Registry
    run: az acr login -n $ACR_NAME
```

In the above step, you execute the command `az acr login` with the ACR_NAME workflow environment variable to specify which container registry to log in to.

Subsequently, you perform steps to prepare the image tag by counting existing tags of the people.webapp image (stored in the IMAGE_NAME environment variable). To retrieve the list of tags, use the following command:

```
az acr repository show-tags -n people --repository people.webapp -o tsv
```

As shown in Figure 11-2, this command returns the list of tags. You use the **wc -l** command to count the number of tags.

```
% az acr repository show-tags -n people --repository people.webapp -o tsv
v1
v2
v3
%
%
% az acr repository show-tags -n people --repository people.webapp -o tsv | wc -l
       3
%
```

FIGURE 11-2 Retrieving the List of Image Tags.

Based on the number of tags, create a new image tag by constructing a string consisting of the letter v followed by the number of tags plus one. Store the resulting string in the new IMAGE_TAG workflow environment variable. Here is the updated list of job steps (Listing 11-4):

LISTING 11-4 Automatic Tagging Based on Azure Container Registry Image Count.

```
steps:
  - name: Checkout code
    uses: actions/checkout@v4

  - name: Login to Azure
    uses: azure/login@v1
    with:
      creds: ${{ secrets.AZURE_CREDENTIALS }}

  - name: Login to Azure Container Registry
    run: az acr login -n $ACR_NAME

  - name: Count existing tags and configure the image tag
    run: |
      COUNT=$(az acr repository show-tags -n $ACR_NAME --repository $IMAGE_NAME
        -o tsv | wc -l)
      IMAGE_TAG=v$(expr $COUNT + 1)
      echo "IMAGE_TAG=$IMAGE_TAG" >> $GITHUB_ENV
```

Now, proceed to build and push the Docker image. First, construct the fully qualified Docker image name by combining environment variables and storing the result in a new variable named FQ_IMAGE_NAME:

```
FQ_IMAGE_NAME=$ACR_LOGIN_SERVER/$IMAGE_NAME:$IMAGE_TAG
echo "FQ_IMAGE_NAME=$FQ_IMAGE_NAME" >> $GITHUB_ENV
```

With the fully qualified image name in hand, you can build and push the Docker image. The updated list of job steps demonstrates this process (Listing 11-5):

LISTING 11-5 Docker Image Build, Tagging, and Push to Azure Container Registry.

```
steps:
  - name: Checkout code
    uses: actions/checkout@v4

  - name: Login to Azure
    uses: azure/login@v1
    with:
      creds: ${{ secrets.AZURE_CREDENTIALS }}

  - name: Login to Azure Container Registry
    run: az acr login -n $ACR_NAME

  - name: Count existing tags and configure the image tag
    run: |
      COUNT=$(az acr repository show-tags -n $ACR_NAME --repository $IMAGE_NAME ↵
        -o tsv | wc -l)
      IMAGE_TAG=v$(expr $COUNT + 1)
      echo "IMAGE_TAG=$IMAGE_TAG" >> $GITHUB_ENV

  - name: Build and push Docker image
    run: |
      FQ_IMAGE_NAME=$ACR_LOGIN_SERVER/$IMAGE_NAME:$IMAGE_TAG
      echo "FQ_IMAGE_NAME=$FQ_IMAGE_NAME" >> $GITHUB_ENV
      docker build -t $FQ_IMAGE_NAME .
      docker push $FQ_IMAGE_NAME
```

Finally, execute two steps to log out from ACR and remove the image from the virtual machine. To achieve this, use the **docker logout** and **docker image rm** commands. Listing 11-6 shows the updated workflow declaration in its final form.

> **Note** You can find the complete declaration at *raw.githubusercontent.com/dawidborycki/ People.WebApp.Declarations/main/Workflows/people-webapp-ci-cd.yml*.

LISTING 11-6 GitHub Actions Configuration: Dynamic Image Versioning and Container Deployment to Azure.

```
name: CI/CD Pipeline

on: push:
    branches:
      - ci-cd

env:
  IMAGE_NAME: people.webapp
  ACR_NAME: people
```

```yaml
  ACR_LOGIN_SERVER: people.azurecr.io

jobs:
  build-and-push-docker-image:
    runs-on: ubuntu-latest

    steps:
    - name: Checkout code
      uses: actions/checkout@v4

    - name: Login to Azure
      uses: azure/login@v1
      with:
        creds: ${{ secrets.AZURE_CREDENTIALS }}

    - name: Login to Azure Container Registry
      run: az acr login -n $ACR_NAME

    - name: Count existing tags and configure the image tag
      run: |
        COUNT=$(az acr repository show-tags -n $ACR_NAME --repository $IMAGE_NAME ↵
            -o tsv | wc -l)
        IMAGE_TAG=v$(expr $COUNT + 1)
        echo "IMAGE_TAG=$IMAGE_TAG" >> $GITHUB_ENV

    - name: Build and push Docker image
      run: |
        FQ_IMAGE_NAME=$ACR_LOGIN_SERVER/$IMAGE_NAME:$IMAGE_TAG
        echo "FQ_IMAGE_NAME=$FQ_IMAGE_NAME" >> $GITHUB_ENV
        docker build -t $FQ_IMAGE_NAME .
        docker push $FQ_IMAGE_NAME

    - name: Logout from Azure Container Registry
      run: docker logout $ACR_LOGIN_SERVER

    - name: Cleanup Docker images
      run: docker image rm $FQ_IMAGE_NAME
```

This script is a complete demonstration of how to automate the building and pushing of a Docker image using GitHub Actions. It encompasses authentication, dynamic image tagging, image building, and pushing, as well as cleanup. This approach drastically simplifies and secures the process of updating applications in a production environment.

Configuring the Secret

After creating the workflow, the next step is to provide the credentials necessary to enable the workflow to access Azure resources. This access is required for actions such as listing existing Docker image tags and pushing images to Azure Container Registry.

To begin, you'll create a service principal with access to Azure services. This involves using the **az ad sp create-for-rbac** command with additional parameters to specify the access scope for specific resources. For the example, you will set the access scope to the Azure subscription used for deploying all the Azure services.

Here's how you can perform this in the first step. Open the terminal or command prompt and execute the following command:

```
az account list --query "[].{Name:name, SubscriptionId:id, TenantId:tenantId}" -o table
```

This command will provide a table of available subscriptions as seen in Figure 11-3. Take note of the values from the SubscriptionId and TenantId columns for the Azure subscription you are using.

```
% az account list --query "[].{Name:name, SubscriptionId:id, TenantId:tenantId}" -o table
Name        SubscriptionId                              TenantId
----------  ------------------------------------------  ------------------------------------------
                           3c319c                                          20b6ec
                           c87e77                                          20b6ec
%
```

FIGURE 11-3 Retrieving the subscription and tenant identifiers.

Now, proceed to create the actual service principal with an Owner role for the selected subscription using the following command:

```
az ad sp create-for-rbac -n sp-people-aks --role Owner --scopes ↵
    /subscriptions/<REPLACE_WITH_YOUR_SUBSCRIPTION_ID>
```

The **-n** parameter is used to set the friendly name of the service principal. After executing this command, you will receive a JSON-formatted string that appears as follows (Listing 11-7):

LISTING 11-7 Azure Service Principal Configuration for Kubernetes Deployment.

```
{
  "appId": "<YOUR_APP_ID_APPEARS_HERE>",
  "displayName": "sp-people-aks",
  "password": "<YOUR_PASSWORD_APPEARS_HERE>",
  "tenant": "<YOUR_TENANT_ID_APPEARS_HERE>"
}
```

Note Assigning the Owner role at the subscription level grants extensive permissions, which exceeds the requirements for most scenarios. As a best practice, assign only the minimal necessary privileges by scoping permissions down to a specific resource or resource group. For example, using the Contributor role scoped to a resource group is typically sufficient and more secure.

You will use the values above to construct the `creds` JSON object in the following format (Listing 11-8):

LISTING 11-8 Azure Credentials JSON Template for Application Authentication.

```
{
    "clientSecret": "<TYPE_YOUR_PASSWORD_HERE>",
    "subscriptionId": "<TYPE_YOUR_SUBSCRIPTION_HERE>",
    "tenantId": "<TYPE_YOUR_TENANT_ID_HERE>",
    "clientId": "<TYPE_YOUR_APP_ID_HERE>"
}
```

Next, return to Visual Studio Code and open the GitHub Actions extension. Click Sign In To GitHub, as shown in Figure 11-4. This Action will launch your web browser and direct you to the GitHub login page. Follow the provided instructions, and once complete, return to Visual Studio Code.

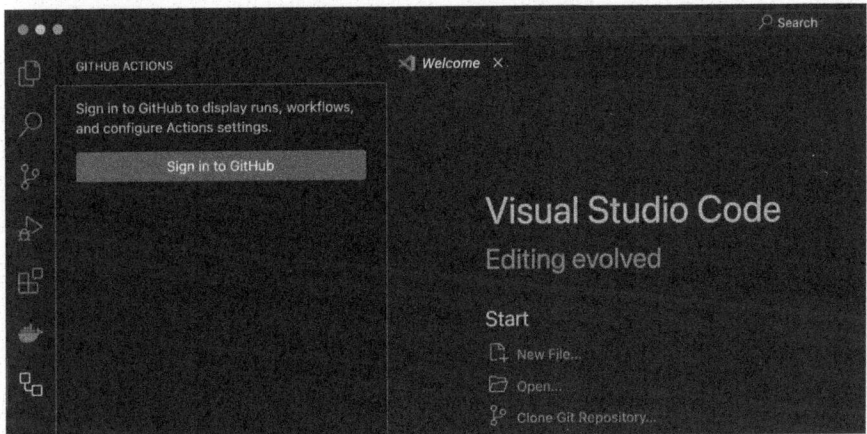

FIGURE 11-4 Sign in to GitHub from Visual Studio Code.

Within the GitHub Actions extension, you will now find three elements (see Figure 11-5): Current Branch, Workflows, and Settings. Expand Settings, then Secrets, and click the + icon located next to Repository Secret. In the pop-up window that appears, enter the name of the Secret: **AZURE_CREDENTIALS**. Afterward, paste the JSON `creds` string into the provided field.

Alternatively, you can create repository Secret in GitHub as follows:

1. Go to your GitHub repository on the GitHub website.
2. Click the Settings tab in the top navigation bar.
3. In the Security section (left sidebar), click Actions under Secrets And Variables.
4. Click the New Repository Secret button.
5. Enter the name (**AZURE_CREDENTIALS**) and paste the JSON string you created earlier into the value field. Then click the Add Secret button (see Figure 11-6).

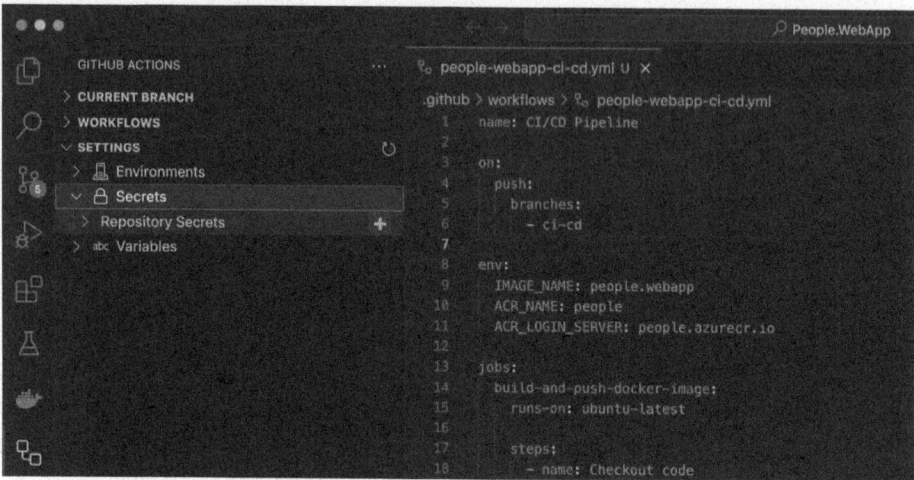

FIGURE 11-5 Creating a repository Secret in Visual Studio Code.

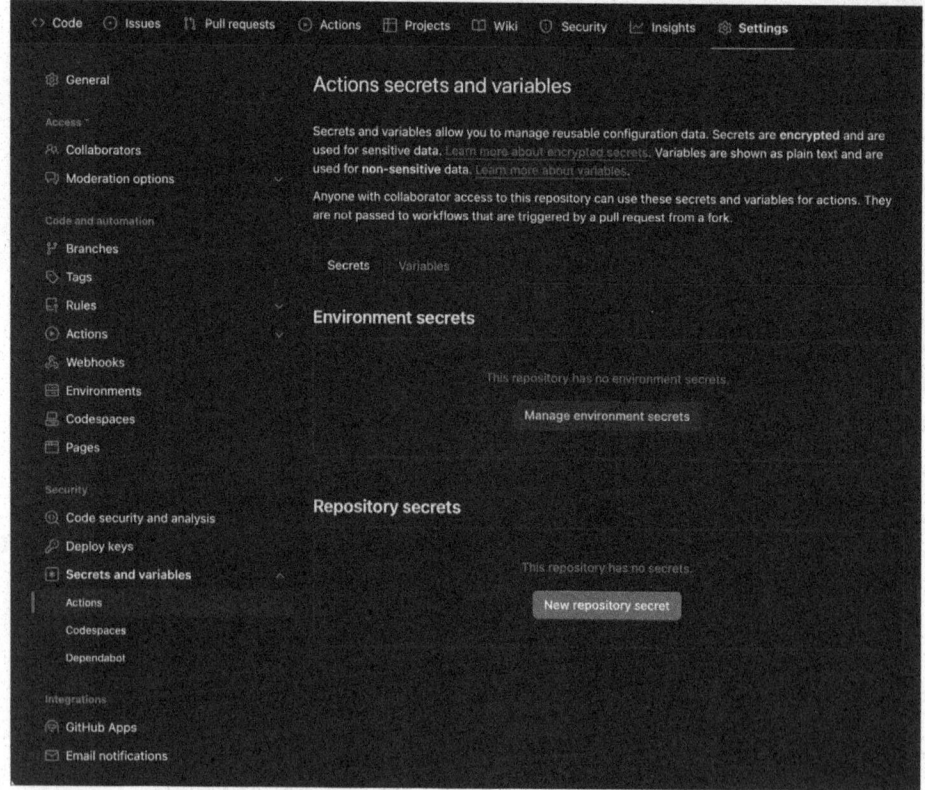

FIGURE 11-6 Creating a repository Secret in GitHub.

Testing the workflow

Now that you have all the necessary tools in place, you can trigger the workflow you just created. To do this, simply commit your source code to the GitHub repository following these steps:

1. Open the terminal or command prompt.

2. Change the working directory to the location of the People.WebApp sources.

3. Enter the following commands:

   `git add .`

   `git commit -am "CI-CD"`

   `git push`

4. Afterward, observe that the workflow has started. You can check its status using Visual Studio Code:

   a. Open the GitHub Actions extension.

   b. Expand the Workflows section, where you will see the CI/CD pipeline workflow (named as specified in the people-webapp-ci-cd.yml file).

   c. Expand the build-and-push-docker-image job.

   You will then see each step of the job, as shown in Figure 11-7.

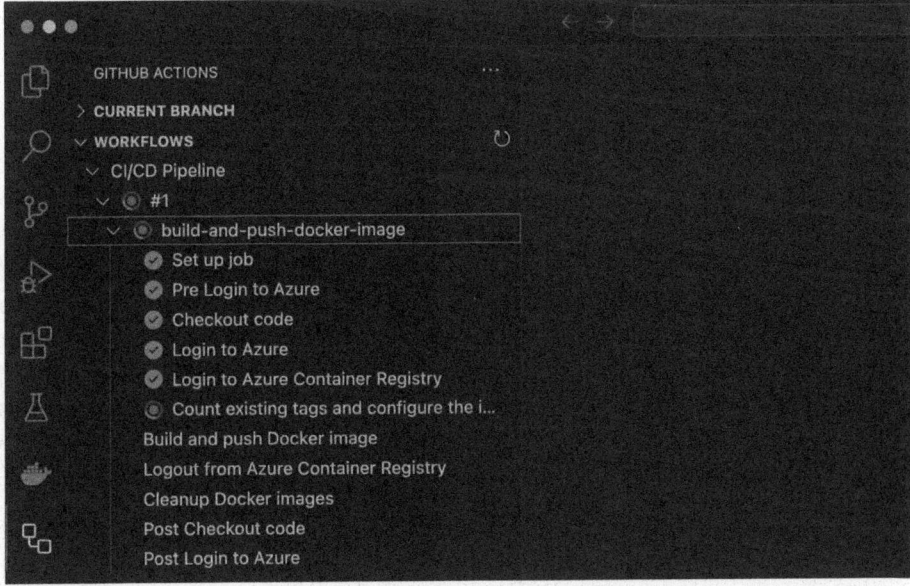

FIGURE 11-7 A workflow status in the GitHub Actions extension of Visual Studio Code.

For more detailed information about the workflow status, you can check it on the GitHub page:

1. Navigate to your GitHub repository on the GitHub website.
2. Click the Actions tab in the top navigation bar.
3. Click the workflow run, and then select the build-and-push-docker-image job.

    Job details will appear on the right, as shown in Figure 11-8.

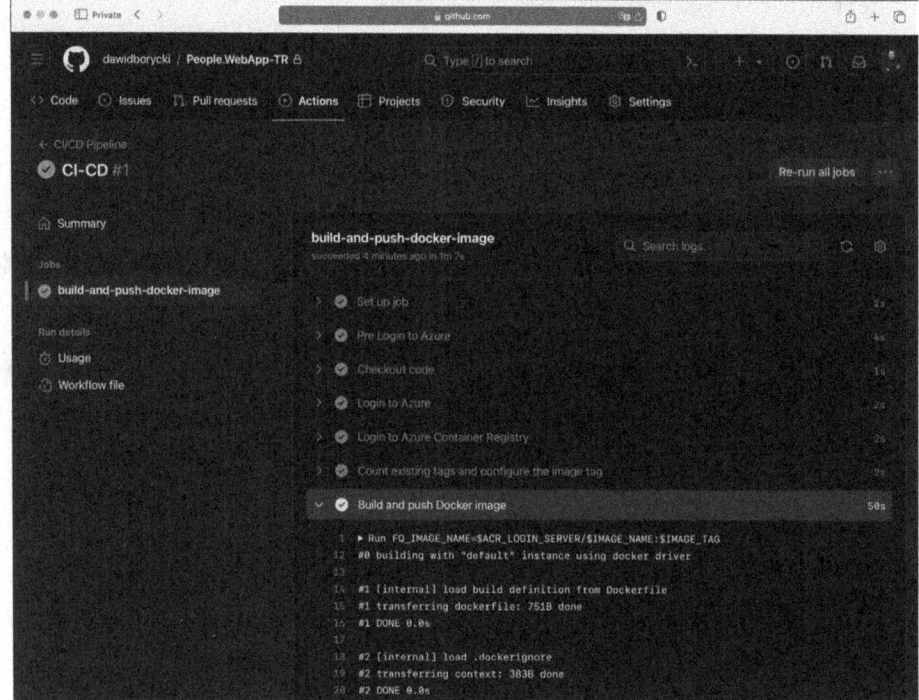

FIGURE 11-8 Workflow status of the GitHub repository.

As depicted in Figures 11-7 and 11-8, the job encompasses all the steps previously defined in the people-webapp-ci-cd.yml file. Specifically, the job begins by checking out the source code. It then logs in to Azure and Azure Container Registry. After that, the job retrieves the list of images in the people.webapp Docker repository. Based on this information, it configures the tag of the Docker image to be built. Following this, the job invokes the Build And Push Docker Image step, which builds and pushes the Docker image. As shown in Figure 11-8, the output of this job resembles what you observed when building the image locally. Finally, the job logs out from Azure and cleans up the Docker images.

In the end, the workflow has successfully created a new Docker image with the v4 tag. You can confirm this by entering the following command in the terminal or command prompt:

```
az acr repository show-tags -n people --repository people.webapp -o tsv
```

Note Automating your image build and deployment process with CI/CD pipelines significantly reduces manual errors and saves time, especially as your application grows. Ensure that your workflows always incorporate proper security practices, however, such as scoping permissions narrowly, storing credentials securely as Secrets, and regularly auditing access privileges.

Tip When dynamically tagging Docker images within a CI/CD pipeline, make sure the tagging strategy you choose (such as incrementing versions) aligns with your application's deployment and rollback strategy.

Alternatively, consider using semantic versioning tags or commit-based tags for more explicit version control and traceability.

Updating the deployment in Azure Kubernetes Service

You've successfully automated the process of building and pushing the Docker image whenever a new version of the application is pushed to the selected Git branch. Next, you will modify the workflow declaration to use the built Docker image for updating the application running in Azure Kubernetes Service. Specifically, you will introduce a second job named deploy-to-aks into the workflow declaration. This job will use the fully qualified name of the Docker image generated by the first job (build-and-push-docker-image).

The deploy-to-aks job will encompass the following tasks:

1. Authenticate to Azure and configure the kubectl context to target the previously created cluster using the `az aks get-credentials` command.

2. Dynamically modify the Kubernetes manifest file. Specifically, it will update the deployment declaration file to incorporate the fully qualified name of the Docker image created by the build-and-push-docker-image job.

3. Execute the `kubectl apply` command to enact the update on the Kubernetes deployment.

Begin by introducing three environment variables into the people-webapp-ci-cd.yml file (Listing 11-8):

LISTING 11-8 GitHub Actions Workflow Definition for AKS Deployment.

```
name: CI/CD Pipeline
on:
  push:
    branches:
      - ci-cd
env:
```

```
IMAGE_NAME: people.webapp
ACR_NAME: people
ACR_LOGIN_SERVER: people.azurecr.io

RG_NAME: rg-aks-people
CLUSTER_NAME: aks-people
AKS_POOL_NODE_NAME: aks-people-agentpool
```

These variables serve the following purposes:

- **RG_NAME** Stores the name of the resource group where you've deployed the Azure Kubernetes cluster, which in this case is rg-aks-people
- **CLUSTER_NAME** Stores the name of the Azure Kubernetes cluster, which is aks-people
- **AKS_POOL_NODE_NAME** Holds the name of the node pool, specifically aks-people-agentpool

To address the challenge of passing the fully qualified name of the Docker image from the build-and-push-docker-image job to the deploy-to-aks job, you need to make a few modifications. Because different workflow jobs run on separate virtual machines hosted by GitHub, you cannot rely on environment variables for this purpose. Therefore, once the build-and-push-docker-image job completes, the environment variables are no longer accessible.

To adapt the build-and-push-docker-image job, follow these steps (Listing 11-9):

1. Introduce an outputs section within the job configuration. Define a single output named `fq_image_name`. This output will capture the FQ_IMAGE_NAME value generated during the `Build and push Docker image` step.

2. Uniquely identify this step. Assign it the job identifier `build-image` using the `id` field in the YAML file.

3. Output the fully qualified image name. Within the `Build and push Docker image` step, output the FQ_IMAGE_NAME variable, which holds the fully qualified image name, to the $GITHUB_OUTPUT.

LISTING 11-9 Workflow Job for Docker Image Creation and Output Handling in GitHub Actions.

```
build-and-push-docker-image:
  runs-on: ubuntu-latest

  outputs:
    fq_image_name: ${{steps.build-image.outputs.FQ_IMAGE_NAME}}

  steps:
    # Check out, login to Azure, and Count existing tags steps...

    - name: Build and push Docker image
      id: build-image
      run: |
```

```
            FQ_IMAGE_NAME=$ACR_LOGIN_SERVER/$IMAGE_NAME:$IMAGE_TAG
            echo "FQ_IMAGE_NAME=$FQ_IMAGE_NAME" >> $GITHUB_ENV
            echo "FQ_IMAGE_NAME=$FQ_IMAGE_NAME" >> $GITHUB_OUTPUT
            docker build -t $FQ_IMAGE_NAME
            docker push $FQ_IMAGE_NAME

      # Logout and clean up steps
```

Next, define the deploy-to-aks job, as highlighted in Listing 11-10:

LISTING 11-10 Deploying Docker Image to Azure Kubernetes Service.

```
name: CI/CD Pipeline

on:
  push:
    branches:
      - ci-cd

env:
  IMAGE_NAME: people.webapp
  ACR_NAME: people
  ACR_LOGIN_SERVER: people.azurecr.io
  RG_NAME: rg-aks-people
  CLUSTER_NAME: aks-people
  AKS_POOL_NODE_NAME: aks-people-agentpool

jobs:
  build-and-push-docker-image:
    # Job declaration is omitted here for clarity.

  deploy-to-aks:
    runs-on: ubuntu-latest
    needs: build-and-push-docker-image

    steps:
      - name: Checkout code
        uses: actions/checkout@v4

      - name: Login to Azure
        uses: azure/login@v1
        with:
          creds: ${{ secrets.AZURE_CREDENTIALS }}

      - name: Configure Kubernetes context
        run: az aks get-credentials -g $RG_NAME -n $CLUSTER_NAME
      - name: Configure Kubernetes Manifest
        env:
          FQ_IMAGE_NAME: ${{ needs.build-and-push-docker-image.outputs.fq_image_name }}
        run: |

          MANAGED_CLIENT_ID=$(az identity list --query "[?contains(name,⤶
              '$AKS_POOL_NODE_NAME')].clientId" -o tsv)
          sed -i "s|<FQ_IMAGE_NAME>|$FQ_IMAGE_NAME|g" ./aks/deployment.yml
```

```
            sed -i "s|<MANAGED_CLIENT_ID>|$MANAGED_CLIENT_ID|g" ./aks/deployment.yml
            cat ./aks/deployment.yml

      - name: Update Deployment
        run: kubectl apply -f ./aks/deployment.yml
```

The deploy-to-aks job uses the needs section to indicate that it should be executed after the build-and-push-docker-image job. It performs five steps, starting with checking out the source code and logging in to Azure—similar actions taken in the build-and-push-docker-image job.

In the third step, the `az aks get-credentials` command is executed to configure the context for the kubectl tool, enabling communication with the previously created Azure Kubernetes cluster using the RG_NAME and CLUSTER_NAME environment variables.

The fourth step involves updating the Kubernetes manifest file, deployment.yml (you need to store this file under the aks/deployment.yml of the People.WebApp project).

Here, you make slight modifications to the declaration, specifically to include two placeholders (Listing 11-11): <FQ_IMAGE_NAME> and <MANAGED_CLIENT_ID>.

LISTING 11-11 Deploying Containerized Application to AKS with Environment Variables.

```yaml
apiVersion: apps/v1
kind: Deployment
metadata:
  name: people-webapp-deployment
  spec:
  replicas: 2
  selector:
      matchLabels:
        app: people-webapp
  template:
      metadata:
        labels:
            app: people-webapp
      spec:
        containers:
        - name: people-webapp
          image: <FQ_IMAGE_NAME>
          imagePullPolicy: Always
          ports:
          - containerPort: 5000
          env:
          - name: UseInMemoryDatabase
            value: "False"
          - name: KeyVaultName
            value: kv-people
          - name: ManagedIdentityClientId
            value: <MANAGED_CLIENT_ID>
```

These placeholders are dynamically replaced within the workflow. Specifically, <FQ_IMAGE_NAME> holds the fully qualified image name, while <MANAGED_CLIENT_ID> stores the managed identity associated with the node pool. To retrieve this identity, the workflow uses the `az identity list` command, as described in Chapter 8. Essentially, the output of `az identity list` is filtered to find an item that corresponds to the identity of the resource named aks-people-agentpool. The resultant identity is then substituted for <MANAGED_CLIENT_ID> using the `sed` command. Similarly, `sed` is used to replace the <FQ_IMAGE_NAME> placeholder with the fully qualified image name generated by the first workflow job.

To facilitate this step, you should save the declarations provided in the above discussion to the aks/deployment.yml file within the People.WebApp source folder. For your convenience, the declarations can be found at these links:

raw.githubusercontent.com/dawidborycki/People.WebApp.Declarations/main/Workflows/people-webapp-ci-cd-aks.yml

raw.githubusercontent.com/dawidborycki/People.WebApp.Declarations/main/Kubernetes/people_deployment_ci_cd.yml

After updating the manifest file, the final step in the deploy-to-aks job executes the command `kubectl apply -f aks/deployment.yml` to apply the changes to the cluster.

Running an updated workflow

To trigger the updated workflow in your GitHub repository, follow these steps:

1. Open the terminal or command prompt.
2. Navigate to the directory containing the People.WebApp sources.
3. Enter the following commands:
    a. `git add .`
    b. `git commit -m "AKS CI/CD"`
    c. `git push`

After executing these commands, navigate to the Actions tab within your GitHub repository. You will see the workflow execution, as depicted in Figure 11-9. The workflow consists of two jobs: build-and-push-docker-image and deploy-to-aks, following the sequence specified in the workflow declaration. The deploy-to-aks job executes after build-and-push-docker-image because it depends on the Docker image updated by the first job.

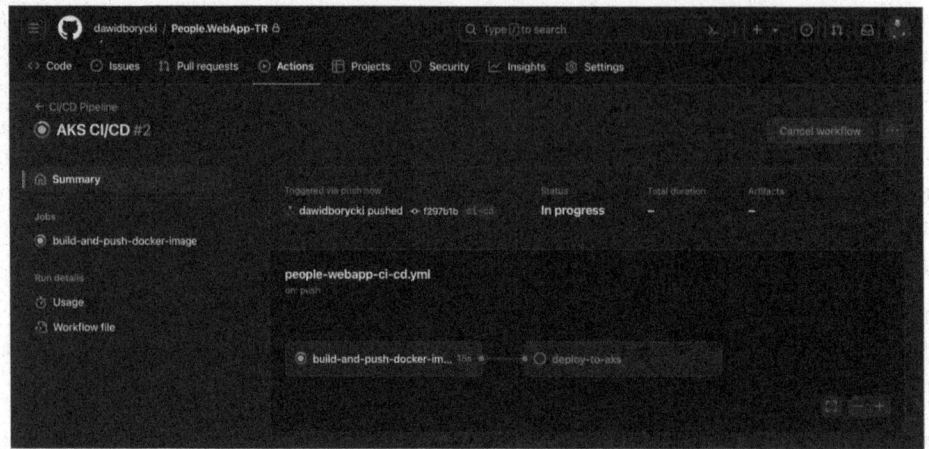

FIGURE 11-9 The workflow now Comprises two sequential jobs.

You can monitor the progress of each job by clicking it. Specifically, observe the deploy-to-aks job, and wait for the Configure Kubernetes Manifest step to complete. Watch for updates to the deployment.yml file, which will now reference the people.webapp Docker image tagged as v5 (see Figure 11-10).

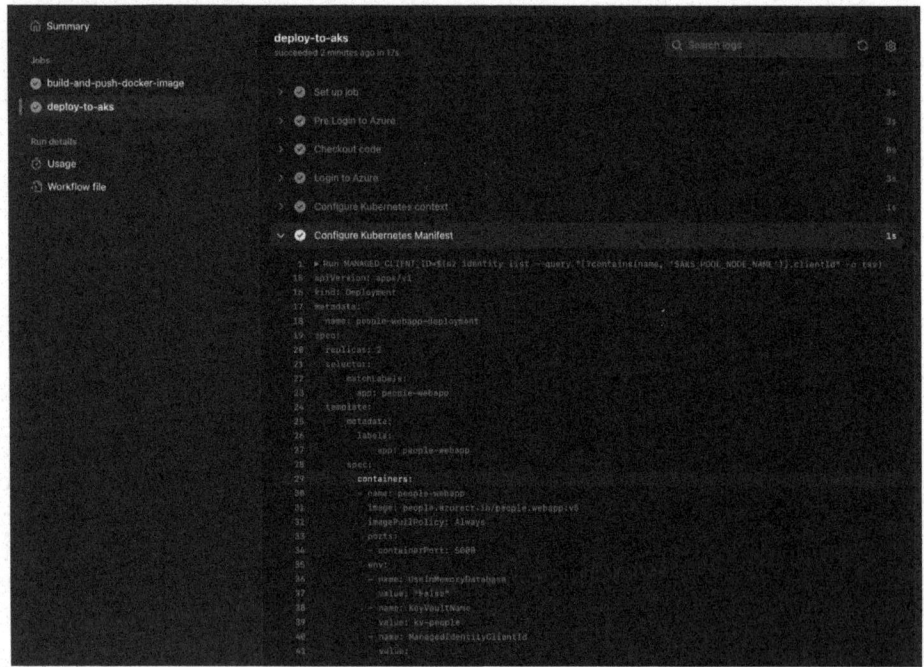

FIGURE 11-10 A representative output from the deploy-to-aks job.

Automatic updates of the application

The final step demonstrates the practicality of the configured workflow. While the initial setup required some effort, you can now reap the benefits of automated application updates. Consider a real-world scenario: Your manager requests an update to the application for deployment to the production Kubernetes cluster. For instance, they may ask you to modify the welcome message on the initial view of People.WebApp.

To accommodate this request, you will make a modification to the Index.cshtml file within the Views/Home folder of People.WebApp. Specifically, you'll replace "Welcome" with "AKS and CI/CD are great!" with the following code (Listing 11-12):

LISTING 11-12 Displaying Host Machine Name.

```
@{
    ViewData["Title"] = "Home Page";}

<div class="text-center">
    <h1 class="display-4">AKS and CI/CD are great!</h1>
    <p>The request was processed by: @Environment.MachineName</p>
</div>
```

After making this change, commit it to the GitHub repository (as described in the previous sections). This action will trigger the workflow, leading to the creation of a new Docker image (tagged as v6) for People.WebApp. This image will then be deployed to the Kubernetes cluster. When you open People.WebApp in your web browser, you will see the updated message, as in Figure 11-11.

FIGURE 11-11 An updated view of the People.WebApp application.

This example demonstrates how the time invested in setting up automation pays dividends by enabling faster delivery of new features or changes to the application, compared to manual processes that involve Docker image builds, pushes, and updates to the Kubernetes manifest file.

Summary

In this chapter, you streamlined the process of updating and deploying a containerized application, showcasing the power of automation in expediting development and deployment tasks.

You began by establishing a GitHub repository for the People.WebApp application. Subsequently, you created a GitHub Actions workflow designed to automate several tasks: building, tagging, and pushing Docker images to Azure Container Registry (ACR), as well as updating deployments in an Azure Kubernetes Service (AKS) cluster.

The workflow was organized into two distinct jobs:

- **build-and-push-docker-image** This job managed Docker image creation, tagging, and ACR pushing. It dynamically generated image tags and stored them as workflow environment variables.

- **deploy-to-aks** In this job, you configured the kubectl context for the AKS cluster, updated the Kubernetes manifest file to use the latest Docker image tag, and applied these changes to the AKS cluster.

In the final step, you took advantage of the workflow's efficiency by making a code change (modifying the welcome message), committing it to the GitHub repository, and observing how the workflow seamlessly built, pushed, and deployed the updated Docker image to the AKS cluster.

CHAPTER 12

Load Testing, Horizontal Pod Autoscaling, and Cluster Autoscaling

When architecting environments in the cloud, striking the right balance in provisioning hardware resources is crucial to both performance and cost efficiency. Over-provisioning can lead to unnecessary expenses as unused resources still incur costs, whereas under-provisioning risks performance bottlenecks, potentially leading to slow response times and a poor user experience during peak demand. The ideal scenario involves dynamically adjusting hardware resources to align with the current load, ensuring that the infrastructure scales to meet demand without wastage. In this chapter, I will demonstrate this principle in action, using load testing and the HorizontalPodAutoscaler (HPA) in Kubernetes. Through practical examples, you'll explore how these technologies enable efficient resource use, ensuring that applications remain responsive under varying loads while optimizing costs.

I will first demonstrate how to use the Hey tool to test People.WebApp under the load of numerous concurrent users. Following that, you'll explore the process of containerizing the load tests to enhance portability and ease of use. Subsequently, you'll delve into the methodology for automatically scaling the application using the HPA.

Load testing with Hey

Hey is an open-source, lightweight tool used for load testing web applications and APIs. Its primary purpose is to send a specified number of requests over a defined period to a target web server and then provide a detailed report on the performance metrics. Hey is favored for its simplicity and effectiveness, featuring a straightforward command-line interface that easily integrates into various development workflows and CI/CD pipelines. Its output includes valuable information such as response times, status code distribution, and request success/failure rates, which are crucial for performance tuning and capacity planning.

In this section, you will learn how to use Hey to perform stress testing on People.WebApp, starting with an introduction to the tool using Azure Cloud Shell. The choice of Azure Cloud Shell ensures a consistent environment, guaranteeing that commands and their outputs will be the same.

To perform your first load test using Hey, proceed as follows:

1. Open Azure Cloud Shell.

2. Enter the following commands to download the Hey binaries for Linux and make them executable (see Figure 12-1):

   ```
   wget https://hey-release.s3.us-east-2.amazonaws.com/hey_linux_amd64
   chmod +x hey_linux_amd64
   ```

3. Execute the test by sending 100 requests (-c parameter) for 30 seconds (-z parameter):

   ```
   ./hey_linux_amd64 -z 30s -c 100 http://<TYPE_IP_OF_PEOPLE_WEBAPP_HERE>
   ```

The final command generates a report like the one shown in Figure 12-2. This report summarizes the load test, detailing the web app's response times and the total duration of the test. Below the summary, you will find a response time histogram, illustrating the frequency of various response times and indicating the number of responses received during a specific period.

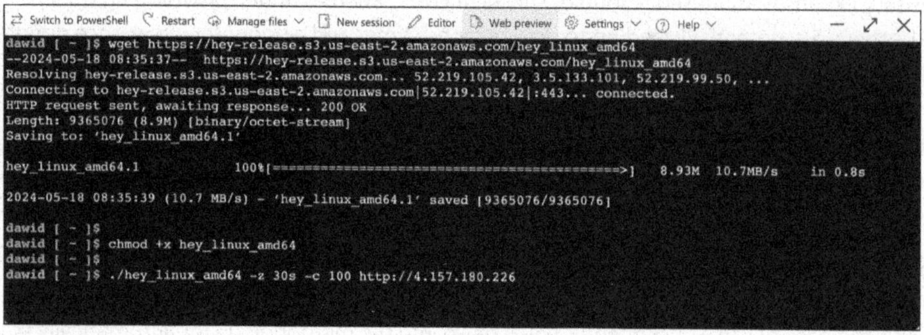

FIGURE 12-1 Downloading and executing the Hey tool.

The histogram's vertical axis is divided into 11 bins, each representing a range of response times. Hey calculates the bin spacing by subtracting the fastest from the slowest response time and dividing by 10. For example, in Figure 12-2, if the response time range is 0.31 seconds, this range is divided into 10 intervals (yielding 11 boundaries), giving a bin size of approximately 0.031 seconds after division. The first bin starts from the fastest response time (0.08 seconds) and spans up to approximately 0.111 seconds. This pattern continues sequentially, with each subsequent bin covering an additional 0.031 seconds until the last bin is reached.

Each response time is categorized into one of these bins based on its value. For instance, a response time that falls between the lower and upper limits of the first bin goes into the first bin, continuing similarly for each subsequent bin.

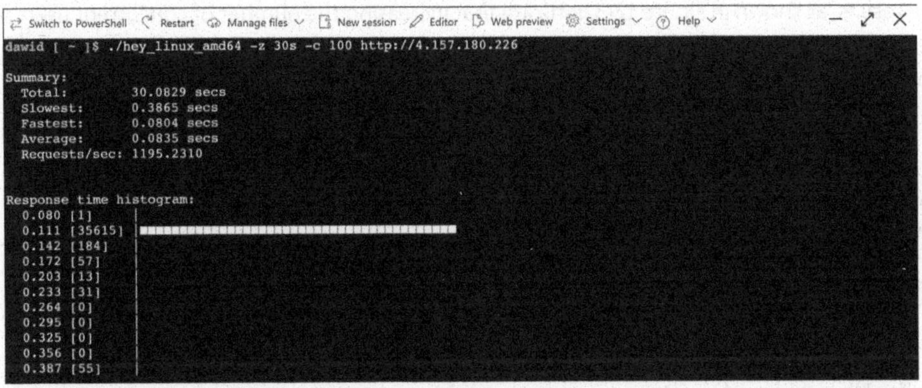

FIGURE 12-2 A fragment of Hey's output.

The horizontal axis shows the proportion of responses for each bin. The length of each line in the histogram corresponds to the number of responses received within that specific time frame, thus visualizing the distribution and concentration of response times. For instance, Figure 12-2 indicates that the largest concentration of responses occurs between 0.08 and 0.111 seconds, with most responses falling within this second bin.

You can now compare these results to the response times for the People endpoint. Invoke the following command:

```
./hey_linux_amd64 -z 30s -c 100 ://<TYPE_IP_OF_PEOPLE_WEBAPP_HERE>/people
```

To observe changes in response times under a larger load, increase the number of clients to 200 (see Figure 12-3):

```
./hey_linux_amd64 -z 30s -c 200 ://<TYPE_IP_OF_PEOPLE_WEBAPP_HERE>/people
```

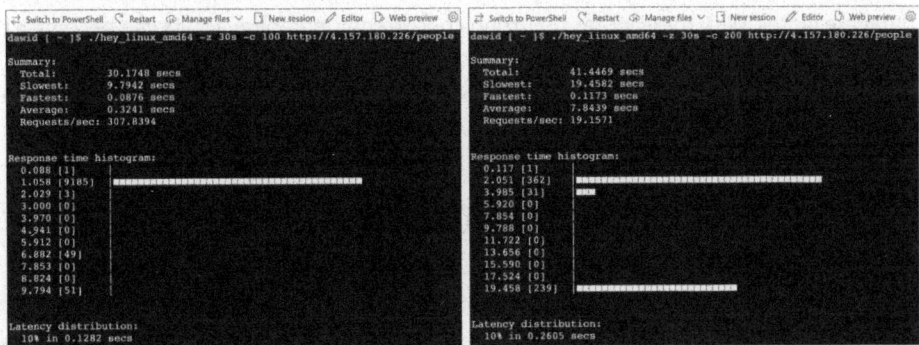

FIGURE 12-3 Load testing of the People endpoint with a variable number of users.

The results, as shown in Figure 12-3, indicate that increasing the number of concurrent users shifts the response time histogram towards longer durations. Specifically, for 100 users, the histogram peak is around 1.058 seconds, but for 200 users, it shifts to 2.051 seconds.

Finally, you will test the API endpoint that allows adding users to the database. As discussed in this chapter, sending **POST** requests to the /api/people endpoint requires including JSON-formatted data of the person to be added. Using curl, the command to send the **POST** request is as follows:

```
curl -X 'POST' \
  'http://<IP_OF_YOUR_WEB_APP>/api/people' \
  -H 'accept: text/plain' \
  -H 'Content-Type: application/json' \
  -d '{
  "id": "",
  "firstName": "FirstName",
  "lastName": "LastName",
  "birthDate": "2000-01-01"
}'
```

Similarly, to load test the /api/people endpoint using Hey, use the command below:

```
./hey_linux_amd64 -z 30s \
                  -c 100 \
                  -H 'accept: text/plain' \
                  -H 'Content-Type: application/json' \
                  -d '{
                    "id": "",
                    "firstName": "FirstName",
                    "lastName": "LastName",
                    "birthDate": "2000-01-01"}' \
                  -m POST http://<IP_OF_YOUR_WEB_APP>/api/people
```

Executing this command in Azure Cloud Shell yields results as depicted in Figure 12-4. Notice that processing **POST** requests takes significantly longer, which is expected as these requests involve additional database writes. With these writes occurring concurrently, database access can become a bottleneck, especially when handling multiple concurrent database writes that challenge the preservation of database consistency. In Figure 12-4, the histogram's peak is at 1.1 second, with a broader distribution indicating that more than 50 requests were processed by the application in at least 10 seconds.

Automating the load test using Docker

After learning about the Hey tool, you will now automate your load tests. These tests will include commands to test the API endpoint by sending **POST** requests from a variable number of users, and you will also stress test the GET API endpoint to compare results. The script will be embedded inside a Docker image, allowing it to be executed anywhere Docker is available.

To create the Docker image, start by creating a new folder named LoadTest outside the People. WebApp project folder. Then, within the LoadTest folder, create two files: Dockerfile and load-test.sh.

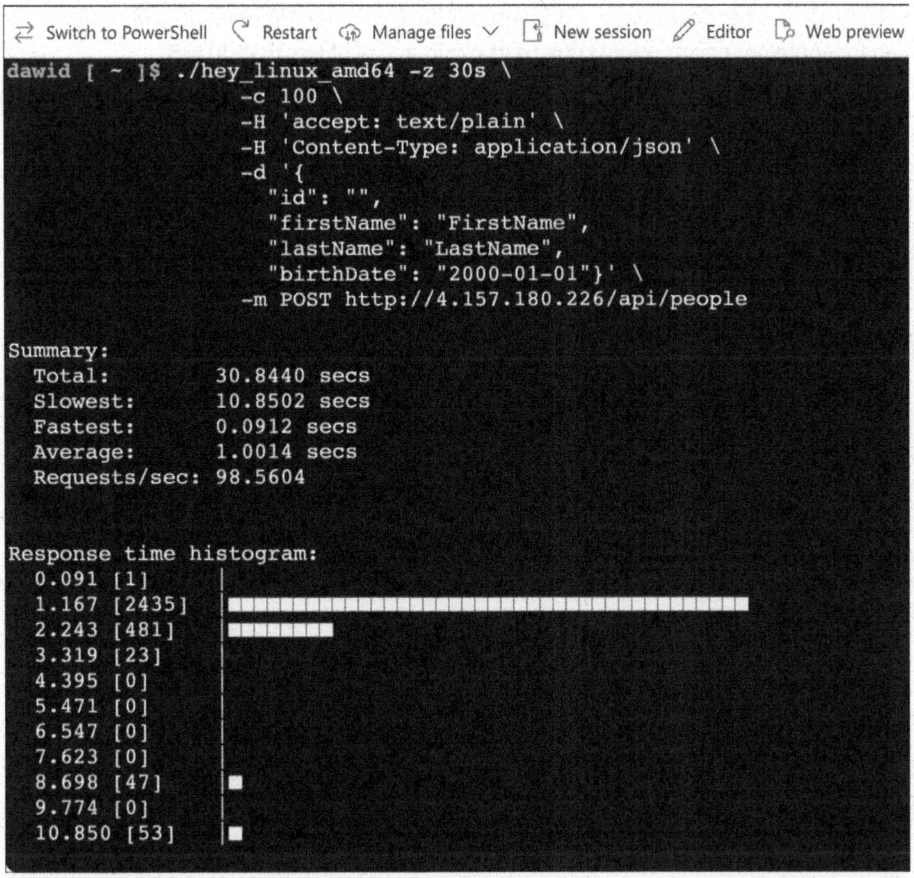

```
dawid [ ~ ]$ ./hey_linux_amd64 -z 30s \
              -c 100 \
              -H 'accept: text/plain' \
              -H 'Content-Type: application/json' \
              -d '{
                "id": "",
                "firstName": "FirstName",
                "lastName": "LastName",
                "birthDate": "2000-01-01"}' \
              -m POST http://4.157.180.226/api/people

Summary:
  Total:        30.8440 secs
  Slowest:      10.8502 secs
  Fastest:      0.0912 secs
  Average:      1.0014 secs
  Requests/sec: 98.5604


Response time histogram:
  0.091 [1]     |
  1.167 [2435]  |■■■■■■■■■■■■■■■■■■■■■■■■■■■■■■■■■■■■■■■■
  2.243 [481]   |■■■■■■■■
  3.319 [23]    |
  4.395 [0]     |
  5.471 [0]     |
  6.547 [0]     |
  7.623 [0]     |
  8.698 [47]    |■
  9.774 [0]     |
  10.850 [53]   |■
```

FIGURE 12-4 Load testing the People API endpoint.

First, declare the Dockerfile as follows (Listing 12-1):

LISTING 12-1 Dockerfile Declaration.

```
# Start from Alpine Linux
FROM alpine:latest

# Add Hey
ADD https://hey-release.s3.us-east-2.amazonaws.com/hey_linux_amd64 /usr/local/bin/hey
RUN chmod +x /usr/local/bin/hey

# Copy the load test script and make it executable
WORKDIR /app
COPY load-test.sh /app/load-test.sh
RUN chmod +x /app/load-test.sh

# Set the entry point to Hey
ENTRYPOINT ["/app/load-test.sh"]
```

The first line specifies the base image, using Alpine Linux, which is a lightweight Linux distribution often chosen for container environments due to its minimal size of less than 10 MB.

Given this base image, you use the ADD instruction to download the Hey binary, then you make the binary executable, similar to procedures performed in Azure CloudShell. Next, you change the working directory to /app, copy the load-test.sh script into this folder, make the script executable, and set it as the Docker container's entry point.

Before building the Docker image, you need to prepare the load-test.sh script. Open it in Visual Studio Code, and add the following statements (Listing 12-2):

LISTING 12-2 Preparing the load-test.sh Script.

```sh
#!/bin/sh

export ACCEPT_PLAIN="accept: text/plain"
export CONTENT_TYPE="Content-Type: application/json"
export PAYLOAD='{
    "id": "",
    "firstName": "FirstName",
    "lastName": "LastName",
    "birthDate": "2000-01-01"
}'

export ENDPOINT=http://$SERVICE_IP/api/people

printf "\nTesting the People.WebApp with IP (POST): %s\n" "$SERVICE_IP"
```

The first line, the shebang, indicates that the script should be executed using the ash shell (Almquist shell), provided by the Alpine base image. The script defines four environment variables: ACCEPT_PLAIN and CONTENT_TYPE for the headers of POST and GET requests, PAYLOAD containing the JSON-formatted data of a person to be added to the database, and ENDPOINT, which stores the API endpoint and is configured using the SERVICE_IP environment variable passed to the Docker container. The script concludes by echoing the SERVICE_IP address, which should point to your People.WebApp (in my case, 4.157.180.226).

With the script defined, you can now execute the load test for a variable number of users (100, 500, 1000, 2000, 4000, and 8000) using the for loop shown in Listing 12-3:

LISTING 12-3 For Loop to Execute a Load Test.

```sh
for users in 100 500 1000 2000 4000 8000; do
    printf "\n%s users.\n" "${users}"

    hey -z 30s -c ${users} -d "$PAYLOAD" -H "$ACCEPT_PLAIN" \
        -H "$CONTENT_TYPE" -m POST "$ENDPOINT"

    echo "Pause for 15 seconds"

    sleep 15
done
```

Afterward, proceed to test the GET request of the People API (Listing 12-4). You use almost the same statements as before, with the only difference being that you do not need to set the **-d**, **-H**, or **-m** parameters in the Hey command:

LISTING 12-4 For Loop to Test a GET Request of the People API.

```
printf "\nTesting the People.WebApp with IP (GET): %s\n" "$SERVICE_IP"

for users in 100 500 1000 2000 4000 8000; do
    printf "\n%s users.\n" "${users}"
    hey -z 30s -c $users "$ENDPOINT"

    echo "Pause for 15 seconds"
    sleep 15
done
```

That's it! You are now ready to build and run the containerized load tests. For your convenience, the Dockerfile and the load-test.sh script are available in the following repository:

github.com/dawidborycki/People.WebApp.Declarations/tree/main/LoadTest

Building and running the containerized load tests

After defining the Dockerfile, you can build and run the prepared load tests. First, change the working directory to the LoadTest folder. Then, execute the following command:

docker build -t load-test:v1 .

This command generates the load-test:v1 Docker image, as confirmed by the output resembling Figure 12-5.

With the Docker image ready, it's time execute the containerized load tests with the command:

docker run --rm -e SERVICE_IP=<TYPE_YOUR_IP_HERE> load-test:v1

This command runs a container using the load-test:v1 Docker image and automatically removes it after exit (using the **--rm** parameter). The **-e** parameter sets the SERVICE_IP environment variable, which the automated stress test uses to configure the endpoint under test.

The initial containerized load test for 100 users is shown in Figure 12-6. The response time histogram indicates that most requests are processed within approximately 1.5 seconds.

Upon increasing the user count to 500, the histogram shifts to longer response times. Notably, the histogram in Figure 12-7 only includes data for two responses; all other responses resulted in timeouts, which is detailed at the end of Hey's report in Figure 12-8. This suggests the API becomes unresponsive under the strain of 500 concurrent users. To address this, you will explore the application scaling, utilizing monitoring tools discussed in Chapter 9, "Diagnosing and Monitoring the Cluster."

```
% docker build -t load-test:v1 .
[+] Building 1.4s (12/12) FINISHED                                docker:desktop-linux
 => [internal] load .dockerignore                                                 0.0s
 => => transferring context: 2B                                                   0.0s
 => [internal] load build definition from Dockerfile                              0.0s
 => => transferring dockerfile: 407B                                              0.0s
 => [internal] load metadata for docker.io/library/alpine:latest                  0.8s
 => https://hey-release.s3.us-east-2.amazonaws.com/hey_linux_amd64                0.4s
 => [internal] load build context                                                 0.0s
 => => transferring context: 877B                                                 0.0s
 => [1/6] FROM docker.io/library/alpine:latest@sha256:c5b1261d6d3e43071626931fc004f70149ba  0.0s
 => CACHED [2/6] ADD https://hey-release.s3.us-east-2.amazonaws.com/hey_linux_amd64 /usr/l  0.0s
 => CACHED [3/6] RUN chmod +x /usr/local/bin/hey                                  0.0s
 => CACHED [4/6] WORKDIR /app                                                     0.0s
 => [5/6] COPY load-test.sh /app/load-test.sh                                     0.0s
 => [6/6] RUN chmod +x /app/load-test.sh                                          0.1s
 => exporting to image                                                            0.0s
 => => exporting layers                                                           0.0s
 => => writing image sha256:d6aabd5deb2b1ab8dbc7d7d6a9a352d4454a19af4377cf95766a341a958687  0.0s
 => => naming to docker.io/library/load-test:v1                                   0.0s
```

FIGURE 12-5 Building the Docker image for load testing.

```
% docker run --rm -e SERVICE_IP=4.157.180.226 load-test:v1

Testing the People.WebApp with IP (POST): 4.157.180.226

100 users.

Summary:
  Total:        40.2430 secs
  Slowest:      19.7826 secs
  Fastest:      0.3127 secs
  Average:      2.1989 secs
  Requests/sec: 18.2641


Response time histogram:
  0.313 [1]    |
  2.260 [558]  |■■■■■■■■■■■■■■■■■■■■■■■■■■■■■■■■■■■■■■■■
  4.207 [44]   |■■■
  6.154 [0]    |
  8.101 [0]    |
  10.048 [0]   |
  11.995 [0]   |
  13.942 [0]   |
  15.889 [0]   |
  17.836 [0]   |
  19.783 [34]  |■■
```

FIGURE 12-6 Stress test results for 100 users.

```
● ● ●   LoadTest — com.docker.cli ‹ docker run --rm -e SERVICE_IP=4.157.180.226 load-test:v1 — 80×26
500 users.

Summary:
  Total:        40.6361 secs
  Slowest:      11.7314 secs
  Fastest:       0.5357 secs
  Average:       4.2716 secs
  Requests/sec: 24.7071


Response time histogram:
  0.536 [1]   |■■■■■■■■■■■■
  1.655 [3]   |■■■■■■■■■■■■■■■■■■■■■■■■■■■■■■■■■■■■■
  2.775 [0]   |
  3.894 [0]   |
  5.014 [0]   |
  6.134 [0]   |
  7.253 [0]   |
  8.373 [0]   |
  9.492 [0]   |
 10.612 [0]   |
 11.731 [2]   |■■■■■■■■■■■■■■■■■■■■■■■■■


Latency distribution:
  10% in 0.5376 secs
```

FIGURE 12-7 Stress test results for 500 users.

```
● ● ●   LoadTest — com.docker.cli ‹ docker run --rm -e SERVICE_IP=4.157.180.226 load-test:v1 — 80×26
Latency distribution:
  10% in 0.5376 secs
  25% in 0.5459 secs
  50% in 0.5557 secs
  75% in 11.7314 secs
  0% in 0.0000 secs
  0% in 0.0000 secs
  0% in 0.0000 secs

Details (average, fastest, slowest):
  DNS+dialup:   0.1922 secs, 0.5357 secs, 11.7314 secs
  DNS-lookup:   0.0000 secs, 0.0000 secs, 0.0000 secs
  req write:    0.0222 secs, 0.0103 secs, 0.0347 secs
  resp wait:    4.0510 secs, 0.3130 secs, 11.5145 secs
  resp read:    0.0045 secs, 0.0003 secs, 0.0115 secs

Status code distribution:
  [201] 6 responses

Error distribution:
  [37]  Post "http://4.157.180.226/api/people": EOF
  [961] Post "http://4.157.180.226/api/people": context deadline exceeded (Clien
t.Timeout exceeded while awaiting headers)
```

FIGURE 12-8 Latency, status, and error distributions.

> **Note** When performing load tests, gradually increase the user load to identify specific thresholds at which your application performance begins to degrade. This allows precise tuning of autoscaling parameters, ensuring optimal resource use without overspending.

Horizontal Pod autoscaling

The HorizontalPodAutoscaler (HPA) automatically adjusts the number of Pods in a Deployment or replication controller based on observed CPU utilization. Implemented as a control loop, the HPA periodically checks the CPU utilization of Pods (every 15 seconds by default) and updates the number of Pod replicas according to the following formula:

desiredReplicas = [currentReplicas × (currentMetricValue / desiredMetricValue)]

which uses the variables:

- **currentReplicas** Number of currently running Pods
- **currentMetricValue** Observed CPU metric
- **desiredMetricValue** Target CPU utilization

For example, if you have two replicas of a specific pod, with a desired CPU utilization of 40%, and the current CPU utilization increases to 80%, the equation becomes:

desiredReplicas = [2 × (80 / 40)] = 4

Thus, the HPA will scale out by adding two additional pod replicas. Similarly, if the CPU utilization reaches 95%, the desired number of replicas would be five, assuming the starting point was running two replicas.

Importantly, to calculate current resource utilization, the HPA uses the resource requests specified in the Pod declaration. Specifically, for CPU utilization, the current utilization is represented as a percentage of the requested CPU over all pods. For instance, if you have two Pods, each requesting 20% of the CPU, the total CPU utilization would be 40%.

The HPA gathers information about the target CPU utilization from the Kubernetes Metrics Server, which is installed by default in the Azure Kubernetes cluster. The Metrics Server collects resource metrics from kubelets and exposes them via the Kubernetes API server.

Configuring horizontal Pod autoscaling?

To configure horizontal Pod autoscaling, you need to create a HorizontalPodAutoscaler (HPA) resource in Kubernetes. The minimal declaration of the HPA for People.WebApp is shown in Listing 12-5.

LISTING 12-5 A Declaration of the HorizontalPodAutoscaler for the people-webapp-deployment.

```
apiVersion: autoscaling/v1
kind: HorizontalPodAutoscaler
metadata:
  name: people-webapp-hpa
spec:
  scaleTargetRef:
```

```
    apiVersion: apps/v1
    kind: Deployment
    name: people-webapp-deployment
minReplicas: 1
maxReplicas: 20
targetCPUUtilizationPercentage: 25
```

The above declaration applies to the `people-webapp-deployment`, as indicated by the `scale-TargetRef.name` field. The HPA will adjust the number of replicas to maintain the target CPU utilization at 25%. It will create up to 20 replicas, as specified by the `maxReplicas` field. Similarly, the HPA will maintain at least one replica, even when the CPU utilization falls below the target value. Importantly, the HPA can also be configured to monitor other metrics, such as memory utilization.

To examine the current CPU and memory utilization of the cluster, proceed as follows:

1. Open the Azure portal, and navigate to your AKS cluster (aks-people).

2. Click Metrics under the Monitoring section.

3. From the Metrics page, select CPU Usage Percentage from the Metric dropdown.

4. Click the Add Metric button, and select the Memory Working Set Percentage metric.

5. Click Add Metric again, and select Number of Pods by Phase.

6. Click the Time Picker (top-right corner), to set a time range for your data. In this case, select Last 30 Minutes.

The resulting plot should resemble the one shown in Figure 12-9.

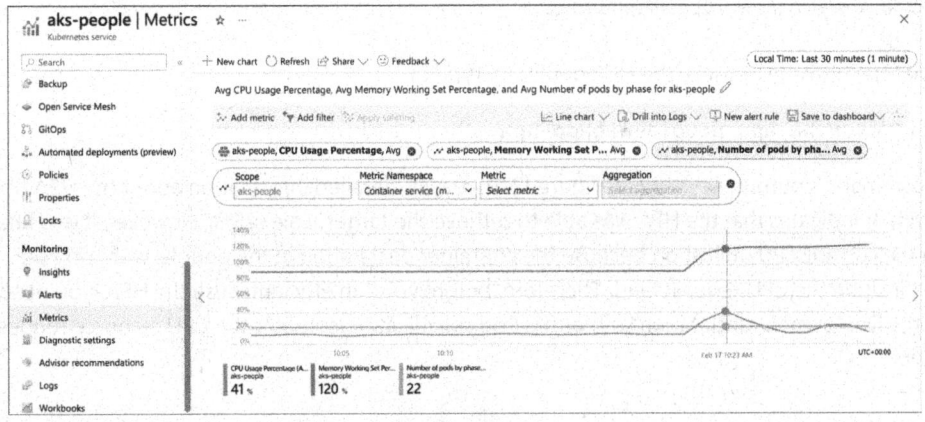

FIGURE 12-9 Using metrics to monitor the status of the cluster under the load test.

The spike observed in the metrics plots from Figure 12-9 corresponds to the load test. Note that during the load test, the CPU Usage Percentage increased from approximately 10% to almost 40%.

Similarly, memory use rose from around 90% to 120%. This indicates that under significant load, the API cannot accommodate all incoming requests due to insufficient resources.

Applying horizontal Pod autoscaling?

You will now use the HorizontalPodAutoscaler to scale the application under load:

1. Open Azure Cloud Shell.

2. Apply the HorizontalPodAutoscaler declaration (which was presented earlier in Listing 12-5):

    `kubectl apply -f https://raw.githubusercontent.com/dawidborycki/↵`

    `People.WebApp.Declarations/main/Kubernetes/people_hpa.yml`

3. Wait a a minute or two for the HPA to configure, and then check the status of the HPA by typing:

    `kubectl get hpa people-webapp-hpa`

The commands above are summarized in Figure 12-10. As observed, the HPA was created and is configured to create at least one and up to a maximum of 20 pods, depending on the load. The HPA aims to maintain the target CPU usage at 25%. However, the current CPU usage cannot be retrieved.

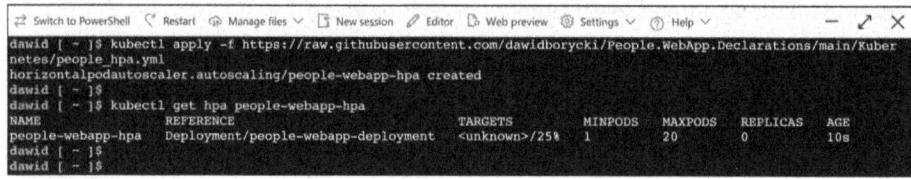

FIGURE 12-10 Applying the HorizontalPodAutoscaler.

To analyze this issue, retrieve the HPA details by typing:

`kubectl describe hpa people-webapp-hpa`

The command's output, as shown in Figure 12-11, reveals detailed information about the HPA object. Specifically, it indicates that the HPA was able to retrieve the target scale (25%). However, it was unable to fetch the current CPU utilization because the container declaration in the people-webapp Pod does not include the CPU request field. Therefore, before you can efficiently use the HPA, you need to modify the Deployment declaration so that the Pod specification contains the CPU resource request for containers.

```
dawid [ ~ ]$ kubectl describe hpa people-webapp-hpa
Name:                                                     people-webapp-hpa
Namespace:                                                default
Labels:                                                   <none>
Annotations:                                              <none>
CreationTimestamp:                                        Sun, 19 May 2024 15:57:54 +0000
Reference:                                                Deployment/people-webapp-deployment
Metrics:                                                  ( current / target )
  resource cpu on pods  (as a percentage of request):     <unknown> / 25%
Min replicas:                                             1
Max replicas:                                             20
Deployment pods:                                          2 current / 0 desired
Conditions:
  Type            Status  Reason                  Message
  ----            ------  ------                  -------
  AbleToScale     True    SucceededGetScale       the HPA controller was able to get the target's current scale
  ScalingActive   False   FailedGetResourceMetric the HPA was unable to compute the replica count: failed to get c
pu utilization: missing request for cpu in container people-webapp of Pod people-webapp-deployment-94968bd4b-888hn
Events:
  Type     Reason                        Age                From                       Message
  ----     ------                        ----               ----                       -------
  Warning  FailedGetResourceMetric       39s                horizontal-pod-autoscaler  failed to get cpu utilizatio
n: missing request for cpu in container people-webapp of Pod people-webapp-deployment-94968bd4b-v8x96
  Warning  FailedComputeMetricsReplicas  39s                horizontal-pod-autoscaler  invalid metrics (1 invalid o
ut of 1), first error is: failed to get cpu resource metric value: failed to get cpu utilization: missing request
for cpu in container people-webapp of Pod people-webapp-deployment-94968bd4b-v8x96
  Warning  FailedGetResourceMetric       9s (x3 over 54s)   horizontal-pod-autoscaler  failed to get cpu utilizatio
n: missing request for cpu in container people-webapp of Pod people-webapp-deployment-94968bd4b-888hn
  Warning  FailedComputeMetricsReplicas  9s (x3 over 54s)   horizontal-pod-autoscaler  invalid metrics (1 invalid o
ut of 1), first error is: failed to get cpu resource metric value: failed to get cpu utilization: missing request
for cpu in container people-webapp of Pod people-webapp-deployment-94968bd4b-888hn
dawid [ ~ ]$
```

FIGURE 12-11 Investigating the status of the HorizontalPodAutoscaler.

Resource requests and limits for Pods and containers

A Pod declaration can include resource specifications for containers, encompassing both resource requests and limits. *Resource requests* specify how much CPU and memory (RAM) the containers in your Pod require, and *limits* dictate the maximum amount of resources your Pod is allowed to use. Resource requests and limits are essential for ensuring that your applications run efficiently and reliably. They also play a significant role in scheduling and resource allocation within the cluster.

Given the resource requests, the kube-scheduler determines the node for deploying the Pod. It analyzes each node's utilization and places newly created Pods on nodes with sufficient resources. Conversely, the kubelet ensures that your Pods do not consume more resources than specified in their limit declarations. Limits prevent a single Pod or application from consuming too much of a node's available resources, which could negatively affect other Pods on the same node.

If a Pod exceeds its memory limit, Kubernetes may terminate it and possibly restart it, depending on the Pod's restart policy. For CPU, if a Pod attempts to use more resources than its limit allows, Kubernetes throttles the Pod's CPU usage to prevent it from exceeding the specified limit.

Limits and requests are specified in units of CPU and memory. In Kubernetes, one CPU unit corresponds to one physical or virtual core. CPU requests and limits are typically expressed in millicpu or millicores (1 CPU = 1000 m), allowing for the specification of fractional CPU values. For example, 200 m means 0.2 CPU or 20% of one CPU.

Memory is measured in bytes and can be expressed as either integers or fixed-point numbers, followed by suffixes like k, M, G, and T for decimal units or Ki, Mi, Gi, and Ti for binary units (power-of-two equivalents), the latter of which is commonly used in Kubernetes declarations.

For each container, you can specify resource limits and requests using the `resources.limits` and `resources.requests` fields within `spec.containers`. For example, the declaration in Listing 12-6 specifies that the people-webapp container requests 250 millicpu and 256 mebibytes of memory, with resource usage limits set to 500 millicpu and 512 mebibytes of memory.

LISTING 12-6 Deployment Declaration for the people-webapp Container.

```yaml
apiVersion: apps/v1
kind: Deployment
metadata:
  name: people-webapp-deployment
spec:
  replicas: 2
  selector:
    matchLabels:
      app: people-webapp
  template:
    metadata:
      labels:
        app: people-webapp
    spec:
      containers:
      - name: people-webapp
        image: people.azurecr.io/people.webapp:v1
        imagePullPolicy: Always
        ports:
        - containerPort: 5000
        resources:
          requests:
            cpu: "250m"
            memory: "256Mi"
          limits:
            cpu: "500m"
            memory: "512Mi"
```

To determine how much your Pods and nodes consume, you can use the **kubectl top** command, which retrieves resource usage from the Metrics Server. For example, to retrieve the resource utilization of Pods, type:

kubectl top pods

The sample result of this command during the load test is shown in Figure 12-12. You can see that two pods of People.WebApp consume about 1 m CPU and 848 Mi of memory on average,. This provides insight into how to configure resource requests and limits for People.WebApp. Based on the results shown in Figure 12-12, you will configure the requests at 500 m and 768 Mi, with limits set to 750 m and 1024 Mi for CPU and memory, respectively.

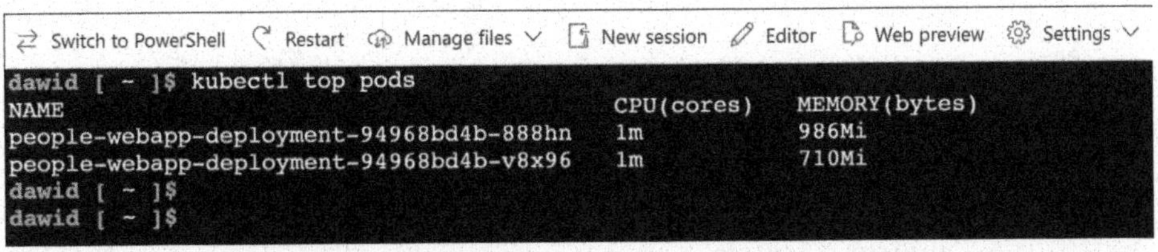

```
dawid [ ~ ]$ kubectl top pods
NAME                                          CPU(cores)   MEMORY(bytes)
people-webapp-deployment-94968bd4b-888hn      1m           986Mi
people-webapp-deployment-94968bd4b-v8x96      1m           710Mi
dawid [ ~ ]$
dawid [ ~ ]$
```

FIGURE 12-12 Analyzing resource utilization.

To apply resource requests and limits, proceed as follows. First, open Azure Cloud Shell and delete the existing Deployment of People.WebApp:

kubectl delete deployment people-webapp-deployment

This step is necessary because the node is short on memory. If you attempt to deploy new Pods with the requested memory values, Kubernetes will be unable to do so. Instead, it will request Azure to provision an additional node (because you enabled autoscaling in Chapter 7, "Azure Kubernetes Service"). However, provisioning a new node can take some time.

Next, return to the source of People.WebApp and modify the aks/deployment.yml file to specify container requests and limits as indicated in Listing 12-7.

LISTING 12-7 An Updated Deployment.yml that Includes Resource Requests and Limits.

```yaml
apiVersion: apps/v1
kind: Deployment
metadata:
  name: people-webapp-deployment
spec:
  replicas: 2
  selector:
    matchLabels:
      app: people-webapp
  template:
    metadata:
      labels:
        app: people-webapp
    spec:
      containers:
      - name: people-webapp
        image: <FQ_IMAGE_NAME>
        imagePullPolicy: Always
        ports:
        - containerPort: 5000
          resources:
            requests:
              cpu: "500m"
              memory: "768Mi"
            limits:
              cpu: "750m"
              memory: "1024Mi"
```

```
        env:
        - name: UseInMemoryDatabase
          value: "False"
        - name: KeyVaultName
          value: kv-people
        - name: ManagedIdentityClientId
          value: <MANAGED_CLIENT_ID>
```

Afterward, commit and push the changes to the repository:

```
git commit -am "Resource requests and limits"
git push
```

This action triggers the CI/CD pipeline, and after a few minutes, the new version of the Pod will be used to deploy new containers.

Confirm the Deployment is ready:

```
kubectl get deployments
```

Then, recheck the HPA status:

```
kubectl get hpa people-webapp-hpa
```

Figure 12-13 summarizes the commands above. You can see that the HPA successfully retrieves the current CPU utilization. Becasue the utilization is significantly below the target value, the HPA automatically reduced the Pod replicas from 2 to 1, as determined by the formula shown earlier. Thus, you just confirmed that the HPA works as expected. You are now ready to see how the HPA performs under the stress test.

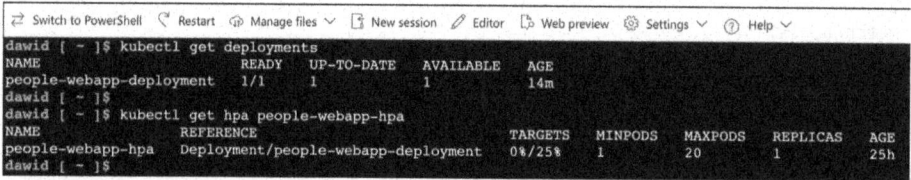

FIGURE 12-13 Analyzing the updated Deployment and the status of the Horizontal Pod Autoscaler.

> **Tip** Always define appropriate resource requests and limits for your Pods. Accurate requests help Kubernetes efficiently schedule workloads, and reasonable limits protect your applications from unexpected resource exhaustion, providing stability and predictability during high-traffic periods.

Performance of the HorizontalPodAutoscaler under load test conditions

To analyze the performance of the HorizontalPodAutoscaler under load, start by running the load test from your local terminal:

```
docker run --rm -e SERVICE_IP=<IP_OF_YOUR_WEB_APP> load-test:v1
```

Then, proceed to Azure Cloud Shell, and enter the following command:

```
kubectl get hpa people-webapp-hpa -w
```

The **-w** parameter enables you to watch the status of the HPA, updating every 15 seconds. This allows you to observe the current CPU usage and the number of replicas in real time. During the stress test, the output from the **kubectl get hpa** command will appear as shown in Figure 12-14.

```
dawid [ ~ ]$ kubectl get hpa people-webapp-hpa -w
NAME                REFERENCE                              TARGETS    MINPODS   MAXPODS   REPLICAS   AGE
people-webapp-hpa   Deployment/people-webapp-deployment    0%/25%     1         20        1          15m
people-webapp-hpa   Deployment/people-webapp-deployment    74%/25%    1         20        1          16m
people-webapp-hpa   Deployment/people-webapp-deployment    74%/25%    1         20        3          17m
people-webapp-hpa   Deployment/people-webapp-deployment    98%/25%    1         20        3          17m
people-webapp-hpa   Deployment/people-webapp-deployment    59%/25%    1         20        4          17m
people-webapp-hpa   Deployment/people-webapp-deployment    98%/25%    1         20        4          18m
people-webapp-hpa   Deployment/people-webapp-deployment    59%/25%    1         20        4          18m
people-webapp-hpa   Deployment/people-webapp-deployment    56%/25%    1         20        4          18m
people-webapp-hpa   Deployment/people-webapp-deployment    56%/25%    1         20        7          19m
people-webapp-hpa   Deployment/people-webapp-deployment    47%/25%    1         20        7          19m
people-webapp-hpa   Deployment/people-webapp-deployment    19%/25%    1         20        7          19m
people-webapp-hpa   Deployment/people-webapp-deployment    19%/25%    1         20        7          20m
```

FIGURE 12-14 Monitoring the status of the HorizontalPodAutoscaler.

Notice the increase in CPU usage and its impact on the number of Pod replicas. The HPA progressively scales up the number of Pod replicas to manage the increased load. More available Pods allow the processing of incoming requests in parallel. Consequently, as shown in Figure 12-15, the API becomes responsive, evidenced by the response time histogram. Notably, with 100 concurrent users, you now receive timely responses, with most response times around 1 second (instead of 2 seconds as before). The peak is at 1.043.

You can also revisit the Metrics page for the aks-people cluster to observe that the number of Pods corresponds with the increased resource usage. This demonstrates that the API can now automatically adjust to incoming traffic, as shown in Figure 12-16.

However, as the HPA requests more Pods to be scheduled, the node size becomes insufficient to accommodate them all. Therefore, the kube-scheduler requests additional nodes through the cloud-controller-manager. This is possible because you configured the Cluster Autoscaler when provisioning the Azure Kubernetes Service cluster. Your initial configuration set the minimum and maximum node counts at 1 and 3, respectively. However, this range can be adjusted to accommodate more pods if needed.

```
LoadTest — com.docker.cli • docker run --rm -e SERVICE_IP=4.157.180.226 load-test:v1 — 80×26
Testing the People.WebApp with IP (POST): 4.157.180.226

100 users.

Summary:
  Total:         31.1370 secs
  Slowest:       9.3866 secs
  Fastest:       0.1162 secs
  Average:       2.0818 secs
  Requests/sec:  47.1144


Response time histogram:
  0.116 [1]    |
  1.043 [517]  |██████████████████████████████████████████
  1.970 [363]  |█████████████████████████████
  2.897 [222]  |██████████████████
  3.824 [141]  |███████████
  4.751 [79]   |██████
  5.678 [64]   |█████
  6.605 [52]   |████
  7.533 [19]   |█
  8.460 [4]    |
  9.387 [5]    |
```

FIGURE 12-15 Load testing.

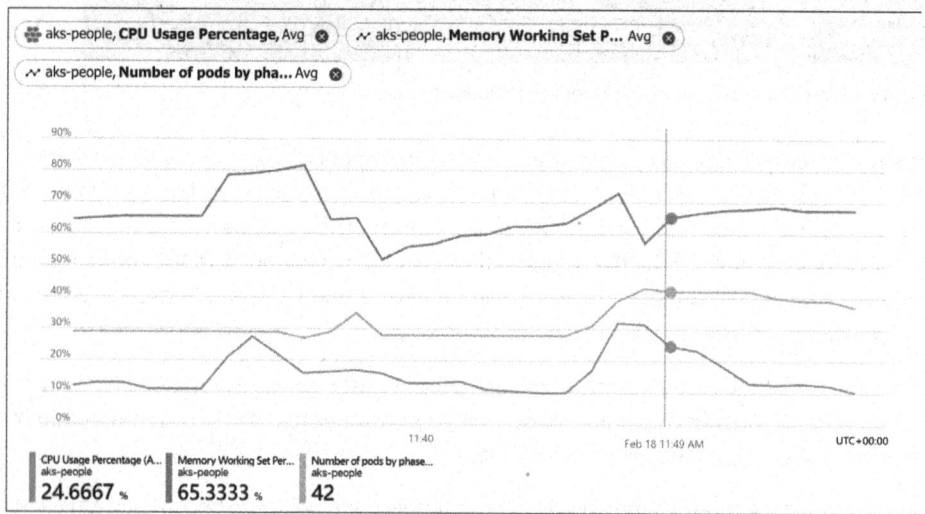

FIGURE 12-16 Monitoring the cluster.

To verify that additional nodes were created, use the following commands:

```
kubectl get nodes
kubectl top nodes
```

As illustrated in Figure 12-17, these commands will show you the list of nodes and their resource usage.

```
dawid [ ~ ]$ kubectl get nodes
NAME                              STATUS   ROLES   AGE     VERSION
aks-agentpool-38167470-vmss000009 Ready    agent   3d11h   v1.27.7
aks-agentpool-38167470-vmss00000g Ready    agent   15m     v1.27.7
aks-agentpool-38167470-vmss00000h Ready    agent   4m55s   v1.27.7
dawid [ ~ ]$
dawid [ ~ ]$ kubectl top nodes
NAME                              CPU(cores)  CPU%  MEMORY(bytes)  MEMORY%
aks-agentpool-38167470-vmss000009 263m        13%   4339Mi         95%
aks-agentpool-38167470-vmss00000g 298m        15%   2942Mi         64%
aks-agentpool-38167470-vmss00000h 265m        13%   1982Mi         43%
dawid [ ~ ]$
dawid [ ~ ]$
```

FIGURE 12-17 An increased application load triggered the Cluster Autoscaler.

Note Combining the HorizontalPodAutoscaler (HPA) with the Kubernetes Cluster Autoscaler ensures your infrastructure scales efficiently at both the application and hardware levels. However, regularly review and adjust autoscaling parameters to align with actual workload demands and avoid unexpected scaling behavior or excessive costs.

Summary

This chapter delved into the implementation and optimization of the Kubernetes HorizontalPodAutoscaler (HPA) to enhance application scalability under variable loads. Your journey began with an introduction to load testing using the Hey tool, followed by containerizing the load test for ease of use and portability. You then configured the HPA to dynamically adjust the number of Pod replicas based on CPU utilization, promoting efficient resource usage and responsive application performance.

A crucial step in ensuring the HPA's effective operation involved setting appropriate resource requests and limits for Pods and containers. This required modifying the deployment specifications to reflect CPU and memory requests and limits aligned with observed resource utilization metrics.

You further explored the deployment and monitoring of these adjustments within a Kubernetes environment, emphasizing the use of kubectl commands to apply HPA configurations, remove existing Deployments, and revise Deployment specifications with updated resource requests and limits.

By monitoring HPA performance and resource utilization with **kubectl top** and **kubectl get hpa**, you ensured that the application scaled effectively during load tests. The hands-on examples illustrated the process of fine-tuning resource parameters to accommodate the demands of numerous concurrent users, thereby enhancing application responsiveness and stability. Additionally, the chapter highlighted the role of the Kubernetes Cluster Autoscaler in dynamically provisioning extra nodes to support the increased load, emphasizing the need to tailor autoscaling parameters to the application's requirements.

Overall, this exploration provided a thorough understanding of how to leverage Kubernetes features such as HPA, resource requests, and limits to sustain optimal application performance and scalability in a cloud-native setting.

CHAPTER 13

Deploying and Managing Kubernetes Applications with Helm

In previous chapters, you learned that deploying applications using Kubernetes declarations is an effective method for achieving a declarative approach to container orchestration. This method ensures consistency, repeatability, and automation in deploying and managing containerized applications. However, as you venture into more complex multi-container, multi-service solutions, the simplicity of Kubernetes manifests begins to diminish. In typical real-world scenarios, this includes a vast number of declarations you need to manage. Each application component requires its own set of declarations, encompassing deployments, services, the HorizontalPodAutoscaler, and more, leading to substantial management overhead.

In response to this challenge, Helm emerges as a vital tool in the Kubernetes ecosystem. Helm is essentially a package manager for Kubernetes that enables developers and operations teams to package, configure, and deploy applications and services on Kubernetes clusters more efficiently (see Figure 5-1 in Chapter 5, "Azure Container Registry"). It introduces the concept of charts, which are pre-configured Kubernetes resources that can be shared, making it easier to define, install, and upgrade even the most complex Kubernetes applications. Helm charts help in modularizing Kubernetes workloads, allowing for the reuse of code and simplifying the management of multi-component solutions. This not only enhances productivity but also significantly reduces the potential for human error, ensuring that complex deployments are handled with the same ease as simpler, single-container applications.

In this chapter, you will learn how to use Helm, beginning with a straightforward example that lays the foundation for understanding its core functionalities. As you progress, you'll delve into managing the application lifecycle using Helm, from deployment to updates and rollbacks, demonstrating how Helm streamlines Kubernetes operations. Next, you will create Helm charts for People.WebApp. Finally, you'll explore how to seamlessly integrate Helm into your continuous integration/continuous deployment (CI/CD) pipelines, enhancing the automation and efficiency of your development workflow.

By the end of this chapter, you'll be well-equipped with the knowledge and skills to leverage Helm in optimizing your Kubernetes deployments.

Introduction to Helm

Helm is a package manager for Kubernetes, designed to streamline the installation and management of applications within Kubernetes clusters. By encapsulating detailed application configurations into reusable charts, Helm simplifies the Kubernetes application lifecycle, facilitating more efficient development workflows and deployment strategies.

A *Helm chart* is a collection of files that describe a related set of Kubernetes resources, serving as a package for Kubernetes applications. This package enables users to define, install, and upgrade complex Kubernetes applications, containing any number of Kubernetes objects necessary to run an application, tool, or service within a Kubernetes cluster.

This packaging simplifies the deployment and management of applications on Kubernetes by encapsulating all necessary components into a single, manageable entity. This approach supports easy sharing, versioning, and customization, enhancing the distribution and maintenance of applications.

Helm charts are collected and shared through *Helm repositories*, which act as libraries or storage spaces for Helm charts. These repositories enable you to share and distribute your packaged applications or services. Repositories can be either public, offering broad access to the community, or private, restricted to an organization or specific group of users.

Helm repositories support versioning, which is essential for maintaining and updating applications deployed on Kubernetes clusters. This feature facilitates controlled upgrades and rollbacks, allowing for the efficient management of chart versions.

When a chart is deployed using Helm, the resulting set of deployed Kubernetes resources is termed a release. This release is central to Helm's application deployment and management capabilities. Each release is uniquely named within a Kubernetes namespace, allowing multiple deployments of the same chart—with potentially different configurations—to coexist without conflict. Helm tracks the deployment history of each release, including upgrades and rollbacks, enabling visibility into deployed versions and the capability to revert to a previous release if necessary.

Creating a Helm chart

You're about to create your first Helm chart. To unify the working environment, you will use Azure Cloud Shell. First, open Azure Cloud Shell, and type:

`helm create people-web-app-helm`

The command will respond with the message: "Creating people-web-app-helm." This command generates the chart, which, as shown in Figure 13-1, has the following structure:

- **Chart.yaml** A YAML file containing metadata about the chart such as its name, version, and description
- **values.yaml** A YAML file that specifies the default configuration values for the chart

- **templates** A directory containing template files that generate valid Kubernetes manifest files when combined with values from the `values.yaml` file
- **charts** A directory containing any charts upon which people-web-app-helm depends
- **.helmignore** A file that specifies patterns to ignore when packaging the chart (similar to `.gitignore`)

A Helm chart can optionally include:

- **crds** An optional directory for Custom Resource Definitions that should be installed as part of the chart
- **README.md** and **LICENSE** Optional files that can contain documentation for the chart and the chart's license, respectively

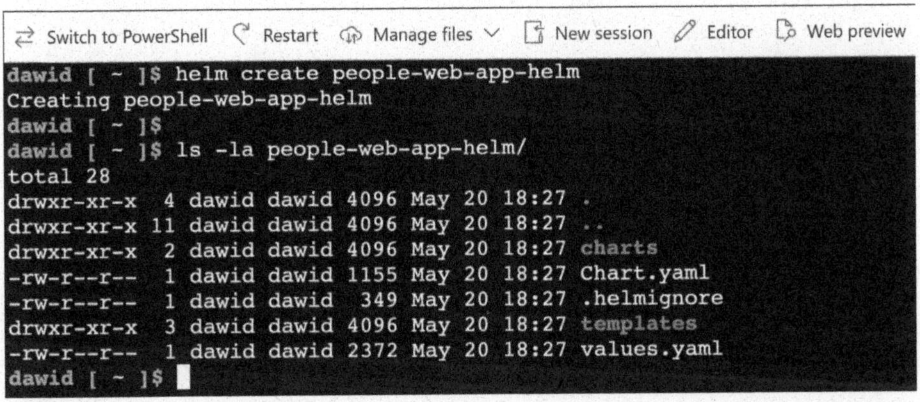
Switch to PowerShell
Restart
Manage files
New session
Editor
Web preview
dawid [~]$ helm create people-web-app-helm
Creating people-web-app-helm
dawid [~]$
dawid [~]$ ls -la people-web-app-helm/
total 28
drwxr-xr-x 4 dawid dawid 4096 May 20 18:27 .
drwxr-xr-x 11 dawid dawid 4096 May 20 18:27 ..
drwxr-xr-x 2 dawid dawid 4096 May 20 18:27 charts
-rw-r--r-- 1 dawid dawid 1155 May 20 18:27 Chart.yaml
-rw-r--r-- 1 dawid dawid 349 May 20 18:27 .helmignore
drwxr-xr-x 3 dawid dawid 4096 May 20 18:27 templates
-rw-r--r-- 1 dawid dawid 2372 May 20 18:27 values.yaml
dawid [~]$

FIGURE 13-1 Creating a Helm chart.

To proceed further, you will need to modify values.yaml as follows:

1. Open the values.yaml file in the text editor by using the following command (see Figure 13-2). If prompted with the Switch to Classic Cloud Shell window, click Confirm:

   ```
   code people-web-app-helm/values.yaml
   ```

2. Go to line 8, and set the repository to the one where you keep your Docker images (Listing 13-1):

   LISTING 13-1 Defining the Container Image Repository Hosted in Azure Container Registry.

   ```
   repository: people.azurecr.io/people.webapp
   ```

3. On line 11, change the image tag to **v1** (Listing 13-2):

   LISTING 13-2 Setting the Container Image Version Tag (v1).

   ```
   tag: "v1"
   ```

4. On line 19, disable **serviceAccount** creation (Listing 13-3):

   LISTING 13-3 Configuration for Kubernetes Service Account.

   ```
   serviceAccount:
     create: false
     automount: false
   ```

5. Under line 43, change the service type from **ClusterIP** to **LoadBalancer**, and add the target and container port (Listing 13-4):

   LISTING 13-4 Defining the Kubernetes Service Type as a LoadBalancer.

   ```
   service:
     type: LoadBalancer
     port: 80
     targetPort: 5000
     containerPort: 5000
   ```

6. Configure resource limits and requests (lines 69–74). Make sure to remove braces after `resources` (Listing 13-5):

   LISTING 13-5 Specification of Kubernetes Resource Allocation.

   ```
   resources:
     limits:
       cpu: 750m
       memory: 1000Mi
     requests:
       cpu: 500m
       memory: 768Mi
   ```

7. Configure the `livenessProbe` and `readinessProbe` (lines 76–83 of values.yaml, Listing 13-6):

   LISTING 13-6 Configuration of Kubernetes Liveness and Readiness Probes.

   ```
   resources:
     livenessProbe:
       httpGet:
         path: /api/people
         port: http
     readinessProbe:
       httpGet:
         path: /api/people
         port: http
   ```

8. Enable horizontal pod autoscaling (lines 85–89 of values.yaml, Listing 13-7):

   LISTING 13-7 Enabling Kubernetes HorizontalPodAutoscaler (HPA).

   ```
   autoscaling:
     enabled: true
     minReplicas: 1
     maxReplicas: 10
     targetCPUUtilizationPercentage: 80
   ```

9. Save the changes, and close the file.

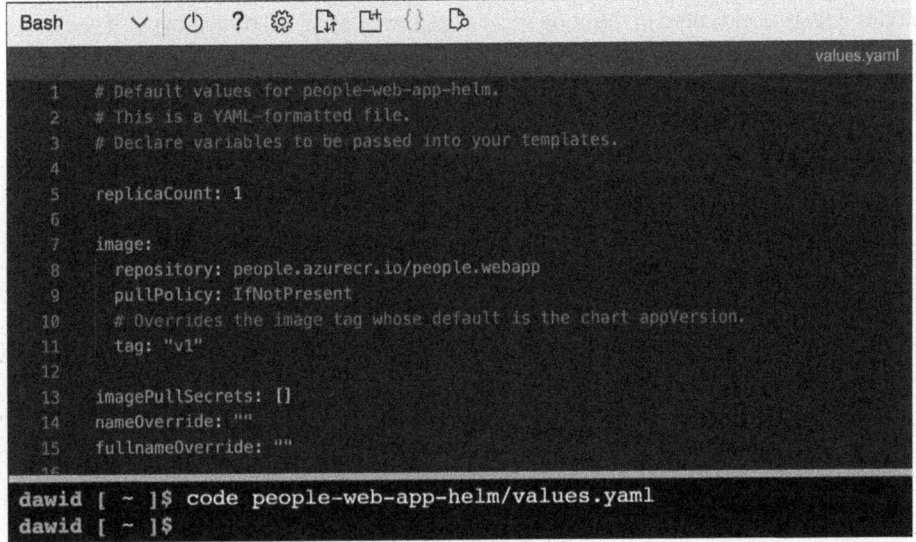

FIGURE 13-2 Modifying the Values.yaml file.

The values you specified will now be used to configure the chart. In this configuration, you used the first version of the People.WebApp's Docker image. You opted to expose the application using a LoadBalancer service, which makes it accessible from outside the cluster. Additionally, you configured both readiness and liveness probes to ensure the health and availability of the containers within a Pod. The liveness probe checks if a container is running properly, and Kubernetes restarts the container if this probe fails. The readiness probe, on the other hand, checks if the container is ready to accept traffic. If a readiness probe fails, Kubernetes stops routing traffic to the Pod until it passes the probe again. Both probes are configured to send HTTP requests to the People API endpoint. Because explicit thresholds were not set, Kubernetes applies the following default thresholds: an initial delay of 0 seconds, a period of 10 seconds between checks, a timeout of 1 second, a success threshold of 1 (the probe needs to succeed once to be considered healthy), and a failure threshold of 3 (the probe must fail three consecutive times to be considered unhealthy).

Finally, you enabled horizontal pod autoscaling to ensure that Kubernetes dynamically adjusts the number of Pod replicas to maintain target CPU usage at 80%. To support this autoscaling, you carefully configured resource limits and requests.

There is one more thing you need to modify: the Deployment template file. The automatically generated template does not fully support our initial configuration, where the container listens on port 5000 and you redirect incoming traffic from port 80 to 5000. Although you added the `containerPort` property to `values.yaml` (under `service`), this value is not yet mapped to any value in the templates. To account for that, proceed as follows:

1. Open the templates/deployment.yaml file in the text editor:

   code people-web-app-helm/templates/deployment.yaml

2. Modify line 41 as indicated in the code snippet below (lines 33–41 of deployment.yaml, Listing 13-8):

   LISTING 13-8 Container Definition Template in Helm.

   ```
   containers:
     - name: {{ .Chart.Name }}
       securityContext:
         {{- toYaml .Values.securityContext | nindent 12 }}
       image: "{{ .Values.image.repository }}:{{ .Values.image.tag | 
           default .Chart.AppVersion }}"
       imagePullPolicy: {{ .Values.image.pullPolicy }}
       ports:
         - name: http
           containerPort: {{ .Values.service.containerPort }}
   ```

3. Save, and close the file.

To validate the chart, use the **helm lint** command as shown below:

```
helm lint people-web-app-helm/
```

This command will analyze your chart and report any warnings or potential errors. Go ahead and validate your chart to ensure everything is correct (Figure 13-3).

```
dawid [ ~ ]$ helm lint people-web-app-helm/
==> Linting people-web-app-helm/
[INFO] Chart.yaml: icon is recommended

1 chart(s) linted, 0 chart(s) failed
dawid [ ~ ]$
dawid [ ~ ]$
```

FIGURE 13-3 Linting the Helm chart.

> **Note** If probe intervals, resource limits, or requests are not explicitly defined in the values.yaml file, Kubernetes will apply default settings. Explicitly specifying these values helps ensure clarity and predictability in your application deployments.

Rollouts and rollbacks

After preparing the chart, you are ready to install the application using Helm. In Azure Cloud Shell, type the following command:

```
helm install people-helm people-web-app-helm/
```

The command installs the people-web-app-helm chart as the people-helm release. The Helm release name is set using the first argument of the **helm install** command (**people-helm**). After invoking that command, the deployment status will be provided, looking similar to what is shown in Figure 13-4. Then, retrieve the application's IP using the provided command or by typing:

```
kubectl get svc
```

Afterward, retrieve the value under the EXTERNAL-IP column for the people-helm-people-web-app-helm row. Copy the IP (here, it is 51.8.218.83) to the address bar of your web browser, and you will see the first version of People.WebApp (shown in Figure 13-5).

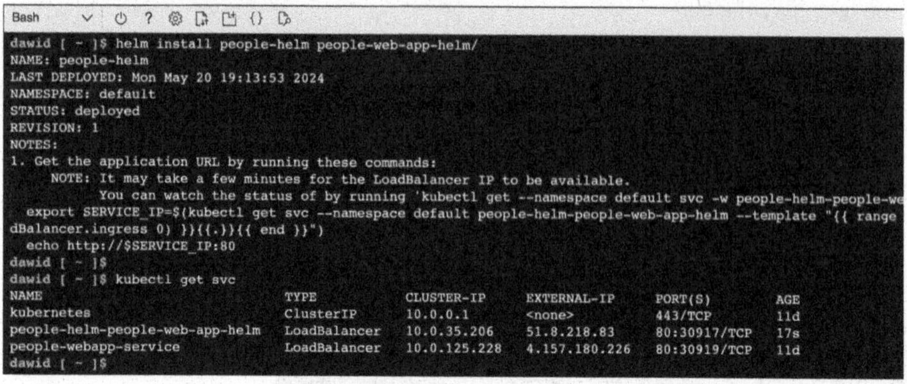

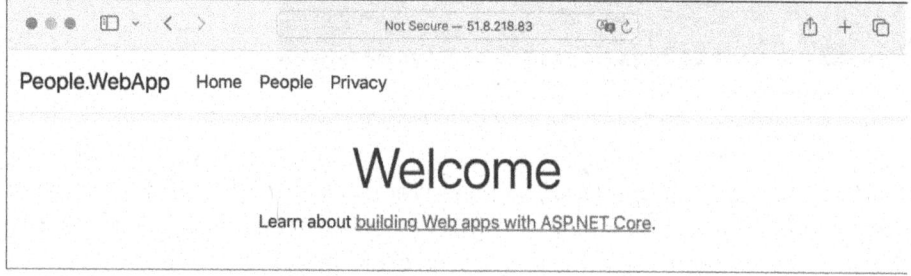

FIGURE 13-4 Installing the Helm chart.

FIGURE 13-5 People.WebApp deployed using Helm.

You have just deployed People.WebApp using Helm. To view all active Helm releases, type:

`helm ls`

As shown in Figure 13-6, this displays a list including the people-helm release, which you just deployed. Now, if you need to upgrade the application to a more recent version, you first update the image tag in `people-web-app-helm/values.yaml` from v1 to a newer version of the People.WebApp Docker image. For this example, use v4, which includes functionality to display the name of the Pod processing requests.

After saving the values.yaml file, apply the change with the following command:

`helm upgrade people-helm people-web-app-helm/`

To confirm the upgrade, rerun **helm ls** and notice that the revision column now indicates 2 instead of 1, confirming that Helm accurately tracks release versions.

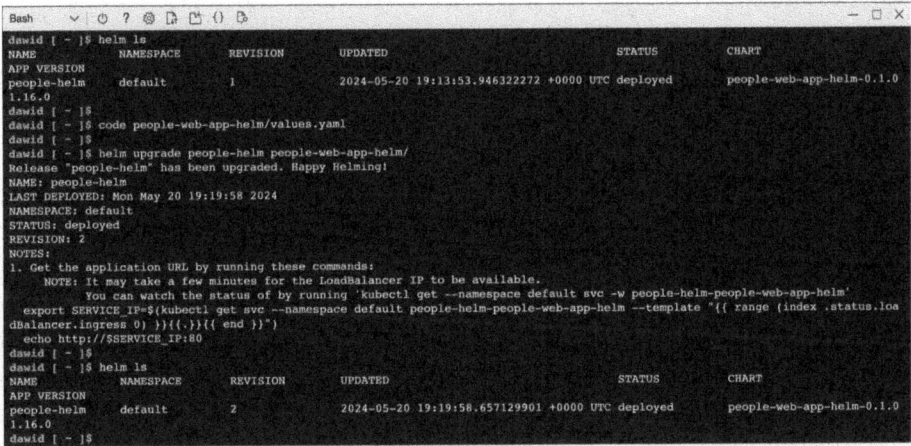

FIGURE 13-6 Upgrading an application using Helm.

Wait a few moments for the application to update, then navigate to its public IP to view the new version of the application (see Figure 13-7).

FIGURE 13-7 An updated People.WebApp.

Helm, similar to the **kubectl rollout** command, enables you to roll back to the previous version. To do so, invoke the following command:

`helm rollback people-helm`

Then, check the list of releases by typing:

`helm ls`

You will see that the revision has changed to 3 (see Figure 13-8) and the application has reverted to its original version.

Finally, to uninstall the application, type:

`helm uninstall people-helm`

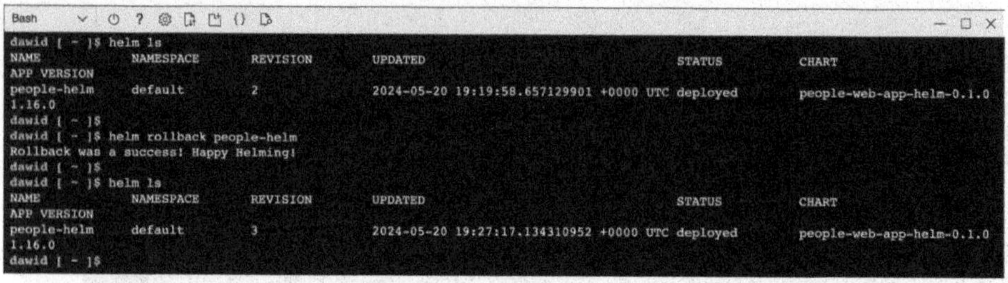

FIGURE 13-8 A reverted People.WebApp.

This section provided a walkthrough for deploying, upgrading, and rolling back an application using Helm within a Kubernetes environment. Through the example of People.WebApp, it demonstrated Helm's ability to effectively manage application versions. Additionally, the section highlighted Helm's lifecycle management capabilities, covering everything from initial deployment to eventual removal. In the next step, you will integrate Helm with your CI/CD pipeline.

Integration with the CI/CD pipeline

You just explored using Helm to deploy applications to a Kubernetes cluster. However, you did not delve into every detail of how the individual components of the Helm chart were created. The focus was primarily on modifying the values.yaml file and making a single change in the deployment.yaml file.

Furthermore, you deployed the application and managed its lifecycle using the Helm command-line interface. However, similar to how you use kubectl, you can integrate the deployment process with the continuous integration/continuous deployment (CI/CD) pipeline you established in Chapter 11, "Automating Image Builds and Deployment Using CI/CD Pipelines." This integration ensures that any change made to the source code and committed to the Git repository triggers the re-creation and pushing of the application's Docker image to Azure Container Registry. Subsequently, the updated Docker image will be used to refresh the application in the Kubernetes cluster using the Helm chart.

To become familiar with the chart's structure and integrate Helm with the CI/CD pipeline, you first will create a new Git branch and the chart files, then, define the required chart files (Chart.yaml and values.yaml) and template files (deployment.yaml, service.yaml, hpa.yaml, and _helpers.tpl).

Git branch and chart files

To prepare the repository branch and chart files, follow these steps:

1. Open your local terminal or command prompt, and change the working directory to the location of People.WebApp's repository.

2. Type the following commands to create a new branch named ci-cd-helm from the ci-cd branch:

    ```
    git checkout ci-cd
    ```

    ```
    git checkout -b ci-cd-helm
    ```

3. Within the People.WebApp folder, create a new subfolder named helm.

4. In the helm subfolder, create the following files:

    Chart.yaml

    values.yaml

5. Inside the helm subfolder, create another folder named **templates**.

6. Add the following files to the helm/templates folder:

    deployment.yaml

    service.yaml

    hpa.yaml

    _helpers.tpl

The Git branch and chart structure are now ready. You could proceed to define the files now, but before you do, let me explain the _helpers.tpl file, as it introduces a new component to the discussion. The _helpers.tpl file is commonly used to define and manage reusable template snippets and helper functions. Helm uses these templates to generate Kubernetes manifest files from the chart's configuration values. You use _helpers.tpl to avoid duplication and promote consistency across the different Kubernetes resources defined within the chart. In your previously created chart, _helpers.tpl contained definitions for deployment and service names, various labels, and so on. Here, you will also use this file to methodically define those names.

Chart and values files

Start by modifying the helm/Chart.yaml file as shown below (Listing 13-9):

LISTING 13-9 Helm Chart Metadata Specifying Chart and Application Version Information.

```
apiVersion: v2
name: people-web-app
description: A Helm chart for Kubernetes
type: application
version: 0.1.0
appVersion: "1.0.0"
```

The above declaration specifies the following:

- **apiVersion** The API version of the chart. v2 indicates that this chart is designed for Helm 3, whereas Helm 2 uses `apiVersion: v1`.

- **name** Indicates the name of the Helm chart (here, it is named people-web-app). This name is used when referencing the chart from commands or dependencies.

- **description** A brief description of what the chart is and what it contains or represents.
- **type** Specifies the type of the chart. The value `application` indicates that this chart is intended to deploy an application. Another possible value is `library`, which would indicate the chart provides utilities or functions for use by other charts but does not deploy an application by itself.
- **version** The version of the Helm chart. This follows semantic versioning (semver), and in this case, it's 0.1.0. This version should be incremented based on changes to the chart itself, following semver rules (`major` for breaking changes, `minor` for new features that are backward compatible, and `patch` for backward-compatible bug fixes).
- **appVersion** The version of the application that this chart deploys. This does not need to adhere to the semver rules of the chart itself and is meant to indicate which version of the underlying application (people-web-app) is being deployed.

Next, open the values.yaml file, and update it as follows (Listing 13-10):

LISTING 13-10 Complete Helm Chart Values Configuration.

```yaml
replicaCount: 1

image:
  repository: <FQ_IMAGE_NAME>
  pullPolicy: IfNotPresent

app:
  env:
    UseInMemoryDatabase: "False"
    KeyVaultName: "kv-people"
    ManagedIdentityClientId: <MANAGED_CLIENT_ID>

service:
  type: LoadBalancer
  port: 80
  targetPort: 5000
  containerPort: 5000

resources:
  limits:
    cpu: 750m
    memory: 1000Mi
  requests:
    cpu: 500m
    memory: 768Mi

livenessProbe:
  httpGet:
    path: /api/people
    port: http
```

```
readinessProbe:
  httpGet:
    path: /api/people
    port: http

autoscaling:
  enabled: true
  minReplicas: 1
  maxReplicas: 10
  targetCPUUtilizationPercentage: 80
```

The above configuration outlines how the application should be deployed, managed, and scaled within a Kubernetes cluster, leveraging Helm's templating capabilities for easy customization and deployment. Additionally, you modified the declaration to include two placeholders: <FQ_IMAGE_NAME> and <MANAGED_CLIENT_ID>. These will be replaced with actual values when the GitHub Actions workflow is executed. The first will be retrieved from the job that builds the Docker image, while the second will be dynamically retrieved.

The declaration defines the following:

- **replicaCount** Specifies the number of replicas of the Pod that should be running. In this case, it's set to 1, meaning only one instance of the Pod will be deployed by default.

- **image** Contains details about the Docker image to be used.
  - **repository** Specifies the fully qualified image name (<FQ_IMAGE_NAME>) of the Docker image for the Pod. This will be updated during the workflow execution.
  - **pullPolicy** Determines the image pull policy. **IfNotPresent** means Kubernetes will use the local image if it exists, rather than pulling it from the repository again.

- **app** Defines application-specific configurations, used here to configure the environment variables in the container, as before:
  - **UseInMemoryDatabase** Configures the application to use (or not use) an in-memory database. Set to False to indicate that an external SQL Server database will be used.
  - **KeyVaultName** Specifies the name of an Azure Key Vault instance (**kv-people**) for storing Secrets, used here to retrieve the SQL connection string.
  - **ManagedIdentityClientId** Placeholder for the managed identity client ID used for authenticating with Azure services. This will be replaced by the actual value when the workflow is executed.

- **service**: Describes the Kubernetes Service to expose the application.
  - **type** The type of service, **LoadBalancer** in this case, which makes the service accessible through an external IP.
  - **port** The port on which the service is exposed externally.

- **targetPort** The port on the container that the service forwards traffic to.
- **containerPort** The port that the container listens on.

- **resources limits** and **requests** Specifies the CPU and memory (RAM) limits and requests for the container.
- **livenessProbe** and **readinessProbe** Define health checks for the container. Both probes use an HTTP GET request to the /api/people path to check the container's health (Liveness-Probe) and readiness (ReadinessProbe) on the HTTP port.
- **autoscaling** Configuration for automatically scaling the number of Pod replicas based on CPU utilization.
  - **enabled** Indicates whether autoscaling is enabled (true).
  - **minReplicas** and **maxReplicas** The minimum and maximum number of Pod replicas.
  - **targetCPUUtilizationPercentage** The target CPU utilization percentage that triggers autoscaling. Set to 80%, meaning if the CPU utilization exceeds 80%, Kubernetes will start creating more replicas until the maximum is reached.

Deployment

You will now create the Helm template for defining a Kubernetes Deployment resource to deploy People.WebApp. Begin by opening the helm/templates/deployment.yaml file and modify it with the following declaration (Listing 13-11):

LISTING 13-11 Helm Deployment Template (deployment.yaml) Dynamivally Generating Kubernetes Deployment Definitions.

```yaml
apiVersion: apps/v1
kind: Deployment
metadata:
  name: {{ include "people-web-app.name" . }}
  labels:
    {{- include "people-web-app.labels" . | nindent 4 }}
spec:
  {{- if not .Values.autoscaling.enabled }}
  replicas: {{ .Values.replicaCount }}
  {{- end }}
  selector:
    matchLabels:
      {{- include "people-web-app.selectorLabels" . | nindent 6 }}
  template:
    metadata:
      {{- with .Values.podAnnotations }}
      annotations:
        {{- toYaml . | nindent 8 }}
      {{- end }}
```

```yaml
      labels:
        {{- include "people-web-app.labels" . | nindent 8 }}
        {{- with .Values.podLabels }}
        {{- toYaml . | nindent 8 }}
        {{- end }}
    spec:
      containers:
        - name: {{ .Chart.Name }}
          image: {{ .Values.image.repository }}
          imagePullPolicy: {{ .Values.image.pullPolicy }}
          ports:
            - name: http
              containerPort: {{ .Values.service.containerPort }}
              protocol: TCP
          env:
            {{- range $key, $value := .Values.app.env }}
            - name: {{ $key }}
              value: "{{ $value }}"
            {{- end }}
          livenessProbe:
            {{- toYaml .Values.livenessProbe | nindent 12 }}
          readinessProbe:
            {{- toYaml .Values.readinessProbe | nindent 12 }}
          resources:
            {{- toYaml .Values.resources | nindent 12 }}
```

This declaration, similar to previous Kubernetes deployment configurations, contains the `apiVersion`, `kind`, `metadata`, and `spec` fields. However, their values are dynamically generated using Helm's templating syntax, denoted by `{{ }}`. This approach allows for the deployment to be customized without directly altering the template, enabling various configurations of the same application. It adapts to different environments or manages releases through Helm charts.

Helm templates, leveraging the Go programming language's templating engine, enable the use of functions, pipelines, variables, and control structures within these `{{ }}` brackets. For instance, the `{{ include "people-web-app.name" . }}` statement dynamically generates a resource name based on the logic defined in the people-web-app.name named template and the current rendering context (denoted by the `.` before the close brackets).

The `include` function injects the content from one named template into another, promoting the reusability of logic across templates. Here, it's used to insert the people-web-app.name template, defined elsewhere in the Helm chart, typically within the _helpers.tpl file. By passing the current context (.) to the `include` function, all data associated with the chart's rendering process, including values from the values.yaml file and built-in Helm and Kubernetes objects, are made available to the named template.

The people-web-app.name template is designed to generate a clean, Kubernetes-friendly name for resources based on the Helm chart's name while ensuring it does not exceed 63 characters and does not end with a hyphen. It is defined as follows in the _helpers.tpl file (Listing 13-12):

LISTING 13-12 Helm Helper Template Function (people-web-app.name) that Generates a Kubernetes-Compliant Resource Name.

```
{{- define "people-web-app.name" -}}
{{- printf "%s" .Chart.Name | trunc 63 | trimSuffix "-" }}
{{- end }}
```

This template uses the `printf` function for formatting the `.Chart.Name` value, followed by the `trunc` function to limit the name to 63 characters and the `trimSuffix` function to remove any trailing hyphens. Such conventions ensure adherence to Kubernetes' DNS-compliant naming requirements.

Additionally, the template demonstrates Helm's flow control capabilities, such as the conditional inclusion of the `replicas` field based on the `autoscaling.enabled` value, and dynamic environment variable construction using a loop over `.Values.app.env`. These features allow for significant flexibility in how deployments are configured and managed. Specifically, `{{- if not .Values.autoscaling.enabled }}` checks if autoscaling is not enabled and, if so, includes the replicas: `{{ .Values.replicaCount }}` line in the generated YAML file.

Furthermore, the environment variables section is dynamically constructed as follows (Listing 13-13):

LISTING 13-13 Environment Variables Section of Helm Helper Template Function (people-web-app.name).

```
env:
  {{- range $key, $value := .Values.app.env }}
  - name: {{ $key }}
    value: "{{ $value }}"
  {{- end }}
```

This snippet uses Helm's templating syntax to iterate over the key-value pairs defined under `.Values.app.env` in the values.yaml file. Each pair represents an environment variable to be set in the container, showcasing how Helm templates can dynamically inject configuration data into Kubernetes resource definitions.

Service

With the Deployment declaration ready, you can now proceed to the Service declaration. Open the helm/templates/service.yaml file and modify it as follows (Listing 13-14):

LISTING 13-14 Helm Template Defining a Kubernetes Service Configuration.

```
apiVersion: v1
kind: Service
metadata:
  name: {{ include "people-web-app.name" . }}
```

```
    labels:
      {{- include "people-web-app.labels" . | nindent 4 }}
  spec:
    type: {{ .Values.service.type }}
    ports:
      - port: {{ .Values.service.port }}
        targetPort: http
        protocol: TCP
    selector:
      {{- include "people-web-app.selectorLabels" . | nindent 4 }}
```

This declaration configures a Kubernetes Service resource using Helm's templating syntax. It dynamically retrieves the service name and its labels from the _helpers.tpl file. Additionally, it sets the service type and port based on the values specified in the values.yaml file (`service.type` and `service.port`). Finally, the service is associated with the deployment using selector labels, which are defined in the _helpers.tpl file. You will define these named templates shortly.

HorizontalPodAutoscaler

The next step is to define the HorizontalPodAutoscaler using Helm's templating approach. Open the helm/templates/hpa.yaml file and modify it as follows (Listing 13-15):

LISTING 13-15 Helm Helper for Generates a Kubernetes HorizontalPodAutoscaler (HPA).

```
{{- if .Values.autoscaling.enabled }}
apiVersion: autoscaling/v2
kind: HorizontalPodAutoscaler
metadata:
  name: {{ include "people-web-app.name" . }}
  labels:
    {{- include "people-web-app.labels" . | nindent 4 }}
spec:
  scaleTargetRef:
    apiVersion: apps/v1
    kind: Deployment
    name: {{ include "people-web-app.name" . }}
  minReplicas: {{ .Values.autoscaling.minReplicas }}
  maxReplicas: {{ .Values.autoscaling.maxReplicas }}
  metrics:
    {{- if .Values.autoscaling.targetCPUUtilizationPercentage }}
    - type: Resource
      resource:
        name: cpu
        target:
          type: Utilization
          averageUtilization: {{ .Values.autoscaling.targetCPUUtilizationPercentage }}
    {{- end }}
{{- end }}
```

This Helm snippet defines a Kubernetes HorizontalPodAutoscaler (HPA) resource, conditional on the `autoscaling.enabled` setting from the values.yaml file. The HPA will be associated with the Deployment, identified by the people-web-app.name template. It configures the minimum and maximum number of Pod replicas, and the target CPU utilization percentage that triggers autoscaling, according to the values specified in values.yaml (Listing 13-10), which were:

```
autoscaling:
  enabled: true
  minReplicas: 1
  maxReplicas: 10
  targetCPUUtilizationPercentage: 80
```

With these settings, autoscaling is enabled, allowing the HPA to adjust the number of pod replicas between 1 and 10 to maintain a target CPU utilization of 80%.

Helpers

Next, you need to define the named templates that were used in the previous declarations. As discussed, these named templates are located in the helm/templates/_helpers.tpl file. This file already includes the definition for the people-web-app.name template. You will now extend the _helpers.tpl file by adding the named templates highlighted in the following listing (Listing 13-16):

LISTING 13-16 Helm Helper Templates (_helpers.tpl).

```
{{- define "people-web-app.name" -}}
{{- printf "%s" .Chart.Name | trunc 63 | trimSuffix "-" }}
{{- end }}

{{/*
Create chart name and version as used by the chart label.
*/}}
{{- define "people-web-app.chart" -}}
{{- printf "%s-%s" .Chart.Name .Chart.Version | replace "+" "_" | ↵
    trunc 63 | trimSuffix "-" }}
{{- end }}

{{/*
Common labels
*/}}
{{- define "people-web-app.labels" -}}
helm.sh/chart: {{ include "people-web-app.chart" . }}
{{ include "people-web-app.selectorLabels" . }}
{{- if .Chart.AppVersion }}
app.kubernetes.io/version: {{ .Chart.AppVersion | quote }}
{{- end }}
app.kubernetes.io/managed-by: {{ .Release.Service }}
{{- end }}
```

```
{{/*
Selector labels
*/}}
{{- define "people-web-app.selectorLabels" -}}
app.kubernetes.io/name: {{ include "people-web-app.name" . }}
app.kubernetes.io/instance: {{ .Release.Name }}
{{- end }}
```

This Helm configuration introduces three additional named templates: people-web-app.chart, people-web-app.labels, and people-web-app.selectorLabels. These templates are used for generating labels and chart information for Kubernetes resources within the people-web-app Helm chart.

The people-web-app.chart named template creates a string combining the chart's name and version, replacing any plus signs (+) with underscores (_). This string is truncated to 63 characters and ensures it does not end with a hyphen. This value is typically used to tag resources with the chart version they are deployed with, aiding in tracking and management.

The people-web-app.labels template generates common labels for Kubernetes resources. It includes labels indicating the chart name and version (using the people-web-app.chart template), selector labels (using the people-web-app.selectorLabels template), the application version (if available), and the tool used to manage the release (`managed-by`). These labels help standardize resource identification and management within Kubernetes.

The people-web-app.selectorLabels template defines the basic labels used to associate resources with a particular instance of the Deployment and the application name. It sets labels for the application's name (from the people-web-app.name template) and instance (using the release name). These selector labels are used to select the correct Pods to manage and route traffic to.

You can find the final declaration files at:

github.com/dawidborycki/People.WebApp.Declarations/tree/main/helm

GitHub Actions

Finally, you need to update the GitHub Actions workflow declaration found in .github/workflows/people-webapp-ci-cd.yml. This file was initially created in the ci-cd branch you created in Chapter 11. Begin by adjusting the workflow's name and the branch it triggers on, as highlighted in the code snippet below (Listing 13-17):

LISTING 13-17 GitHub Actions Workflow Definition Triggered by Commits to the ci-cd-helm Branch.

```
name: CI/CD Pipeline (Helm)

on:
  push:
    branches:
      - ci-cd-helm
```

The declaration of the environment variables and the first job do not require any changes. Scroll down to the `deploy-to-aks` job, and rename it **deploy-to-aks-with-helm** (Listing 13-18):

LISTING 13-18 GitHub Actions Workflow Job Definition (deploy-to-aks-with-helm).

```
deploy-to-aks-with-helm:
  runs-on: ubuntu-latest
  needs: build-and-push-docker-image
```

Keep the first three job steps unchanged: Checkout code, Login to Azure, and Configure Kubernetes context. Next, remove the declarations for the Configure Kubernetes Manifest and Update Deployment steps (Listing 13-19):

LISTING 13-19 GitHub Actions Steps for Configuring and Applying Kubernetes Manifests.

```
- name: Configure Kubernetes Manifest
  env:
    FQ_IMAGE_NAME: ${{ needs.build-and-push-docker-image.outputs.fq_image_name }}
  run: |
    MANAGED_CLIENT_ID=$(az identity list --query "[?contains(name, '$AKS_POOL_NODE_
        NAME')].clientId" -o tsv)
    sed -i "s|<FQ_IMAGE_NAME>|$FQ_IMAGE_NAME|g" ./aks/deployment.yml
    sed -i "s|<MANAGED_CLIENT_ID>|$MANAGED_CLIENT_ID|g" ./aks/deployment.yml
    cat ./aks/deployment.yml

- name: Update Deployment
  run: kubectl apply -f ./aks/deployment.yml
```

Next, add the following three steps (Listing 13-20):

LISTING 13-20 GitHub Actions Steps.

```
- name: Update values.yaml
  env:
    FQ_IMAGE_NAME: ${{ needs.build-and-push-docker-image.outputs.fq_image_name }}
  run: |
    MANAGED_CLIENT_ID=$(az identity list --query "[?contains(name, '$AKS_POOL_NODE_
        NAME')].clientId" -o tsv)
    sed -i "s|<FQ_IMAGE_NAME>|$FQ_IMAGE_NAME|g" ./helm/values.yaml
    sed -i "s|<MANAGED_CLIENT_ID>|$MANAGED_CLIENT_ID|g" ./helm/values.yaml
    cat ./helm/values.yaml

- name: Helm Lint
  run: helm lint ./helm

- name: Deploy with Helm
  run: helm upgrade --install people-web-app-helm ./helm/
```

This approach updates the values.yaml file with the fully qualified image name and the managed client ID, then runs `helm lint` to check the chart for any issues. Finally, it deploys the application using Helm with the `helm upgrade --install` command.

You can find the complete workflow declaration here:

github.com/dawidborycki/People.WebApp.Declarations/blob/main/Workflows/people-webapp-ci-cd-helm.yml

> **Tip** Always integrate `helm lint` into your CI/CD pipelines (for example, GitHub Actions) before deployment. This step validates your Helm chart for syntax or configuration errors, allowing you to identify and fix issues early, which minimizes disruptions and ensures smoother deployments.

Testing the workflow

To commit all the changes to the ci-cd-helm git branch to trigger the workflow defined above, use the following commands:

```
git commit -am "Helm"
git push
```

Next, log in to GitHub, navigate to the repository, and click Actions. Select the Helm workflow from the list of workflow runs. The summary of this workflow run should appear as shown in Figure 13-9. The workflow displays two jobs: build-and-push-docker-image and deploy-to-aks-with-helm, with the second job depending on the first. This setup is similar to what was presented in Chapter 11.

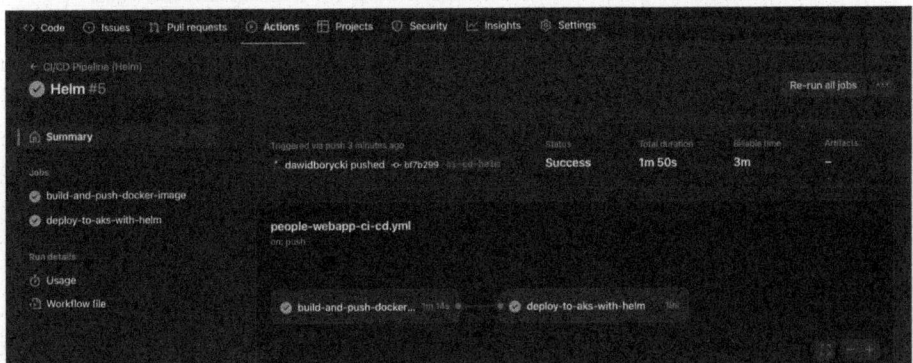

FIGURE 13-9 A summary of the modified workflow.

If you now click deploy-to-aks-with-helm, you will see the job log as depicted in Figure 13-10. This log includes the modified steps: Update values.yaml, Helm Lint, and Deploy with Helm. Specifically, Figure 13-10 shows output generated by the Update values.yaml step. This demonstrates how the values.yaml was dynamically updated during the workflow execution, including the fully qualified image name generated during the first job. Although not explicitly shown, the other Helm template files, including deployment.yaml, service.yaml, and hpa.yaml, are also automatically configured when the `helm upgrade` command is invoked during the last job's step.

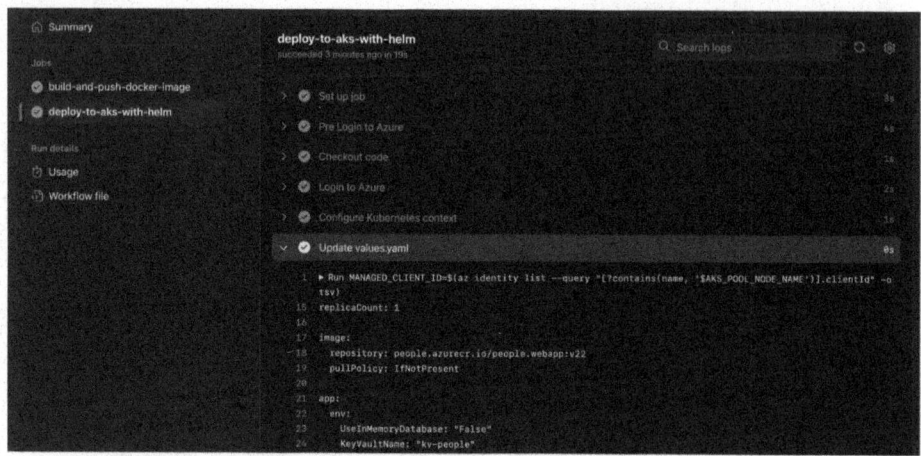

FIGURE 13-10 Output generated by the deploy-to-aks-with-helm job.

You can now verify that the application was deployed. To do so, return to Azure Cloud Shell and type:

`kubectl get svc`

Note that you now have two applications running in the cluster: the one deployed previously and another one deployed with Helm, resulting in two LoadBalancer services. Look for the EXTERNAL-IP of the people-webapp (in Figure 13-11), and then open this IP in a web browser.

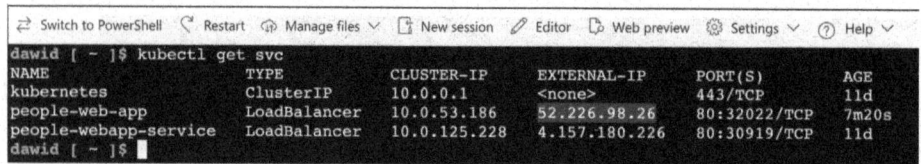

FIGURE 13-11 Finding the EXTERNAL-IP of the people-webapp.

You will see the welcome screen shown in Figure 13-12, which is identical to the one you created in Chapter 11.

FIGURE 13-12 An Application Deployed with Helm.

To test the workflow you created, modify the Views/Home/Index.cshtml file of People.WebApp. Specifically, change line 6 to:

```
<h1 class="display-4">AKS, Helm and CI/CD are great!</h1>
```

Then, save the file and commit the changes to the repository to rerun the workflow:

```
git commit -am "Updated Index.cshtml"
git push
```

Once the workflow completes, return to the web application to see the updated view (Figure 13-13).

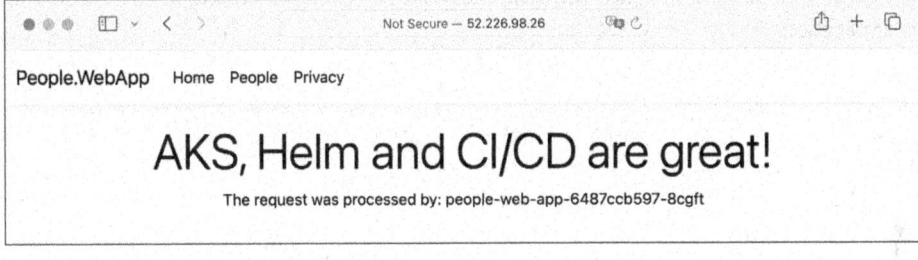

FIGURE 13-13 Testing the CI/CD workflow.

To uninstall the application, type the following command:

```
helm uninstall people-web-app-helm
```

Summary

In this chapter, you learned how to use Helm to deploy applications to Kubernetes. You started by creating a Helm chart using the command line, then modified it to deploy People.WebApp. Next, you built a Helm chart from scratch to fully grasp Helm's approach. By doing so, you established a robust deployment mechanism that leverages Helm's capabilities for managing Kubernetes resources, ensuring your application deployments are consistent, reproducible, and automated. Understanding and utilizing Helm's templating syntax and control structures are crucial for creating flexible and reusable Kubernetes resource definitions. Best practices include maintaining well-documented values.yaml files, testing charts with **helm lint** and **helm template**, and using version control to manage chart versions to ensure smooth deployments and updates.

You have then successfully integrated Helm into your CI/CD pipeline using GitHub Actions, demonstrating a comprehensive approach to automating the deployment and management of a Kubernetes application. You began by modifying the GitHub Actions workflow to include Helm-specific steps, such as updating values.yaml, linting the Helm chart, and deploying the application with Helm. This allowed you to dynamically configure your Deployment settings based on the workflow's execution context, ensuring that your application's deployment is both flexible and controlled.

By committing changes to the ci-cd-helm branch, you triggered the modified workflow, structured to build and push a Docker image, followed by the deployment of the application to Azure Kubernetes Service (AKS) using Helm. This workflow not only streamlines the deployment process but also ensures that changes made to the application are automatically reflected in the deployed version, showcasing the power of continuous deployment.

Furthermore, you verified the deployment by inspecting the Kubernetes services in AKS, highlighting the presence of two applications: one deployed traditionally and the other using Helm. This illustrates the seamless integration of Helm into existing CI/CD pipelines. Finally, you tested the workflow's effectiveness by updating the application's frontend and observing the changes in the deployed application, thereby demonstrating the end-to-end process of code changes leading to automatic updates in the live application.

CHAPTER 14

Infrastructure as Code

Software development is a dynamic field that demands agility to adapt to changing requirements while ensuring applications remain operational without interruptions. The DevOps methodology addresses these challenges, emphasizing key practices such as continuous integration (CI) and continuous delivery (CD).

As you learned, CI enables you to frequently integrate your code into a shared repository, typically using Git. This process involves automated builds each time code is committed. CD builds upon CI, facilitating the deployment of applications immediately after successful builds and tests, thus accommodating swift changes in requirements and minimizing downtime. You have successfully adopted these approaches to deploy the example application, demonstrating that you can use either Kubernetes CLI or Helm.

However, applications depend on an underlying infrastructure of compute, storage, and network services, managed across various environments such as development, staging, and production. Traditional management of these environments can lead to "environment drift," where configurations diverge over time, making them difficult to reproduce automatically and leading to errors that require manual intervention.

Infrastructure as Code (IaC) addresses this issue by allowing the infrastructure to be defined and managed through code, typically in YAML or JSON files, which are stored in a source control system. This approach enables the application of version control practices to infrastructure changes, where updates are committed to a repository, triggering CI/CD processes that validate and automatically provision or decommission resources.

This methodology extends into GitOps when applied to managing Kubernetes clusters, where infrastructure declarations are stored in Git repositories. Git workflows facilitate infrastructure deployments through branch management and pull requests, ensuring changes are reviewed before merging. The CI/CD system then automatically deploys the infrastructure changes, enabling a seamless update process for containerized applications.

In practice, a build pipeline is established, consisting of various jobs and steps. The initial job might provision resources, such as updating a Kubernetes cluster, using command-line scripts. Subsequently, other jobs can build and deploy the application to this prepared environment. This automation streamlines the development and deployment process, allowing teams to concentrate on feature development and adapt to ever-changing requirements efficiently.

By adopting IaC and GitOps, organizations can significantly reduce manual overhead, enhance consistency across environments, and achieve greater operational efficiency, aligning with the goals of DevOps to support rapid and reliable software delivery.

In this chapter, you will learn how to use IaC and incorporate it into your CI/CD workflow to achieve GitOps. Specifically, you will declare your infrastructure, including Azure Container Registry (ACR), Azure Kubernetes Service (AKS), Key Vault, and SQL database instances in text files. These will be added to the repository and subjected to the same development cycle as code, enabling an efficient IaC approach.

For IaC, you will use Terraform, an open-source software tool created by HashiCorp. Terraform allows you to define and provision infrastructure using a high-level configuration language known as HashiCorp Configuration Language (HCL) or JSON. Terraform manages external resources with a plan-and-apply model, efficiently handling the creation, modification, and deletion of resources in a safe and predictable manner.

By the end of this chapter, you will grasp the final component of the comprehensive approach depicted in Figure 5-1 (Chapter 5, "Azure Container Registry").

Introduction to Terraform

Terraform uses declarative configuration files to describe the desired state of your infrastructure, enabling the creation of reproducible and predictable environments across development, staging, and production settings. This approach ensures consistency and compliance. Supporting a multitude of providers, including major cloud platforms like Azure, AWS, and Google Cloud Platform, Terraform allows for the management of a wide variety of services with a single tool. Its ability to manage cross-platform resources and its emphasis on infrastructure as code principles have made it a popular choice among DevOps teams for efficient infrastructure management and automation.

Terraform uses providers to interface seamlessly across various cloud platforms and on-premises data centers. A provider acts as a conduit, connecting the Terraform CLI to the target API, such as the Azure Resource Manager (ARM) for Microsoft Azure. The Terraform Registry hosts an extensive library of publicly available providers, simplifying the integration of Terraform with a broad array of services and platforms.

When configuring Terraform, you typically start by specifying the provider. Then, you declare the resources you intend to provision. Remarkably, a single Terraform configuration file can use multiple providers, enabling the simultaneous deployment of diverse resources across different clouds. To incorporate a provider into your Terraform project, initiate it with the **terraform init** CLI command, which prepares your working directory for further commands.

After outlining your infrastructure in the template file, use the **terraform validate** command to ensure that your configurations are syntactically valid and internally consistent before deployment. The typical workflow involves creating an execution plan with **terraform plan**, offering a preview of the actions Terraform will undertake based on the current state of cloud resources relative to the state defined in your template file. This comparison identifies the necessary actions to align the actual infrastructure with the desired state outlined in your configuration. Subsequently, you use **terraform apply** to apply the planned actions, requiring your approval before proceeding. This transparent and controlled approach to infrastructure management is crucial for preventing unintended modifications and ensuring that changes align precisely with expectations.

In the process of managing your infrastructure, Terraform keeps track of the current state of the resources it manages in a state file. By default, when you run Terraform in a local environment, this state file is stored locally in a file named terraform.tfstate. This local state file contains a serialized representation of your managed infrastructure and configuration, which Terraform uses to map real-world resources to your configuration, keep track of metadata, and improve performance for large infrastructures.

While local state management is the default behavior, it's important to note that storing state locally can pose challenges, especially when working in a team or across different machines. The local state file can become a source of conflicts, and its sensitive contents may not be adequately secured. Furthermore, it does not support state locking to prevent concurrent executions that could potentially corrupt the state file. For these reasons, for any nontrivial or collaborative projects, it's recommended to configure Terraform to use a remote state backend. Remote backends, such as Azure Blob Storage, offer enhanced security, versioning, and state locking, making them suitable for collaborative and production environments.

Terraform's design promotes modular and reusable configurations, enabling teams to share and reuse templates for common infrastructure patterns. This modularity boosts collaboration and efficiency, reducing the likelihood of errors and inconsistencies in infrastructure provisioning.

Moreover, Terraform Cloud and Terraform Enterprise offer advanced features for teams and organizations, providing solutions for collaboration, security, and compliance, further enhancing Terraform's utility in large-scale operations.

In summary, Terraform's use of providers is a foundational aspect of its design, enabling seamless interaction with a multitude of cloud and on-premises platforms. By adhering to Terraform's workflow—from initializing providers and validating configurations to reviewing and applying execution plans—teams can achieve sophisticated, automated, and consistent infrastructure management across their entire technology stack.

In the next steps, you will explore how to use Terraform to deploy the Azure Container Registry. Afterwards, you will extend your infrastructure declaration to include other cloud resources you used earlier in the book.

Deploying Azure Container Registry

To deploy Azure Container Registry, you'll use Terraform within Azure Cloud Shell, where Terraform is pre-installed. This approach eliminates the need for local tool installations.

Creating Terraform declarations for Azure Container Registry

Follow these steps to create your Terraform configuration:

1. Open Azure Cloud Shell.

2. Create a new Terraform configuration file by typing **code people-webapp-iac.tf** in the Cloud Shell.

3. Edit the file with the following content (Listing 14-1):

    LISTING 14-1 Terraform Configuration for Provisioning an Azure Resource Group and Azure Container Registry.

    ```
    provider "azurerm" {
      features {}
    }

    resource "azurerm_resource_group" "rg-tf" {
      name     = "rg-aks-people-tf"
      location = "East US"
    }

    resource "azurerm_container_registry" "container_registry" {
      name = "peopletf"
      resource_group_name = azurerm_resource_group.rg-tf.name
      location = azurerm_resource_group.rg-tf.location
      sku = "Basic"
      admin_enabled = false
    }
    ```

4. Save and close the file.

This declaration encompasses three primary elements. The first specifies the Azure provider. Typically, the provider declaration includes configuration settings. This example includes the `features {}` block, which is mandatory for the Azure provider but does not require any settings to be specified.

The second element establishes the resource group named rg-aks-people-tf, designated for deployment to the East US Azure Region. Analyzing the initial line of this declaration reveals the use of the `resource` keyword, indicating that you are defining a component of your infrastructure managed by Terraform. Following this, you specify the resource type (`azurerm_resource_group`), and then you provide a local name or alias for this resource instance. This alias is how you will refer to this specific Azure Resource Group within your Terraform configuration. Importantly, this name influences the actual name of the resource in Azure, as determined by the name attribute inside the `resource` block. This block contains two properties: name and `location`, with which you define the resource's name within Azure and the Azure Region where the resource will be deployed, respectively.

Finally, the third block delineates the Azure Container Registry instance to be deployed within the previously defined resource group. It aligns the location with that of the resource group, opts for the `Basic` SKU (which dictates the registry's features and cost), and disables the creation of an admin user account for the registry. This setup mirrors the configuration employed during the manual creation of a registry with Azure Container Registry.

Note that you must adhere to Azure's naming conventions. Also, the name of the Azure Container Registry instance has to be globally unique because it forms part of the DNS endpoint.

Remote backend

An important aspect of creating Infrastructure as Code (IaC) is managing the state file. As mentioned above, Terraform keeps track of the current state of the resources it manages in a state file. By default, this state file is stored locally. However, when integrating IaC into the CI/CD pipeline, you encounter a problem: Each job in the workflow run uses a different runner. Once a workflow completes, the Terraform state is lost, rendering Terraform unable to make infrastructure updates in subsequent workflow runs. To address this issue, you will add a remote backend using Azure Blob Storage. In Azure Cloud Shell, create the storage account with the following command:

```
az storage account create -n peoplewebappstore -g rg-aks-people -l eastus ↵
    --sku Standard_LRS --kind StorageV2
```

In the above command, the **-n** parameter configures the storage account name. You then specify the resource group name (in this case, rg-aks-people), the location, SKU, and storage kind. Note that the storage account name must be globally unique and contain 3 to 24 characters, consisting of numbers and lowercase letters only.

Once the storage account is ready, create a blob container named terraform:

```
az storage container create --account-name peoplewebappstore -n terraform
```

With the storage account and blob container now set up, you have a durable and secure place to store your Terraform state. This ensures that your CI/CD pipeline can consistently manage and update your infrastructure across multiple runs, leveraging the remote state to maintain a single source of truth for your Azure resources.

The next step involves configuring Terraform to use this blob as its backend for state management, enabling seamless infrastructure management. To do so, modify the people-webapp-iac.tf in Cloud Shell by adding the following backend configuration below the provider (Listing 14-2):

LISTING 14-2 Terraform Backend Configuration.

```
terraform {
  backend "azurerm" {
    resource_group_name   = "rg-aks-people"
    storage_account_name  = "peoplewebappstore"
    container_name        = "terraform"
    key                   = "terraform.tfstate"
  }
}
```

So, the complete people-webapp-iac.tf file will look as follows (Listing 14-3):

LISTING 14-3 Complete Terraform Configuration Defining the Azure Provider, Backend State Storage Configuration, Resource Group Creation, and Azure Container Registry.

```
provider "azurerm" {
  features {}
}

terraform {
  backend "azurerm" {
    resource_group_name  = "rg-aks-people"
    storage_account_name = "peoplewebappstore"
    container_name       = "terraform"
    key                  = "terraform.tfstate"
  }
}

resource "azurerm_resource_group" "rg-tf" {
  name     = "rg-aks-people-tf"
  location = "East US"
}

resource "azurerm_container_registry" "container_registry" {
  name                = "peopletf"
  resource_group_name = azurerm_resource_group.rg-tf.name
  location            = azurerm_resource_group.rg-tf.location
  sku                 = "Basic"
  admin_enabled       = false
}
```

Make sure to save the file before proceeding further. In the next step, you will deploy the above resources using Terraform.

Deploying the infrastructure

To deploy resources, type the following command in Azure Cloud Shell:

terraform init

This command initializes the Terraform configuration. As illustrated in Figure 14-1, Terraform will initialize the backend and install the hashicorp/azurerm provider, based on your .tf file.

To proceed, follow Terraform's output instructions to create an execution plan by typing:

terraform plan

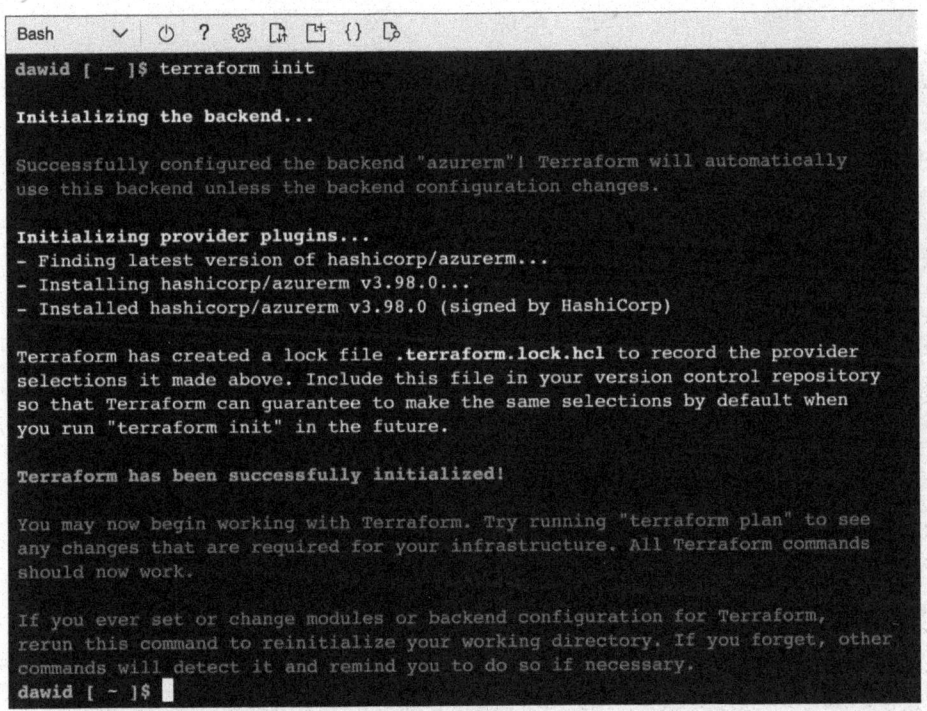

FIGURE 14-1 Initializing Terraform.

This command allows you to review the actions to be performed. Its output, shown in Figure 14-2, will list the resources to be created, updated, or removed. In this specific instance, you will see the creation of two resources (azurerm_container_registry.container_registry and azurerm_resource_group. rg-tf) both declared in the Terraform file. The output will also display a list of attributes and their values for each resource. Note that the plan shows all available attributes, implying that Terraform applies default values for those you do not explicitly specify. Additionally, some attributes, such as id, are marked as "known after applying the declaration," indicating that their values will be generated by Azure upon deployment.

To apply the configuration, type:

`terraform apply`

Terraform will display the plan again and then wait for your confirmation. Type **yes**, and press Enter to approve the deployment. To automatically approve the plan, you can use the `-auto-approve` parameter.

```
dawid [ ~ ]$ terraform plan

Terraform used the selected providers to generate the following execution plan.
  + create

Terraform will perform the following actions:

  # azurerm_container_registry.container_registry will be created
  + resource "azurerm_container_registry" "container_registry" {
      + admin_enabled                 = false
      + admin_password                = (sensitive value)
      + admin_username                = (known after apply)
      + encryption                    = (known after apply)
      + export_policy_enabled         = true
      + id                            = (known after apply)
      + location                      = "eastus"
      + login_server                  = (known after apply)
      + name                          = "peopletf"
      + network_rule_bypass_option    = "AzureServices"
      + network_rule_set              = (known after apply)
      + public_network_access_enabled = true
      + resource_group_name           = "rg-aks-people-tf"
      + retention_policy              = (known after apply)
      + sku                           = "Basic"
      + trust_policy                  = (known after apply)
      + zone_redundancy_enabled       = false
    }

  # azurerm_resource_group.rg-tf will be created
  + resource "azurerm_resource_group" "rg-tf" {
      + id       = (known after apply)
      + location = "eastus"
      + name     = "rg-aks-people-tf"
    }

Plan: 2 to add, 0 to change, 0 to destroy.
```

FIGURE 14-2 Creating an execution plan.

The output, as depicted in Figure 14-3, will confirm that Terraform has deployed the resource group and container registry. These resources can be verified within the Azure portal. Simply type **rg-aks-people-tf** in the search box and navigate to that group. Notice that the group contains one resource, peopletf, which is the Azure Container Registry instance you declared (see Figure 14-4).

Following these steps, you successfully deployed a registry to Azure Container Registry using Terraform, showcasing an efficient and repeatable approach to infrastructure management.

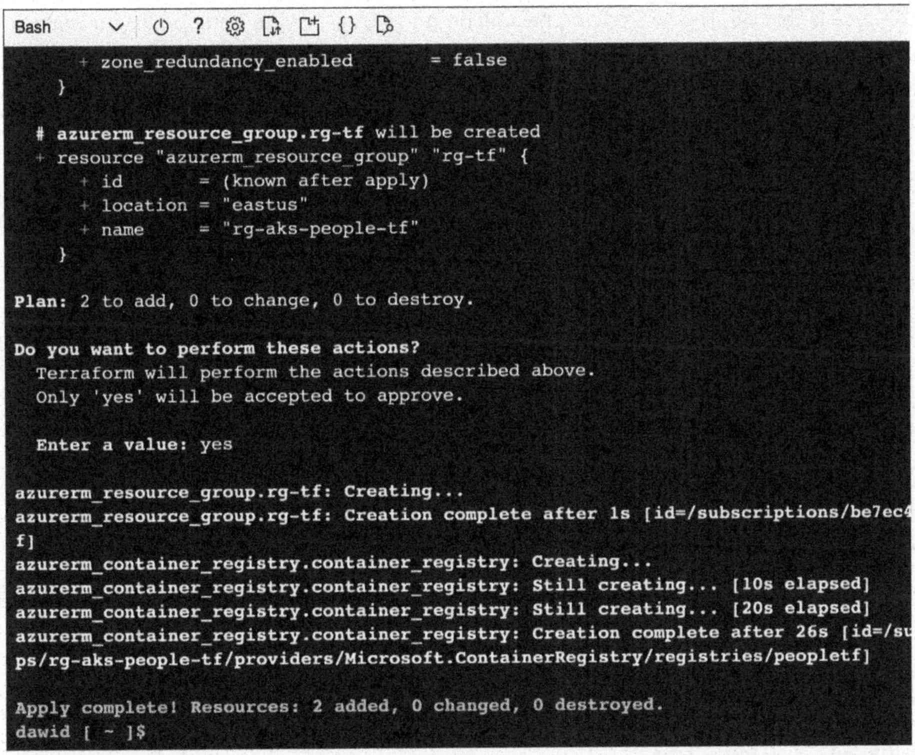
Bash
+ zone_redundancy_enabled = false
}
# azurerm_resource_group.rg-tf will be created
+ resource "azurerm_resource_group" "rg-tf" {
+ id = (known after apply)
+ location = "eastus"
+ name = "rg-aks-people-tf"
}
Plan: 2 to add, 0 to change, 0 to destroy.
Do you want to perform these actions?
Terraform will perform the actions described above.
Only 'yes' will be accepted to approve.
Enter a value: yes
azurerm_resource_group.rg-tf: Creating...
azurerm_resource_group.rg-tf: Creation complete after 1s [id=/subscriptions/be7ec4
f]
azurerm_container_registry.container_registry: Creating...
azurerm_container_registry.container_registry: Still creating... [10s elapsed]
azurerm_container_registry.container_registry: Still creating... [20s elapsed]
azurerm_container_registry.container_registry: Creation complete after 26s [id=/su
ps/rg-aks-people-tf/providers/Microsoft.ContainerRegistry/registries/peopletf]
Apply complete! Resources: 2 added, 0 changed, 0 destroyed.
dawid [~]$

FIGURE 14-3 Deploying Azure resources with Terraform.

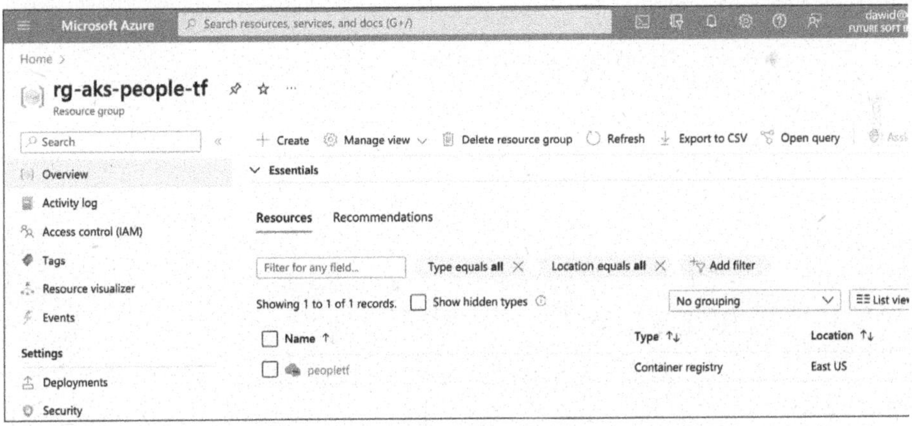
Microsoft Azure
Search resources, services, and docs (G+/)
Home >
rg-aks-people-tf
Resource group
Search
Overview
Activity log
Access control (IAM)
Tags
Resource visualizer
Events
Settings
Deployments
Security
Create
Manage view
Delete resource group
Refresh
Export to CSV
Open query
Essentials
Resources
Recommendations
Filter for any field...
Type equals all
Location equals all
Add filter
Showing 1 to 1 of 1 records.
Show hidden types
No grouping
List view
Name
Type
Location
peopletf
Container registry
East US

FIGURE 14-4 Previewing deployed resources in the Azure portal.

Deploying Azure Kubernetes Cluster

In the next step, you will modify the Terraform declaration to deploy a cluster in Azure Kubernetes Service (AKS), configuring it similarly to what was described in Chapter 7. Specifically, you will set the cluster name to aks-people-tf. The cluster will be deployed in the same region as the resource group, which in this case is East US. The AKS pricing tier will be set to Free. For the node pool, you will use Standard DS2 v2 Virtual Machines. Autoscaling will be enabled for the node pool, with the minimum and maximum node counts set to 1 and 3, respectively. Finally, you will configure the cluster to pull Docker images from the registry you previously created in Azure Container Registry.

To create such a declaration, proceed as follows:

1. Return to Azure Cloud Shell, and open the declaration file by typing:

   code people-webapp-iac.tf

2. Add the following statements, ensuring you place them below the declaration of the container registry (Listing 14-4):

LISTING 14-4 Terraform Configuration Creating an Azure Kubernetes Service Cluster.

```
resource "azurerm_kubernetes_cluster" "kubernetes_cluster" {
  name                = "aks-people-tf"
  resource_group_name = azurerm_resource_group.rg-tf.name
  location            = azurerm_resource_group.rg-tf.location
  dns_prefix          = "aks-people-tf-dns"

  default_node_pool {
    name                = "agentpool"
    vm_size             = "Standard_DS2_v2"
    enable_auto_scaling = true
    min_count           = 1
    max_count           = 3
    os_disk_size_gb     = 30
    os_disk_type        = "Managed"
    type                = "VirtualMachineScaleSets"
  }

  identity {
    type = "SystemAssigned"
  }

  network_profile {
    network_plugin = "kubenet"
  }

  sku_tier = "Free"

  depends_on = [
    azurerm_container_registry.container_registry
  ]
}

resource "azurerm_role_assignment" "acr_pull" {
  principal_id                     = azurerm_kubernetes_cluster.kubernetes_cluster. ⏎
      kubelet_identity[0].object_id
```

```
    role_definition_name             = "AcrPull"
    scope                            = azurerm_container_registry.container_registry.id
    skip_service_principal_aad_check = true
}
```

3. Save and close the file.

This declaration employs the azurerm_kubernetes_cluster Terraform resource and sets the instance name to kubernetes_cluster. It specifies the cluster's name (aks-people-tf), resource group (rg-aks-people-tf), and location (in this instance, East US) using the `name`, `resource_group_name`, and `location` attributes, respectively. Additionally, the `dns_prefix` attribute is used to configure the DNS prefix that constructs the fully qualified domain name of the Kubernetes API server.

The configuration then defines the node pool within the `default_node_pool` block, setting the node pool's name to agentpool, and configuring the initial node count, the size of the virtual machines, autoscaling capabilities, and disk type. Moreover, the nodes are configured to use Virtual Machine Scale Sets.

Subsequently, Managed Identity is enabled, which, as before, facilitates configuring access for applications running within the node pool. The declaration then selects the `kubenet` networking plug-in, sets the SKU tier, and specifies that the Azure Kubernetes Service declaration depends on a prior declaration of the registry in Azure Container Registry. This dependency is crucial for attaching the ACR instance to the cluster, particularly to grant the AKS cluster's kubelet managed identity permission to pull images from ACR, ensuring the AKS cluster has the necessary access permissions.

This attachment is accomplished using the `azurerm_role_assignment` resource, which creates the `AcrPull` role assignment for the cluster. This assignment necessitates specifying the scope at which the role is applied, in this case, set to the ID of the previously defined ACR registry (azurerm_container_registry.container_registry.id). This scope ensures that the role assignment grants permissions specifically for this registry. The `role_definition_name` attribute is set to `AcrPull`, a built-in Azure role that permits image pulling from ACR. Assigning this role thereby grants the specified permissions to the designated principal. The `principal_id` identifies the entity receiving the role assignment; here, it is the managed identity associated with the AKS cluster's kubelet, responsible for running containers on the cluster's nodes. This `principal_id` is derived from the AKS cluster resource (azurerm_kubernetes_cluster.kubernetes_cluster), specifically the object ID of the first kubelet identity (kubelet_identity[0].object_id). As you already saw in previous chapters, AKS utilizes managed identities for the kubelet to interact with other Azure services, including Azure Container Registry.

To deploy the cluster, proceed as follows:

1. Return to Azure Cloud Shell, and validate the Terraform configuration by typing:

    terraform validate

    The output should be: "Success! The configuration is valid." If not, correct the declaration file based on the feedback provided by **terraform validate**.

2. Create an execution plan:

   `terraform plan`

3. Observe the list of resources to be deployed. It will include two key resources: azurerm_kubernetes_cluster and azurerm_role_assignment.acr_pull.

4. Apply the execution plan:

   `terraform apply -auto-approve`

   Wait a few minutes for the deployment to complete. Confirm that the cluster was deployed by typing:

```
az aks list --query "[].{Name:name, Location:location, ↵
    ResourceGroup:resourceGroup, FQDN:fqdn}" -o table
```

This command will display a list of Azure Kubernetes Service clusters (see Figure 14-5). Note that the cluster with the **-tf** suffix was deployed using Terraform.

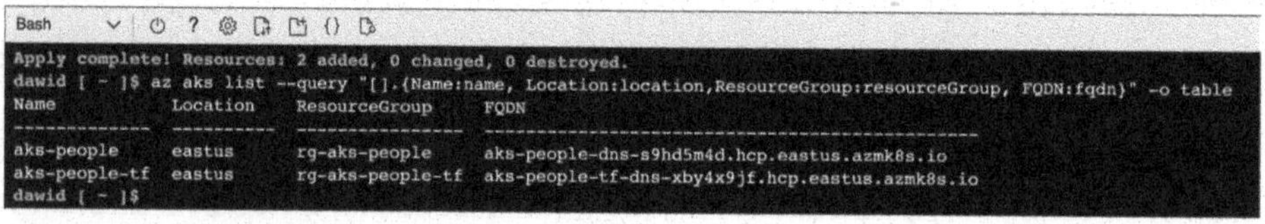

FIGURE 14-5 The List of Azure Kubernetes clusters.

You have now successfully deployed an Azure Kubernetes Service cluster using Terraform. Next, you will extend the declaration to include the deployment of a SQL database.

Deploying a SQL database

To deploy the SQL database, you will modify people-webapp-iac.tf by adding the following declaration right below `acr_pull` (Listing 14-5):

LISTING 14-5 Terraform Configuration for Azure SQL Server (aks-sql-people-tf) with Administrator Credentials

```
resource "azurerm_mssql_server" "sql_server" {
  name                         = "aks-sql-people-tf"
  resource_group_name          = azurerm_resource_group.rg-tf.name
  location                     = azurerm_resource_group.rg-tf.location
  version                      = "12.0"
  administrator_login          = "azure"
  administrator_login_password = "P@ssw0rD"
  public_network_access_enabled = true
}
```

This declaration uses the `azurerm_mssql_server` Terraform resource to deploy an Azure SQL server, named aks-sql-people-tf. As mentioned in Chapter 8, "Azure SQL Database and Azure Key Vault," this name must be globally unique because Azure uses it to set the server's DNS name. The SQL server will be deployed to the same resource group and Azure region as the other Azure services you created earlier in this chapter. The server version specified is 12.0, which corresponds to SQL Server 2014. This is the preferred version for new deployments. Credentials for SQL authentication are configured next, and you enable the public endpoint, allowing the server to be accessed from outside Azure, assuming the appropriate firewall rules are in place to allow incoming traffic.

After you set up the SQL server, you can move on to adding another declaration for deploying the Azure SQL database. Make sure to place the following statements below the SQL server declaration in people-web-app-iac.tf (Listing 14-6):

LISTING 14-6 Terraform Configuration for Azure SQL Database (people) on the SQL Server Instance.

```
resource "azurerm_mssql_database" "sql_database" {
  name       = "people"
  server_id  = azurerm_mssql_server.sql_server.id
  sku_name   = "Basic"
}
```

This declaration creates a SQL database named people. The database will be managed by the SQL server you created previously. Using the `Basic` SKU for the database minimizes costs.

You need to take two final steps. The first is to declare the firewall rule to enable the containers running in the node pool to access the database. As discussed in Chapter 8, you do this by allowing all Azure services to access the SQL server. In practice, however, you might want to adhere to the principle of least privilege and further restrict the firewall.

Therefore, add the following statements to the people-web-app-iac.tf declaration (Listing 14-7):

LISTING 14-7 Terraform Rule Allowing Azure Services Firewall Access to SQL Server.

```
resource "azurerm_mssql_firewall_rule" "sql_firewall_rule" {
  name             = "allow-azure-services"
  server_id        = azurerm_mssql_server.sql_server.id
  start_ip_address = "0.0.0.0"
  end_ip_address   = "0.0.0.0"
}
```

Finally, create a local variable containing the SQL connection string so that it can later be added to Azure Key Vault as a Secret (Listing 14-8):

LISTING 14-8 Terraform Local Defining the SQL Database Connection String Dynamically.

```
locals {
  sql_connection_string="Server=tcp:${azurerm_mssql_server.sql_server.↵
      fully_qualified_domain_name},1433;Initial Catalog=↵
      ${azurerm_mssql_database.sql_database.name};Persist Security Info=False;↵
      User ID=${azurerm_mssql_server.sql_server.administrator_login};↵
      Password=${azurerm_mssql_server.sql_server.administrator_login_password};↵
      MultipleActiveResultSets=False;Encrypt=True;TrustServerCertificate=False;↵
      Connection Timeout=30;"
}
```

To deploy the resources, make sure to save the Terraform declaration file first. Then, validate it by typing:

terraform validate

The command's output should be "Success! The configuration is valid." If not, correct the issues in the declaration based on the feedback provided by **terraform validate**.

Next, regenerate the execution plan with:

terraform plan

Review the list of resources to be deployed. A fragment of this list is depicted in Figure 14-6.

```
# azurerm_mssql_server.sql_server will be created
+ resource "azurerm_mssql_server" "sql_server" {
    + administrator_login                  = "azure"
    + administrator_login_password         = (sensitive value)
    + connection_policy                    = "Default"
    + fully_qualified_domain_name          = (known after apply)
    + id                                   = (known after apply)
    + location                             = "eastus"
    + minimum_tls_version                  = "1.2"
    + name                                 = "aks-sql-people-tf"
    + outbound_network_restriction_enabled = false
    + primary_user_assigned_identity_id    = (known after apply)
    + public_network_access_enabled        = true
    + resource_group_name                  = "rg-aks-people-tf"
    + restorable_dropped_database_ids      = (known after apply)
    + version                              = "12.0"
  }
```

FIGURE 14-6 Deploying Azure SQL Server with Terraform.

Finally, deploy the resources by typing:

terraform apply -auto-approve

Wait for the deployment to complete. Afterwards, utilize Azure portal to verify that the server and database have been successfully created. As illustrated in Figure 14-7, by this stage, you should observe four Azure resources within the rg-aks-people-tf resource group.

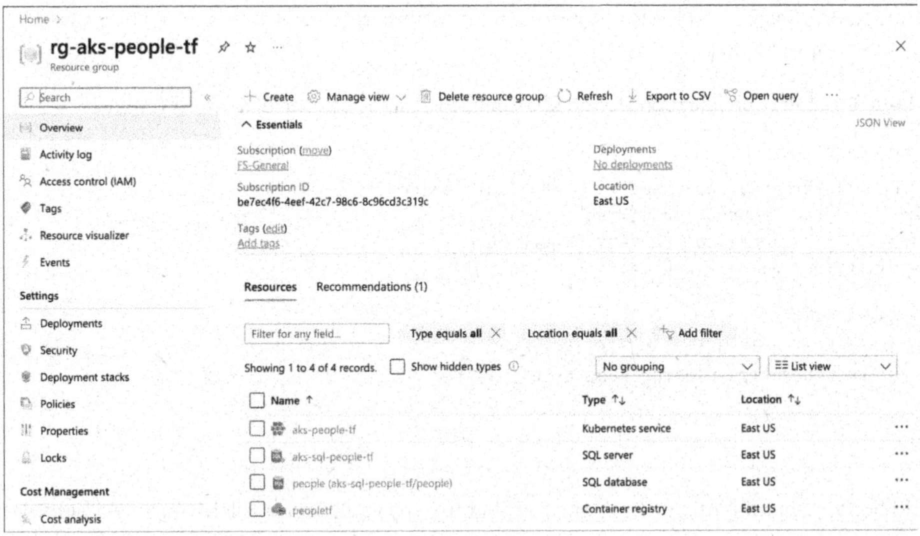

FIGURE 14-7 Azure resources deployed with Terraform.

Deploying a Key Vault

You are now ready to deploy the key vault instance on Azure Key Vault. You will name the vault instance kv-people-tf and deploy it to the same resource group and location as the previous services. To create a Key Vault instance with Terraform, you also need to provide the Azure Active Directory tenant ID, which is used for authenticating requests to your vault. You will set the SKU for the vault to standard.

Listing 14-9 is the declaration of the Azure Key Vault Terraform resource that utilizes the aforementioned parameters. Note that to retrieve the tenant ID, you use the azurerm_client_config data source. This data source allows you to access the configuration of the Azure Resource Manager (ARM) provider.

LISTING 14-9 Terraform Configuration for Azure Key Vault.

```
data "azurerm_client_config" "current" {}

resource "azurerm_key_vault" "key_vault" {
  name                = "kv-people-tf"
  resource_group_name = azurerm_resource_group.rg-tf.name
  location            = azurerm_resource_group.rg-tf.location
  tenant_id           = data.azurerm_client_config.current.tenant_id
  sku_name            = "standard"
}
```

Next, create the Secret to store the SQL connection string value, which was previously saved in a local variable (Listing 14-10):

LISTING 14-10 Terraform Configuration Storing SQL Connection String as a Secret in Azure Key Vault.

```
resource "azurerm_key_vault_secret" "key_vault_secret" {
  name         = "connection-string"
  value        = local.sql_connection_string
  key_vault_id = azurerm_key_vault.key_vault.id

  depends_on = [
    azurerm_key_vault_access_policy.self,
    azurerm_kubernetes_cluster.kubernetes_cluster
  ]
}
```

An additional `depends_on` attribute ensures that the key vault Secret will be removed before the access policy, and the Kubernetes cluster. The access policy is required to remove the Secret itself. To create the access policy, which enables the ARM provider to create, retrieve, and delete Secrets in the created key vault, add the following declaration (Listing 14-11):

LISTING 14-11 Terraform Configuration Granting Current User Secret Management Permissions in Azure Key Vault.

```
resource "azurerm_key_vault_access_policy" "self" {
  key_vault_id = azurerm_key_vault.key_vault.id
  tenant_id    = data.azurerm_client_config.current.tenant_id
  object_id    = data.azurerm_client_config.current.object_id

  secret_permissions = ["Get", "Set", "Delete", "Purge"]
}
```

Finally, define the access policy, which enables applications running in the cluster to retrieve the Secrets from the key vault (Listing 14-12):

LISTING 14-12 Terraform Access Policy Allowing AKS Cluster Identity to Read Azure Key Vault Secrets.

```
resource "azurerm_key_vault_access_policy" "cluster" {
  key_vault_id = azurerm_key_vault.key_vault.id
  tenant_id    = data.azurerm_client_config.current.tenant_id
  object_id    = azurerm_kubernetes_cluster.kubernetes_cluster.↵
                  kubelet_identity[0].object_id

  secret_permissions = ["Get", "List"]

  depends_on = [
    azurerm_key_vault.key_vault,
    azurerm_kubernetes_cluster.kubernetes_cluster
  ]
}
```

Although not strictly necessary in this context, the `depends_on` attribute was added to ensure that the key vault access policy is created after both the vault itself and the Azure Kubernetes cluster.

After placing all the above declarations in the people-web-app-iac.tf file, you can validate the Terraform configuration, regenerate the plan, and deploy all resources:

```
terraform validate
terraform plan
terraform apply -auto-approve
```

For your convenience, the final form of the people-web-app-iac.tf file is at:

github.com/dawidborycki/People.WebApp.Declarations/blob/main/Terraform/people-webapp-iac.tf

Wait a few minutes for Terraform to deploy the key vault, Secret, and access policy. Congratulations: You have now learned how to deploy the entire infrastructure for an application using Terraform. In the next step, you will integrate the Infrastructure as Code (IaC) declaration with the CI/CD pipeline developed in previous chapters, ensuring that People.WebApp can be deployed to the infrastructure set up with Terraform.

Before proceeding, you need to destroy all the resources created here so that they can be re-created by the CI/CD pipeline. To do so, type the following in Azure Cloud Shell:

```
terraform destroy -auto-approve
```

Integration with the CI/CD pipeline

It's time to integrate the Infrastructure as Code (IaC) declarations with your CI/CD pipeline to automate resource provisioning and application deployment. Resource provisioning must occur before application deployment. Therefore, you will create a new job that prepares the Azure infrastructure and then adjust the jobs responsible for building and pushing the Docker image, as well as deploying the application. These jobs will be modified to use the names of resources created by the infrastructure job.

To enhance the manageability of your IaC declarations, you will refine the general structure by splitting them into five files:

- **provider.tf** This file will contain the provider configuration, including your declaration of the Azure Resource Manager.

- **backend.tf** This file will store the backend configuration for the Terraform setup, referencing the Azure Blob Storage container you created earlier.

- **variables.tf** This file is used to define variables, such as the names of the resource group and Azure region.

- **main.tf** This file will contain the resource declarations. You will reference the variables defined in variables.tf instead of hardcoding values. As configurations grow larger, locals and data blocks can be split into separate files (locals.tf and data.tf).

- **outputs.tf** This file will contain Terraform outputs, such as the names of the created cluster and container registry. These outputs will be used to pass information to the application deployment jobs.

Declaration files

You will create the declaration files locally in People.WebApp repository, using a separate Git branch as before. Start by opening your terminal or command prompt and entering the following commands:

```
git checkout ci-cd-helm
git checkout -b ci-cd-iac
```

These commands create a new branch, ci-cd-iac, branching off from ci-cd-helm.

Next, within the People.WebApp directory, create an iac folder. Inside this folder, create the provider.tf file (ensure this file is saved in the iac folder). Add the following statements to the provider.tf file (Listing 14-13):

LISTING 14-13 Terraform Azure Provider Initialization.

```
provider "azurerm" {
  features {}
}
```

Next, add the iac/backend.tf file (Listing 14-14):

LISTING 14-14 Terraform Backend Configuration for Azure State Storage.

```
terraform {
  backend "azurerm" {
    resource_group_name  = "rg-aks-people"
    storage_account_name = "peoplewebappstore"
    container_name       = "terraform"
    key                  = "terraform.tfstate"
  }
}
```

The backend configuration specifies the details of the Azure Blob Storage container. It includes the name of the container, the parent storage account, and the resource group in which the storage account was deployed. The key attribute specifies the name of the blob where Terraform will save its state.

Next, create the iac/variables.tf file (Listing 14-15):

LISTING 14-15 Terraform Variables for Resource Group Name and Azure Region.

```
variable "resource_group_name" {
  description= "Name of the Azure resource group"
  default    = "rg-aks-people-tf"
}

variable "location" {
  description = "Azure region for all resources"
  default     = "East US"
}
```

This file defines two variables, `resource_group_name` and `location`, which are used to configure infrastructure resources in Azure. Each variable block includes a description and a default value. The presence of a default value implies that if no specific value is provided for these variables when executing Terraform commands, rg-aks-people-tf and East US will be adopted as the default values for the resource group name and the Azure region, respectively.

By establishing these variables, the Terraform configuration affords flexibility in deployment locations and naming conventions, while providing sensible defaults. Employing variables in this manner significantly enhances the reusability and maintainability of the Terraform code. It simplifies the process of adapting the configuration for various environments or projects by merely altering the values of the variables.

Next, create the iac/main.tf file, which will contain the declarations of the resource group, container registry, Kubernetes cluster, SQL server, connection string, key vault, and key vault access policies (Listing 14-16):

LISTING 14-16 Complete Terraform Infrastructure Script for AKS Deployment, Including Azure Resources.

```
resource "azurerm_resource_group" "rg-tf" {
  name     = var.resource_group_name
  location = var.location
}

resource "azurerm_container_registry" "container_registry" {
  name                = "peopletf"
  resource_group_name = azurerm_resource_group.rg-tf.name
  location            = azurerm_resource_group.rg-tf.location
  sku                 = "Basic"
  admin_enabled       = false
}

resource "azurerm_kubernetes_cluster" "kubernetes_cluster" {
  name                = "aks-people-tf"
  resource_group_name = azurerm_resource_group.rg-tf.name
  location            = azurerm_resource_group.rg-tf.location
  dns_prefix          = "aks-people-tf-dns"
```

```
  default_node_pool {
    name                  = "agentpool"
    vm_size               = "Standard_DS2_v2"
    enable_auto_scaling.  = true
    min_count             = 1
    max_count             = 3
    os_disk_size_gb       = 30
    os_disk_type          = "Managed"
    type                  = "VirtualMachineScaleSets"
  }

  identity {
    type = "SystemAssigned"
  }

  network_profile {
    network_plugin = "kubenet"
  }

  sku_tier = "Free"

  depends_on = [
    azurerm_container_registry.container_registry
  ]
}

resource "azurerm_role_assignment" "acr_pull" {
  principal_id                     = azurerm_kubernetes_cluster.kubernetes_cluster. ↵
      kubelet_identity[0].object_id
  role_definition_name             = "AcrPull"
  scope                            = azurerm_container_registry.container_registry.id
  skip_service_principal_aad_check = true
}

resource "azurerm_mssql_server" "sql_server" {
  name                         = "aks-sql-people-tf"
  resource_group_name          = azurerm_resource_group.rg-tf.name
  location                     = azurerm_resource_group.rg-tf.location
  version                      = "12.0"
  administrator_login          = "azure"
  administrator_login_password = "P@ssw0rD"
  public_network_access_enabled = true
}

resource "azurerm_mssql_database" "sql_database" {
  name       = "people"
  server_id  = azurerm_mssql_server.sql_server.id
  sku_name   = "Basic"
}

resource "azurerm_mssql_firewall_rule" "sql_firewall_rule" {
  name             = "allow-azure-services"
  server_id        = azurerm_mssql_server.sql_server.id
  start_ip_address = "0.0.0.0"
```

```
    end_ip_address      = "0.0.0.0"
}

locals {
    sql_connection_string="Server=tcp:${azurerm_mssql_server.sql_server.↵
      fully_qualified_domain_name},1433;Initial Catalog=${azurerm_mssql_database. ↵
      sql_database.name};Persist Security Info=False; ↵
    User ID=${azurerm_mssql_server.sql_server.administrator_login};↵
    Password=${azurerm_mssql_server.sql_server.administrator_login_password};↵
    MultipleActiveResultSets=False;Encrypt=True;TrustServerCertificate=False;↵
    Connection Timeout=30;"
}

data "azurerm_client_config" "current" {}

resource "azurerm_key_vault" "key_vault" {
  name                = "kv-people-tf"
  resource_group_name = azurerm_resource_group.rg-tf.name
  location            = azurerm_resource_group.rg-tf.location
  tenant_id           = data.azurerm_client_config.current.tenant_id
  sku_name            = "standard"
}

resource "azurerm_key_vault_secret" "key_vault_secret" {
  name         = "connection-string"
  value        = local.sql_connection_string
  key_vault_id = azurerm_key_vault.key_vault.id

  depends_on = [
    azurerm_key_vault_access_policy.self,
    azurerm_kubernetes_cluster.kubernetes_cluster
  ]
}

resource "azurerm_key_vault_access_policy" "self" {
  key_vault_id = azurerm_key_vault.key_vault.id
  tenant_id    = data.azurerm_client_config.current.tenant_id
  object_id    = data.azurerm_client_config.current.object_id

  secret_permissions = ["Get", "Set", "Delete", "Purge"]
}

resource "azurerm_key_vault_access_policy" "cluster" {
  key_vault_id = azurerm_key_vault.key_vault.id
  tenant_id    = data.azurerm_client_config.current.tenant_id
  object_id    = azurerm_kubernetes_cluster.kubernetes_cluster.↵
    kubelet_identity[0].object_id

  secret_permissions = ["Get", "List"]

  depends_on = [
    azurerm_key_vault.key_vault,
    azurerm_kubernetes_cluster.kubernetes_cluster
  ]
}
```

The declarations above are the same as before; therefore, a detailed description is omitted here. Finally, create the iac/outputs.tf file (Listing 14-17):

LISTING 14-17 Terraform Outputs Exposing Key Azure Resource Details.

```
output "acr_name" {
  value = azurerm_container_registry.container_registry.name
}

output "acr_login_server" {
  value = azurerm_container_registry.container_registry.login_server
}

output "rg_name" {
  value = azurerm_resource_group.rg-tf.name
}

output "cluster_name" {
  value = azurerm_kubernetes_cluster.kubernetes_cluster.name
}

output "aks_pool_node_name" {
  value = azurerm_kubernetes_cluster.kubernetes_cluster.default_node_pool[0].name
}

output "key_vault_name" {
  value = azurerm_key_vault.key_vault.name
}
```

This Terraform file defines a series of output variables related to Azure resources that have been declared in your other Terraform configurations. Outputs are a way to extract information about the resources created, which can be useful for integrating with other tools or systems. Here, you utilize this capability to configure jobs in our CI/CD pipeline. Specifically, this file includes:

- The name of the Azure Container Registry (ACR) instance that has been created (acr_name). This is used to reference the registry in build and deployment GitHub Action jobs that need to push the container image.

- The login server for Azure Container Registry (acr_login_server) for Docker login commands.

- The name of the Azure resource group where these resources have been provisioned (rg_name).

- The name of the Azure Kubernetes Service (AKS) cluster created (cluster_name). This is required to configure the Kubernetes context with the `kubectl` command.

- The name of the default node pool within the AKS cluster (aks_pool_node_name). This is needed to retrieve the managed identity of the node pool, which is later used to access Secrets in the key vault.

- The name of the key vault. This information will be passed to the People.WebApp application so that it knows where to retrieve the SQL connection string from.

By declaring these outputs, the file not only makes critical information about the provisioned resources readily available for further use, but also enhances the visibility of the infrastructure setup, aiding in both manual inspection and automation scenarios. Specifically, you will use the outputs for updating the Helm file and declaring the CI/CD pipeline.

Helm files

First, you update the Helm values.yaml file by introducing the <KEY_VAULT_NAME> placeholder (the values.yaml file is located under the helm subfolder). This placeholder will be automatically substituted with the actual name of the key vault, which is generated by Terraform. To accomplish this, open the helm/values.yaml file and replace the `KeyVaultName` entry with the <KEY_VAULT_NAME> placeholder, as illustrated in Listing 14-18:

LISTING 14-18 Helm Values File Defining Container Image Details, Environment Variables with Key Vault Integration, Kubernetes Service Settings, Resource Limits, Health Checks, and Autoscaling Parameters.

```yaml
replicaCount: 1

image:
  repository: <FQ_IMAGE_NAME>
  pullPolicy: IfNotPresent

app:
  env:
    UseInMemoryDatabase: "False"
    KeyVaultName: <KEY_VAULT_NAME>
    ManagedIdentityClientId: <MANAGED_CLIENT_ID>

service:
  type: LoadBalancer
  port: 80
  targetPort: 5000
  containerPort: 5000

resources:
  limits:
    cpu: 750m
    memory: 1000Mi
  requests:
    cpu: 500m
    memory: 768Mi

livenessProbe:
  httpGet:
    path: /api/people
    port: http
```

```yaml
    readinessProbe:
      httpGet:
        path: /api/people
        port: http

    autoscaling:
      enabled: true
      minReplicas: 1
      maxReplicas: 10
      targetCPUUtilizationPercentage: 80
```

CI/CD declaration

You are now ready to define the CI/CD pipeline using the .github/workflows/people-webapp-ci-cd.yml file, already present in the repository. Given the extensive changes you need to make, start by clearing all the contents of the file.

Next, configure the pipeline's name and specify that it should be triggered when code is pushed to the `ci-cd-iac` branch. Additionally, define an environment variable, IMAGE_NAME, which holds the name of the Docker image being generated by the pipeline (Listing 14-19):

LISTING 14-19 GitHub Actions Workflow Triggering CI/CD Pipeline (Helm and Terraform) on Commits to the ci-cd-iac Branch.

```yaml
name: CI/CD Pipeline (Helm + Terraform)

on:
  push:
    branches:
      - ci-cd-iac

env:
  IMAGE_NAME: people.webapp
```

In the next step, you will define three jobs: infrastructure, build-and-push-docker-image, and deploy-to-aks-with-helm. These jobs will be executed sequentially, as illustrated in Figure 14-8. First, the infrastructure job will deploy or update the Azure resources. Following that, the Docker image will be built and then pushed to the Azure Container Registry. Finally, the application will be deployed to the Azure Kubernetes Service cluster using Helm.

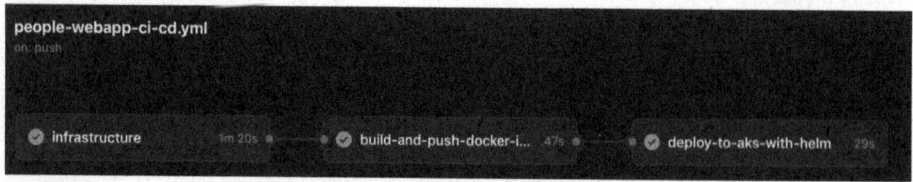

FIGURE 14-8 Jobs in the GitHub Actions workflow.

Start by declaring the infrastructure job (Listing 14-20):

LISTING 14-20 GitHub Actions Job Executing Terraform to Provision Infrastructure and Exporting Outputs for Subsequent Pipeline Steps.

```
jobs:
  infrastructure:
    runs-on: ubuntu-latest
    outputs:
      acr_name: ${{ steps.terraform-apply.outputs.ACR_NAME }}
      acr_login_server: ${{ steps.terraform-apply.outputs.ACR_LOGIN_SERVER }}
      rg_name: ${{ steps.terraform-apply.outputs.RG_NAME }}
      cluster_name: ${{ steps.terraform-apply.outputs.CLUSTER_NAME }}
      aks_pool_node_name: ${{ steps.terraform-apply.outputs.AKS_POOL_NODE_NAME }}
      key_vault_name: ${{ steps.terraform-apply.outputs.KEY_VAULT_NAME }}
```

This job will run on an Ubuntu-based GitHub runner and will generate six outputs. These outputs correspond to the Terraform outputs that will be generated during the terraform-apply step of the infrastructure job. The outputs include the name (`acr_name`) and login server (`acr_login_server`) of Azure Container Registry, the name of the resource group (`rg_name`), the name of the Kubernetes cluster (`cluster_name`) and its node pool (`aks_pool_node_name`), and the name of the key vault (`key_vault_name`).

Next, define the job's steps, ensuring the steps section aligns with the `outputs` section (Listing 14-21):

LISTING 14-21 GitHub Actions Workflow Steps for Checking Out Code, authenticating to Azure, Configuring Terraform, and Applying Infrastructure Changes with Terraform Outputs Captured for Pipeline Reuse.

```
steps:
  - name: Checkout code
    uses: actions/checkout@v4

  - name: Login to Azure
    uses: azure/login@v1
    with:
      creds: ${{ secrets.AZURE_CREDENTIALS }}

  - name: Configure Azure credentials from GitHub Secret
    run: |
      echo "ARM_CLIENT_ID=$(echo '${{ secrets.AZURE_CREDENTIALS }}' ↵
          | jq -r '.clientId')" >> $GITHUB_ENV
      echo "ARM_CLIENT_SECRET=$(echo '${{ secrets.AZURE_CREDENTIALS }}' ↵
          | jq -r '.clientSecret')" >> $GITHUB_ENV
      echo "ARM_SUBSCRIPTION_ID=$(echo '${{ secrets.AZURE_CREDENTIALS }}' ↵
          | jq -r '.subscriptionId')" >> $GITHUB_ENV
      echo "ARM_TENANT_ID=$(echo '${{ secrets.AZURE_CREDENTIALS }}' ↵
          | jq -r '.tenantId')" >> $GITHUB_ENV
    shell: bash
```

```yaml
- name: Setup Terraform
  uses: hashicorp/setup-terraform@v2.0.3
  with:
    terraform_wrapper: false

- name: Terraform Init
  working-directory: ./iac
  run: |
    STORAGE_ACCOUNT_NAME=$(grep 'storage_account_name' ↵
        backend.tf | awk '{print $3}' | tr -d '"')
    RESOURCE_GROUP_NAME=$(grep 'resource_group_name' backend.tf ↵
        | awk '{print $3}' | tr -d '"')

    ARM_ACCESS_KEY=$(az storage account keys list -n $STORAGE_ACCOUNT_NAME ↵
        -g $RESOURCE_GROUP_NAME --query '[0].value' -o tsv)
    echo "ARM_ACCESS_KEY=${ARM_ACCESS_KEY}" >> $GITHUB_ENV

    terraform init

- name: Terraform Plan
  working-directory: ./iac
  run: terraform plan

- name: Terraform Apply
  working-directory: ./iac
  id: terraform-apply
  run: |
    terraform apply -auto-approve
    echo "ACR_NAME=$(terraform output -raw acr_name)" >> $GITHUB_OUTPUT
    echo "acr_login_server=$(terraform output -raw acr_login_server)" >> $GITHUB_OUTPUT
    echo "rg_name=$(terraform output -raw rg_name)" >> $GITHUB_OUTPUT
    echo "cluster_name=$(terraform output -raw cluster_name)" >> $GITHUB_OUTPUT
    echo "aks_pool_node_name=$(terraform output -raw aks_pool_node_name)" ↵
        >> $GITHUB_OUTPUT
    echo "key_vault_name=$(terraform output -raw key_vault_name)" >> $GITHUB_OUTPUT
```

This job comprises the following steps:

1. Checkout code and Login to Azure are standard initial steps that prepare the environment for subsequent actions.

2. Configure Azure credentials from GitHub Secret parses the AZURE_CREDENTIALS Secret to extract Azure credentials' components (client ID, client secret, subscription ID, and tenant ID) using the `jq` command-line processor. These values are set as environment variables in $GITHUB_ENV, making them accessible for subsequent workflow steps.

3. Setup Terraform uses the `hashicorp/setup-terraform` action to install Terraform on the GitHub Actions runner. The `terraform_wrapper` is set to false for direct control over Terraform's output.

4. Terraform Init initializes Terraform configuration, setting up the backend and downloading necessary providers. The storage account name and resource group name are extracted from backend.tf for backend configuration, and the Azure Storage Account access key is retrieved.

5. Terraform Plan outputs the execution plan, showing what Terraform intends to change in the infrastructure without applying those changes.

6. Terraform Apply applies the planned changes and extracts and stores Terraform outputs like the ACR name, login server, resource group name, Kubernetes cluster, and node pool name in $GITHUB_OUTPUT for use in subsequent actions.

Subsequently, you declare the build-and-push-docker-image job (Listing 14-22):

LISTING 14-22 GitHub Actions Workflow Job for Building and Pushing a Docker Image to Azure Container Registry, Dynamically Tagging Images Based on Existing Tags.

```yaml
build-and-push-docker-image:
  runs-on: ubuntu-latest
  needs: infrastructure
  outputs:
    fq_image_name: ${{steps.build-image.outputs.FQ_IMAGE_NAME}}

  steps:
    - name: Checkout code
      uses: actions/checkout@v4

    - name: Login to Azure
      uses: azure/login@v1
      with:
        creds: ${{ secrets.AZURE_CREDENTIALS }}

    - name: Login to Azure Container Registry
      run: az acr login -n ${{ needs.infrastructure.outputs.acr_name }}

    - name: Count existing tags and configure the image tag
      run: |
        COUNT=$(az acr repository show-tags -n ${{ needs.infrastructure. ↵
              outputs.acr_name }} --repository $IMAGE_NAME -o tsv | wc -l)
        IMAGE_TAG=v$(expr $COUNT + 1)
        echo "IMAGE_TAG=$IMAGE_TAG" >> $GITHUB_ENV

    - name: Build and push Docker image
      id: build-image
      run: |
        FQ_IMAGE_NAME=${{ needs.infrastructure.outputs. ↵
              acr_login_server }}/$IMAGE_NAME:$IMAGE_TAG
        echo "FQ_IMAGE_NAME=$FQ_IMAGE_NAME" >> $GITHUB_ENV
        echo "FQ_IMAGE_NAME=$FQ_IMAGE_NAME" >> $GITHUB_OUTPUT
        docker build -t $FQ_IMAGE_NAME .
        docker push $FQ_IMAGE_NAME

    - name: Logout from Azure Container Registry
      run: docker logout ${{ needs.infrastructure.outputs.acr_login_server }}

    - name: Cleanup Docker images
      run: docker image rm $FQ_IMAGE_NAME
```

This job will run after the infrastructure job, as indicated by the needs element. It executes seven steps, proceeding similarly to previous configurations. The primary difference now is the use of outputs from the infrastructure job. The ACR name (acr_name) and login server (acr_login_server) are utilized to log in to the ACR (see the Login to Azure Container Registry step). Utilizing the repository name ($IMAGE_NAME), you count the existing Docker images (in the Count existing tags and configure the image tag step) to determine the new image tag. You then construct the fully qualified image name using the ACR login server and the image tag, and push the Docker image to the ACR (in the Build and push Docker image step). Finally, you log out from the ACR and clean up the Docker images.

In the final step, you declare the deploy-to-aks-with-helm job (Listing 14-23):

LISTING 14-23 GitHub Actions Workflow Steps Configuring Kubernetes Context, Dynamically Updating Helm Values, Linting, and Deploying to AKS with Helm.

```yaml
deploy-to-aks-with-helm:
    runs-on: ubuntu-latest
    needs: [build-and-push-docker-image, infrastructure]

    steps:
      - name: Checkout code
        uses: actions/checkout@v4

      - name: Login to Azure
        uses: azure/login@v1
        with:
          creds: ${{ secrets.AZURE_CREDENTIALS }}

      - name: Configure Kubernetes context
        run: az aks get-credentials -g ${{ needs.infrastructure.outputs.rg_name }} ↵
              -n ${{ needs.infrastructure.outputs.cluster_name }}

      - name: Update values.yaml
        env:
          FQ_IMAGE_NAME: ${{ needs.build-and-push-docker-image.outputs.fq_image_name }}
          KEY_VAULT_NAME: ${{ needs.infrastructure.outputs.key_vault_name }}
        run: |
          MANAGED_CLIENT_ID=$(az identity list --query "[?contains(name, ↵
              '${{ needs.infrastructure.outputs.cluster_name }}-↵
              ${{ needs.infrastructure.outputs.aks_pool_node_name }}')].clientId" -o tsv)
          echo "FQ_IMAGE_NAME=${FQ_IMAGE_NAME}"
          echo "KEY_VAULT_NAME=${KEY_VAULT_NAME}"
          echo "MANAGED_CLIENT_ID=${MANAGED_CLIENT_ID}"
          sed -i "s|<FQ_IMAGE_NAME>|$FQ_IMAGE_NAME|g" ./helm/values.yaml
          sed -i "s|<KEY_VAULT_NAMF>|$KEY_VAULT_NAME|g" ./helm/values.yaml
          sed -i "s|<MANAGED_CLIENT_ID>|$MANAGED_CLIENT_ID|g" ./helm/values.yaml

      - name: Helm Lint
        run: helm lint ./helm

      - name: Deploy with Helm
        run: helm upgrade --install people-web-app-helm ./helm/
```

This job depends on the build-and-push-docker-image and infrastructure jobs, ensuring they complete successfully before starting. After cloning the source code in the Checkout code step, it authenticates to Azure using credentials from the repository's secrets in the Login to Azure step. The Kubernetes configuration (kubeconfig) for kubectl commands to interact with the AKS cluster is set up using resource group and cluster name outputs from the infrastructure job in the Configure Kubernetes context step.

Next, the Update values.yaml step sets environment variables for the Docker image name (FQ_IMAGE_NAME) and key vault name (KEY_VAULT_NAME), retrieved from the build-and-push-docker-image and infrastructure jobs, respectively. This step also fetches the Managed Identity Client ID based on AKS cluster and node pool names, and updates the values.yaml file for Helm deployment with these dynamic values using sed commands.

The Helm Lint step validates the Helm chart's structure and syntax, ensuring there are no configuration errors. Finally, the Deploy with Helm step deploys or updates the application on AKS, referencing the Helm chart in the ./helm directory.

This job effectively orchestrates the deployment of an application to AKS, ensuring that necessary configurations and credentials are dynamically fetched and applied, and using Helm for the deployment process.

You can find the final declaration of this workflow in the repository:

github.com/dawidborycki/People.WebApp.Declarations/blob/main/Workflows/people-webapp-ci-cd-terraform.yml

Additionally, the repository includes Helm and Terraform configurations:

github.com/dawidborycki/People.WebApp.Declarations/tree/main/helm-terraform

github.com/dawidborycki/People.WebApp.Declarations/tree/main/Terraform/people-ci-cd

Testing the pipeline

You can now run the pipeline by committing and pushing all the files to the repository. Open the terminal or command prompt and execute the following commands:

```
git add .
git commit -am "CI/CD with Terraform"
git push
```

This action will trigger the GitHub Action you created. Navigate to your GitHub repository, and click the Actions tab to observe the progress of the CI/CD pipeline. The process should appear similar to Figure 14-9.

Click the infrastructure job to view its details. Here, you will see the list of steps. Click Terraform Apply to observe the output, which should appear similar to when you were executing Terraform commands in Azure Cloud Shell (see Figure 14-10).

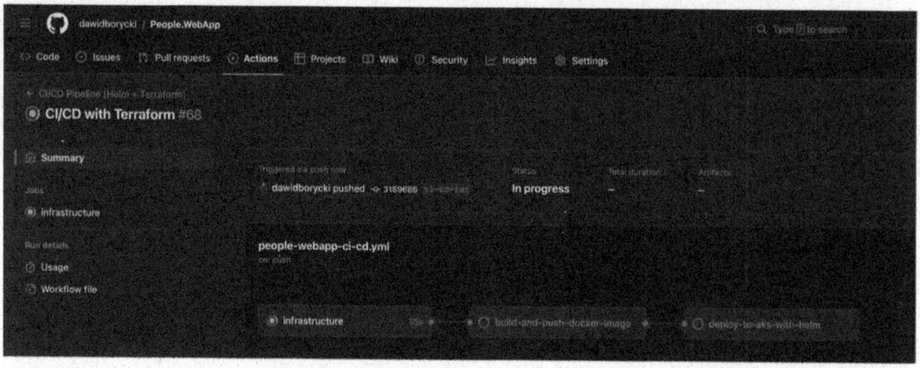

FIGURE 14-9 Jobs in the GitHub Actions workflow.

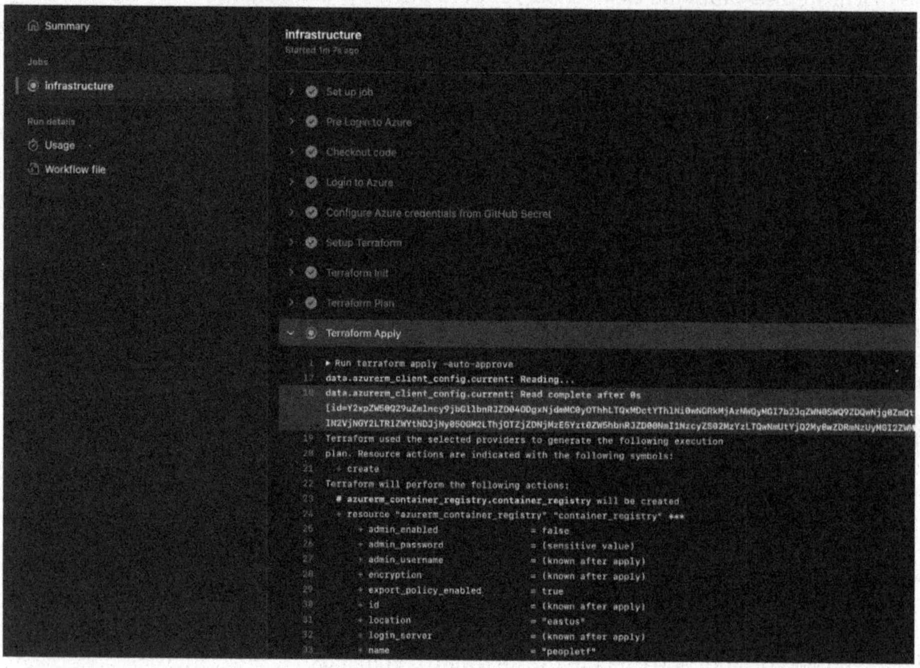

FIGURE 14-10 Previewing the Terraform Apply step.

Wait for the deployment to complete. Once all the jobs have finished, navigate to the Azure portal and search for the aks-people-tf Kubernetes cluster. Then, click Services and Ingresses to find the External IP of the people-web-app service (as shown in Figure 14-11). Use this IP address to access and view the running application (Figure 14-12).

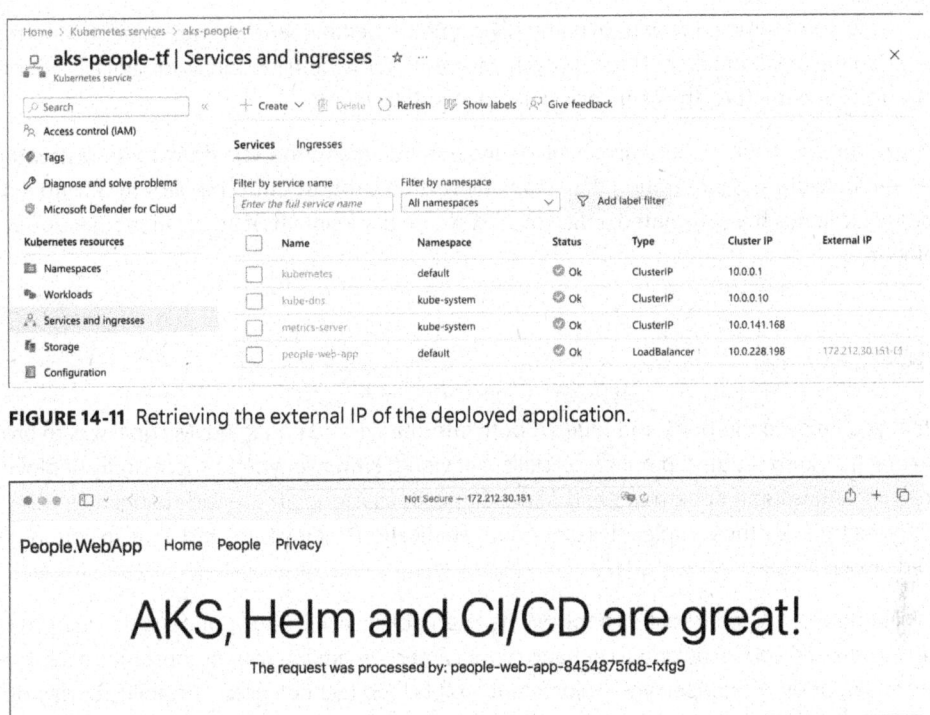

FIGURE 14-11 Retrieving the external IP of the deployed application.

FIGURE 14-12 Previewing the application.

Summary

In this chapter, you delved into the use of Terraform for deploying various Azure resources and integrated this with a CI/CD pipeline in GitHub Actions. You learned how to use Terraform to provision Azure resources, including the Azure Container Registry (ACR), Azure Kubernetes Service (AKS), and other dependent services. This process involved setting up Terraform configurations, initializing the Terraform environment, configuring the backend, and applying infrastructure as code.

The chapter covered the deployment of critical Azure resources essential for a comprehensive cloud-based application infrastructure, including the setup of container registries, Kubernetes clusters, SQL servers and databases, and key vaults. This demonstrated how Terraform can effectively manage complex cloud environments.

Furthermore, you explored how to integrate Terraform with GitHub Actions to automate the deployment process. This involved creating a CI/CD pipeline that executes various jobs such as building and pushing Docker images, deploying infrastructure with Terraform, and deploying applications to AKS using Helm.

You explored optimizing the GitHub Actions workflow for efficiency and security, which included authenticating to Azure, managing Docker images, handling Helm charts, and securely storing and retrieving secrets.

Additionally, you examined how to dynamically configure deployment settings using Terraform outputs within the CI/CD pipeline. This approach ensures that the pipeline can automatically adapt to changes in the infrastructure, thus enhancing deployment flexibility.

In conclusion, you achieved a comprehensive understanding of using Terraform for infrastructure management in Azure and integrating these capabilities into a robust CI/CD pipeline in GitHub Actions. This synergy facilitates the automated, efficient, and secure deployment of applications in a cloud environment.

Conclusion

I hope that you enjoyed this book and found it both informative and engaging. My goal was to provide you with practical knowledge and hands-on skills that would empower you to successfully deploy modern applications using Kubernetes and Azure Cloud. By mastering these technologies, you are well-equipped to tackle the complexities of modern application deployment and excel in your professional endeavors.

The skills you've acquired from this book will be invaluable in achieving your personal and professional goals, whether you're looking to enhance your career, streamline your organization's deployment processes, or simply deepen your understanding of cloud technologies. The ability to deploy and manage applications in a cloud-native environment is a highly sought-after skill in today's tech industry.

To leave you with an inspiring thought, consider this quote from Brendan Burns, one of the creators of Kubernetes:

> *"There are more distributed systems that need to be built than there are people who know how to build them. The development and sharing of patterns for building distributed systems (especially in container orchestration technology like Kubernetes) enables both novice and veteran system builders to rapidly build and deploy reliable distributed systems."* —Brendan Burns.

This should reassure you that you have chosen the correct path in learning about app deployment with Docker, Kubernetes and Microsoft Azure.

Index

A

accessing
    Azure Cloud Shell, 64
    files from other containers, 34
    GET method, Swagger UI, 17
    namespaces, 115
    web API, 15
ACR (Azure Cloud Registry), 92
adding
    Docker Compose files to workspaces, 47
    Microsoft SQL Server to containers, 48–50
    people to databases, POST method, 17–18
AKS (Azure Kubernetes Service), 153–157
    advantages of, 83–84
    clusters, Terraform deployments, 213–216
    cost of, 84
    resource requirements, 84
    role of, 83
alerts
    clusters, 119–120
    rules, 120
Analytics, Log, 123–125
analyzing resource usage, 173–176
annotating deployments, 135
API (Application Programming Interfaces)
    Kubernetes API, 73, 75
    web API
        accessing, 15
        data retrieval, web browser, 16
        testing methods, 19
apps (applications)
    cloning, 14
    configuring settings, 43–46
    containers, importance in app development, 6–7
    database connections, 14–15
    deploying, 92–95
        Helm, 188–189
        listing deployments, 130
        to clusters, 78–82
    in-memory databases, 15
    launching, 14–15
    load-testing
        automated load-testing, Docker, 164–167
        containerized load tests, 167–169
        Hey tool, 161–165
        HPA performance, 177–179
    manual scaling, 137
    modern app workflows, 55
    modern development and deployment workflow
        inner loops, 4
        outer loops, 4
        overview, 4–6
    rollbacks, 135–136
    rollouts
        listing deployments, 130
        load balancing, 132
        status, checking, 130–131
        strategies, 132–134
    running, 14, 50–52
    SQL Server, 15
    tags, listing, 129–130
    testing, 51–53
    uninstalling, Helm, 189–190
    updating, 127–131, 159
    upgrading, Helm, 188–189
    viewing, running apps, 14
    web API
        accessing, 15
        data retrieval, web browser, 16
architectures
    clusters, 73
    Docker, 25–26
attaching volumes to containers, 33
automating
    app updates, 159
    image builds
        building/pushing Docker images, 143–147
        CI/CD branches, 142
        cloning source code, 142

automating *(continued)*
    importing repositories, 141–142
    running updated workflows, 157–158
    Secrets, 147–150
    setting up workflows, 141–143
    testing workflows, 151–152
    triggering workflows with GitHub, 151
    updating deployments, AKS, 153–157
    workflow declaration files, 142–143
  load-testing, Docker, 164–167
autoscaling
  Cluster Autoscaler, 177–179
  HPA, 170
    applying, 172–173
    configuring, 170–172
    Helm charts, 186
    Helm integration, 197–198
    load-testing, 177–179
Azure, subscriptions, 9
Azure CLI (Command-Line Interface), 10
  building
    container registries, building, 63–64
    resource groups, removing, 65
  commands, invoking with Azure Cloud Shell, 64
  Help, 60
  output formats, 61–63
  overview, 59–61
Azure Cloud Shell
  accessing, 64
  Azure CLI commands, 64
  cluster connections, 92
  building
    container registries, 64
    Helm charts, 182–183
  resource groups, displaying, 64
Azure Container Registry, 56–59
  Azure CLI
    building container registries, 56–59
    Help, 60
    invoking commands with Azure Cloud Shell, 65
    output formats, 61–63
    overview, 59–61
    removing resource groups, 65
  Azure Cloud Shell
    accessing, 64
    building container registries, 64
    displaying resource groups, 64
    removing resource groups, 65

  Azure Portal, building container registries, 56–59
  defined, 56
  deploying with Terraform, 208–209
  listing
    images, 68
    repositories, 68
  local images, pushing to container registries, 65–68
Azure Key Vault, 107
  key vaults
    building, 107
    permissions, 110
  Secrets
    displaying, 108
    retrieving, 108–109
Azure Portal
  clusters
    alerts, 119–120
    metrics, 120–121
    monitoring features, 119–125
  commands, running, 119
  Container Insights, 121–125
  container registries, building, 56–59
  namespaces
    accessing, 115
    building, 115
    listing, 115–116
    removing, 115
  services
    ingresses, 116–117
    listing, 116–117
    viewing, 116–117
Azure SQL Database
  Basics tab, 100–101
  building, 98–103
  configuring, 99
  connecting to, 106
  connection strings, 97, 103–105
  dashboard, 98–99
  deploying databases, Terraform, 216–219
  DTU, 97
  elastic data pools, 98
  Networking tab, 101–102
  overview, 103, 106
  People.WebApp example
    modifying deployments, 104–105
    querying data, 106–107
    updating people, 105

previewing, 106–107
pricing options, 97–98
requirements, 97
Review tab, 102
serverless, 98, 103
servers, building, 100
vCore, 97

B

backends, remote, 209–210
balancing loads, Pods, 132
Basics tab, Azure SQL Database, 100–101
branches, CI/CD pipelines, building, 142
building
    Azure SQL Database, 98–103
    branches, CI/CD pipelines, 142
    clusters with AKS, 84–87
    configuration files, 47–48
    container images, 40–42
    container registries
        Azure CLI, 56–59
        Azure Cloud Shell, 64
        Azure Portal, 56–59
    containerized load tests, 167–169
    Docker images, automated image builds, 143–147
    Dockerfiles, 37–40
    Helm charts, 182–187
    images (automating)
        automatic app updates, 159
        building/pushing Docker images, 143–147
        CI/CD branches, 142
        cloning source code, 142
        Docker images, building/pushing, 143–147
        importing repositories, 141–142
        running updated workflows, 157–158
        Secrets, configuring, 147–150
        setting up workflows, 141–143
        testing workflows, 151–152
        triggering workflows with GitHub, 151
        updating deployments, AKS, 153–157
        workflow declaration files, 142–143
    key vaults, 107–108
    namespaces, 115
    services, 81
    volumes, 32, 117
Builds tab, Docker Desktop, 27
Burns, Brendan
    IaC, 236
    Kubernetes operation, 74–75

C

charts, Helm
    building, 182–187
    CI/CD pipeline integration, 190–194
    deployment template files, 186
    HPA, 186
    linting, 187
    modifying, 183–186
    rollbacks, 187–190
    rollouts, 187–190
    structure of, 182–183
checking
    status of rollouts, 130–131
    workflow statuses, GitHub Action extension, 151–152
CI/CD pipelines
    branches, building, 142
    declarations, Terraform, 228–233
    Helm integration, 190
        chart/value files, 191–194
        deployments, 194–196
        Git branches/chart files, 190–191
        GitHub Actions, 199–201
        helpers, 198–199
        HPA, 197–198
        services, 196–197
        testing workflows, 194–196
    IaC integration, 221–222
    testing, Terraform, 233–235
claims, persistent volume, 117
CLI (Command-Line Interfaces)
    Azure CLI, 10
        building container registries, 56–59
        Help, 60
        invoking commands with Azure Cloud Shell, 64
        output formats, 61–63
        overview, 59–61
        removing resource groups, 65
    Docker CLI commands, 25, 32
cloning
    apps, 14
    People.WebApp example app, 14
    source code, automated image builds, 142
closing containers, 36
cloud computing
    benefits of, 3
    role of, 3
Cloud Registry, Azure, 92

Cloud Shell, Azure
    accessing, 64
    Azure CLI commands, 64
    cluster connections, 92
    container registries, building, 64
    resource groups, displaying, 64
cloud-controller-manager, 74
Cluster Autoscaler, 177–179
clusters
    AKS
        building clusters, 84–87
        deploying clusters with Terraform, 213–216
    alerts, 119–120
    app deployments, 92–95
    architectures, 73
    configuring, ConfigMaps, 117–118
    connections, 77
        Azure Cloud Shell, 92
        local machines, 90–91
    Container Insights, 121–125
    containers
        listing, 123
        runtimes, 74
    Create Kubernetes Cluster wizard, 85–86
    defined, 72
    deploying apps to, 78–82
    kubectl
        displaying lists of nodes, 77
        displaying lists of services, 78
        retrieving lists of Pods, 77–78
    kubelets, 74
    kube-proxies, 74
    local clusters
        installing, 75–76
        setting up, 75–77
    metrics, 120–121
    namespaces
        accessing, 115
        building, 115
        listing, 115–116
        removing, 115
    Node pools, configuring, 86–87
    resource groups, listing, 88–90
    running, 81–82
    services
        ingresses, 116–117
        listing, 116–117
        viewing, 116–117
    storage, 117–118

code blocks, notation, 10
Command Palette, Visual Studio Code, 38
commands
    Azure CLI commands, invoking with Azure Cloud Shell, 64
    Docker CLI commands, 25, 32
    notation, 10
    running from Azure Portal, 119
Compose, Docker, 31–32, 35–36
    files, adding to workspaces, 47
    multi-container solutions, provisioning, 46–47
ConfigMaps, storing cluster configuration data, 117–118
configuration files
    building, 47–48
    notation, 10
configuring
    app settings, 43–46
    Azure SQL Database, 99
    clusters
        ConfigMaps, 117–118
        storing cluster configuration data, 117–118
    connection strings, 50, 103–105
    Container Insights, 121
    container settings, 43–46
    Helm charts, 183–186
    HPA, 170–172
    imperative configurations, 21
    key vault permissions, 110
    Node pools, 86–87
    Secrets, automated image builds, 147–150
connecting to
    Azure SQL Database, 106
    clusters
        Azure Cloud Shell, 92
        local machines, 90–91
connection strings
    Azure Key Vault, 107
        key vaults, building, 107
        key vaults, configuring permissions, 110
        Secrets, displaying, 108
        Secrets, retrieving, 108–109
    Azure SQL Database, 97, 103–105
    configuring, 50, 103–105
Container Insights, 121–125
Container Registry, Azure, 56–59
    Azure CLI
        building container registries, 56–59
        Help, 60
        invoking commands with Azure Cloud Shell, 65

creating

output formats, 61–63
    overview, 59–61
    removing resource groups, 65
  Azure Cloud Shell
    accessing, 64
    building container registries, 64
    displaying resource groups, 65
    removing resource groups, 65
  Azure Portal, building container registries, 56–59
  defined, 56
  listing
    images, 68
    repositories, 68
  local images, pushing to container registries, 65–68
containers/containerization
  adding Microsoft SQL Server to, 48–50
  advantages of, 21, 22–23
  closing, 36
  configuring settings, 43–46
  declarative configurations, 35
  defined, 22–23
  files, accessing from other containers, 34
  "Hello from container 1" messages, 33
  identifiers, viewing, 32–33
  images
    building, 40–42
    local images, pushing to container registries, 65–68
    pulling with Docker, 26–28
  importance in app development, 6–7
  listing, Containers Insights, 123
  load tests, 167–169
  logs, People.WebApp example, 125
  managing with Docker, 29–30
  multi-container solutions, provisioning with Docker Compose, 46–47
  multiple containers, stopping, 53
  networking, 34–35
  orchestration tools. *See* Kubernetes
  People.WebApp example
    adding Microsoft SQL Server, 48–50
    building configuration files, 47–48
    building container images, 40–42
    building Dockerfiles, 37–40
    configuring settings, 43–46
    multi-container solutions, provisioning with Docker Compose, 46–47

    running, 50–52
    testing, 51–53
  physical and software container comparisons, 23
  pulling with Docker, 26–28
  registries, building
    Azure CLI, 56–59
    Azure Cloud Shell, 64
    Azure Portal, 56–59
  removing with Docker, 30–31
  role of, 3
  running
    multiple containers, 31–32
    onnec, 44–45
    with Docker, 28–29
    with Docker Desktop, 31
  runtimes, 74
  VM vs., 23–24
  volumes, attaching to containers, 33
Containers tab, Docker Desktop, 27
contents of volumes, listing, 33
control plane (Kubernetes), defined, 72
CPU (Central Processing Units), resource requests/limits, 173–176
Create Kubernetes Cluster wizard, 85–86
creating
  branches, CI/CD pipelines, 142
  clusters with AKS, 84–87
  configuration files, 47–48
  container images, 40–42
  container registries
    Azure CLI, 56–59
    Azure Cloud Shell, 64
    Azure Portal, 56–59
  containerized load tests, 167–169
  Docker images, automated image builds, 143–147
  Dockerfiles, 37–40
  Helm charts, 182–187
  images (automating)
    automatic app updates, 159
    building/pushing Docker images, 143–147
    CI/CD branches, 142
    cloning source code, 142
    importing repositories, 141–142
    running updated workflows, 157–158
    Secrets, 147–150
    setting up workflows, 141–143
    testing workflows, 151–152
    triggering workflows with GitHub, 151

creating *(continued)*
    updating deployments, AKS, 153–157
    workflow declaration files, 142–143
key vaults, 107–108
namespaces, 115
servers, Azure SQL Database, 100
services, 81
volumes, 32, 117

D

dashboard, Azure SQL Database, 98–99
data retrieval (web API), web browser, 16
database connections
    apps, 14–15
    launching apps, 14–15
    People.WebApp example app, 14–15
databases
    adding people to databases, POST method, 17–18
    app connections, 14–15
        launching apps, 14–15
        People.WebApp example app, 14–15
    Azure SQL Database
        Basics tab, 100–101
        building servers, 100
        configuring, 99
        connecting to, 106
        connection strings, 97, m 103–105
        dashboard, 98–99
        databases, deploying with Terraform, 216–219
        Networking tab, 101–102
        overview, 103, 106
        People.WebApp example, modifying deployments, 104–105
        People.WebApp example, querying data, 106–107
        People.WebApp example, updating people, 105
        previewing, 106–107
        Review tab, 102
        vCore, 97
    connections
        apps, 14–15
        launching apps, 14–15
        People.WebApp example app, 14–15
    DTU, 97
    in-memory databases, 15
    SQL Database, Azure
        building, 98–103
        DTU, 97
        elastic data pools, 98
        pricing options, 97–98
        requirements, 97
        serverless, 98, 103
declaration files
    CI/CD pipelines, 228–235
    Terraform, 222–227
    workflows, automated image builds, 142–143
declarative configurations, 21–22, 35
deploying
    AKS clusters, Terraform, 213–216
    annotating deployments, 135
    apps, 92–95
        Helm, 188–189
        modern development and deployment workflow, 4–6
        to clusters, 78–82
    Azure Container Registry, Terraform, 208–209
    Azure SQL Database, People.WebApp example, 104–105
    Dockerfiles, 40
    Helm and CI/CD pipeline integration, 194–196
    infrastructures, Terraform, 210–213
    key vaults, Terraform, 219–221
    modifying deployments, 104–105
    People.WebApp example, 92–95, 104–105
    rapid deployments, declarative configurations, 21
    rollouts, listing deployments, 130
    services, 81
    updating deployments, AKS, 153–157
deployment template files, Helm charts, 186
Deployments, Kubernetes, 74–75
Desktop, Docker, 25–27
    building volumes, 32
    Builds tab, 27
    Containers tab, 27
    Dev Environments tab, 27
    Docker Scout tab, 27
    Images tab, 27
    installing, 8–9
    local Kubernetes clusters, 75–77
    running containers, 31, 43–46
    Volumes tab, 27
Dev Environments tab, Docker Desktop, 27
disaster preparedness, declarative configurations, 21
disk images, advantages of, 6
displaying
    lists of
        nodes, with kubectl, 77
        services, with kubectl, 78
    resource groups, Azure Cloud Shell, 64

Docker
    architecture of, 25–26
    automated load-testing, 164–167
    CLI commands, 25, 32
    Compose, 31–32, 35–36
        adding files to workspaces, 47
        provisioning multi-container solutions, 46–47
    containers
        accessing files from other containers, 34
        attaching volumes to, 33
        closing, 36
        images, 40–42
        managing, 29–30
        networking, 34–35
        pulling, 26–28
        removing, 30–31
        running, 28–29
        running, Docker Desktop, 31
        running, multiple containers, 31–32
    defined, 25
    Docker Desktop, 25–27
        building volumes, 32
        Builds tab, 27
        Containers tab, 27
        Dev Environments tab, 27
        Docker Scout tab, 27
        Images tab, 27
        installing, 8–9
        local Kubernetes clusters, 75–77
        running containers, 31, 43–46
        Volumes tab, 27
    Docker Hub, 25
    Dockerfiles
        building, 37–38
        deploying, 40
    images
        automated image builds, 143–147
        pushing to container registries, 67–68
        updating, 129–131
    volumes, 32
        attaching to containers, 33
        listing contents of, 33
        name conflicts, 33
        removing, 36
        showing with Docker CLI command, 32
DTU (Database Transaction Units), 97

E

elastic data pools, Azure SQL Database, 98
etcd, key-value store, 74

F

files
    accessing from other containers, 34
    configuration files, building, 47–48
    declaration files
        CI/CD pipelines, 228–235
        Terraform, 222–227
        workflows, automated image builds, 142–143
    deployment template files, Helm charts, 186
    Docker Compose files, adding to workspaces, 47
    Dockerfiles, building, 37–38
    Helm chart files
        CI/CD pipeline integration, 190–194
        Terraform, 227–228
    OpenAPI files, exposing with Swagger, 16–17
    state files, managing, 209–210

G

generator (Swagger), activating, 16
GET method, accessing Swagger UI, 17
Git
    Helm and CI/CD pipeline integration, 190–191
    installing, 8
    role of, 3
GitHub
    repositories
        building Secrets, 150
        importing, 141–142
    workflows
        running updated workflows, 157–158
        statuses, 152
        triggering, 151
GitHub Actions
    Helm and CI/CD pipeline integration, 199–201
    workflow statuses, 151–152
GitOps, 205

H

"Hello from container 1" messages, 33
Helm
    apps
        deploying, 188–189
        uninstalling, 189–190
        upgrading, 188–189
    charts
        building, 182–187
        CI/CD pipeline integration, 190–194

Helm *(continued)*
    deployment template files, 186
    HPA, 186
    linting, 187
    modifying, 183–186
    rollbacks, 187–190
    rollouts, 187–190
    structure of, 182–183
  CI/CD pipelines, 190
    chart/value files, 191–194
    deployments, 194–196
    Git branches/chart files, 190–191
    GitHub Actions, 199–201
    helpers, 198–199
    HPA, 197–198
    services, 196–197
    testing workflows, 194–196
  commands, running from Azure Portal, 119
  introduction to, 182
  repositories, 182
  Terraform and Helm files, 227–228
Help, Azure CLI, 60
helpers, Helm and CI/CD pipeline integration, 198–199
Hey tool, load-testing apps, 161–165
histories, rollouts, 134
HPA (HorizontalPodAutoscaler), 170
  applying, 172–173
  configuring, 170–172
  Helm and CI/CD pipeline integration, 197–198
  Helm charts, 186
  load-testing, 177–179
  performance, 177–179

I

IaC (Infrastructure as Code), 205
  role of, 3
  state files, managing, 209–210
  Terraform, 206–207
    AKS clusters, deploying, 213–216
    Azure Container Registry deployments, 208–209
    Azure SQL Databases, deploying, 216–219
    CI/CD pipelines, 221–222, 228–235
    declaration files, 222–227
    Helm files, 227–228
    infrastructures, deploying, 210–213
    key vaults, deploying, 219–221
    remote backends, 209–210

identifiers (containers), viewing, 32–33
images
  automating builds
    automatic app updates, 159
    building/pushing Docker images, 143–147
    CI/CD branches, 142
    cloning source code, 142
    Docker images, building/pushing, 143–147
    importing repositories, 141–142
    running updated workflows, 157–158
    Secrets, configuring, 147–150
    setting up workflows, 141–143
    testing workflows, 151–152
    triggering workflows with GitHub, 151
    updating deployments, AKS, 153–157
    workflow declaration files, 142–143
  container images
    building, 40–42
    pulling with Docker, 26–28
  disk images, advantages of, 6
  docker images, pushing to container registries, 67–68
  listing, Azure Container Registry, 68
  local images, pushing to container registries, 65–68
  updating, 129–131
Images tab, Docker Desktop, 27
imperative configurations, 21
importing repositories, 141–142
in-memory databases, 15
infrastructure deployments, Terraform, 210–213
ingresses
  listing, 116–117
  viewing, 116–117
inner loops, modern app development and deployment workflows, 4
Insights, Container, 121–125
installing
  Docker Desktop, 8–9
  Git, 8
  local Kubernetes clusters, 75–77
  NET 8 SDK, 8
  Visual Studio Code, 9

J - K

k8s. *See* Kubernetes
Key Vault, Azure, 107
  key vaults
    building, 107

configuring permissions, 110
    deploying with Terraform, 219–221
  Secrets
    displaying, 108
    retrieving, 108–109
key-value store, etcd, 74
KQL (Kusto Query Language), 123–125
kubectl
  commands, running from Azure Portal, 119
  namespaces
    accessing, 115
    building, 115
    listing, 115–116
    removing, 115
  services
    ingresses, 116–117
    listing, 116–117
    viewing, 116–117
Kubernetes (k8s)
  advantages of, 72–73
  AKS
    advantages of, 83–84
    cost of, 84
    resource requirements, 84
    role of, 83
    updating deployments, 153–157
  alerts, 119–120
  API, 73
  API Server (kube-api-server), 75
  cloud-controller-manager, 74
  clusters
    app deployments, 92–95
    architectures, 73
    building with AKS, 84–87
    configuring Node pools, 86–87
    connections, Azure Cloud Shell, 92
    connections, local machines, 90–91
    container runtimes, 74
    defined, 72
    deploying apps to, 78–82
    displaying lists of nodes with kubectl, 77
    displaying services of nodes with kubectl, 78
    kubectl, cluster connections, 77
    kubelets, 74
    kube-proxy, 74
    listing resource groups, 88–90
    local clusters, installing, 75–77
    local clusters, setting up, 75–77
    retrieving lists of services with kubectl, 78
    running, 81–82

ConfigMaps, storing cluster configuration data, 117–118
Container Insights, 121–125
control plane, defined, 72
Create Kubernetes Cluster wizard, 85–86
defined, 71–72
Deployments, 74–75
etcd, key-value store, 74
kube-controller-manager, 73–74
kubectl
  cluster connections, 77
  displaying lists of nodes, 77
  displaying lists of services, 78
  retrieving lists of Pods, 77–78
kubelets, 74
kube-proxies, 74
kube-scheduler, 73
load balancing, 132
metrics, 120–121
monitoring, 119–125
operating, 74–75
Pods, 74–75, 132
Secrets, 117–118
Services, 75
services
  building, 81
  deploying, 81

L

launching apps, database connections, 14–15
limits/resource requests, 173–176
linting, Helm charts, 187
listing
  alert rules, 120
  containers in clusters, 123
  contents of volumes, 33
  images, Azure Container Registry, 68
  ingresses in clusters, 116–117
  namespaces, 115–116
  nodes with kubectl, 77
  Pods, 77–78, 131
  ReplicaSets, 130–131
  repositories, Azure Container Registry, 68
  resource groups, 88–90
  rollouts, deployments, 130
  running containers, 44–45
  services
    in clusters, 116–117
    with kubectl, 78
  tags, 129–130

lists, Web API users, retrieving lists of, 53–54
load balancing, Pods, 132
load-testing apps
    automated load-testing, Docker, 164–167
    containerized load tests, 167–169
    Hey tool, 161–165
    HPA performance, 177–179
local clusters
    installing, 75–76
    setting up, 75–77
local images, pushing to container registries, 65–68
local machines, cluster connections, 90–91
Log Analytics, 123–125
logs (container), People.WebApp example, 125

M

managing containers with Docker, 29–30
manual scaling, Pods, 137
memory, resource requests/limits, 173–176
metrics, clusters, 120–121
Microsoft SQL Server, 15, 48–50
modern app development and deployment workflows, 4–6
modern app workflows, 55modifying
    app settings, 43–46
    Azure SQL Database, 99
    clusters
        ConfigMaps, 117–118
        storing cluster configuration data, 117–118
    connection strings, 50, 103–105
    Container Insights, 121
    container settings, 43–46
    Helm charts, 183–186
    HPA, 170–172
    imperative configurations, 21
    key vault permissions, 110
    Node pools, 86–87
    Secrets, automated image builds, 147–150
monitoring features (Azure Portal), 119–125
multi-container solutions, provisioning with Docker Compose, 46–47
multiple containers
    running with Docker, 31–32
    stopping, 53

N

name conflicts, volumes, 33
namespaces
    accessing, 115
    building, 115
    listing, 115–116
    Pod names, retrieving, 127–130
    removing, 115
NET 8 SDK, installing, 8
networking containers, 34–35
Networking tab, Azure SQL Database, 101–102
Node pools, configuring, 86–87
nodes
    listing with kubectl, 77, 78
    usage limits, 173–176
notation
    code blocks, 10
    commands, 10
    configuration files, 10

O

OpenAPI files, exposing with Swagger, 16–17
outer loops, modern app development and deployment workflows, 4
output formats, Azure CLI, 61–63

P

people, adding to databases, POST method, 17–18
People.WebApp example, 13
    automated image builds
        building/pushing Docker images, 143–147
        configuring Secrets, 147–150
        importing repositories, 141–142
        running updated workflows, 157–158
        testing workflows, 151–152
        updating deployments, AKS, 153–157
    automatic app updates, 159
    cloning, 14
    Cluster Autoscaler, 177–179
    connection strings, configuring, 103–105
    containerization
        adding Microsoft SQL Server, 48–50
        building configuration files, 47–48
        building container images, 40–42
        building Dockerfiles, 37–40
        configuring settings, 43–46
        multi-container solutions, provisioning with Docker Compose, 46–47
        running containers, 42–46
    container logs, 125
    database connections, 14–15

deploying, 92–95, 104–105
   Helm and CI/CD pipeline integration
      chart/value files, 191–194
      deployments, 194–196
      Git branches/chart files, 190–191
      GitHub Actions, 199–201
      helpers, 198–199
      HPA, 197–198
      services, 196–197
      testing workflows, 190–191
   HPA, 170
      applying, 172–173
      configuring, 170–172
      load-testing, 177–179
   IaC with Terraform, 228–233
      AKS cluster deployments, 213–216
      Azure Container Registry deployments, 208–209
      Azure SQL Database deployments, 216–219
      CI/CD pipeline integration, 221–222, 228–233
      declaration files, 222–227
      Helm files, 227–228
      infrastructures deployments, 210–213
      key vault deployments, 219–221
      remote backends, 209–210
   load-testing
      automated load-testing, Docker, 164–167
      containerized load tests, 167–169
      Hey tool, 161–165
   local images, pushing to container registries, 65–68
   manual scaling, 137
   namespaces
      accessing, 115
      building, 115
      listing, 115–116
      removing, 115
   Pod names, retrieving, 127–130
   querying data, 106–107
   resource requests/limits, 173–176
   rollbacks, 135–136, 187–190
   rollouts, 130–131
      Helm rollouts, 187–190
      histories, 134
      load balancing, 132
      strategies, 132–134
   running, 14, 50–52, 109
   services
      ingresses, 116–117
      listing, 116–117
      viewing, 116–117
   Swagger
      activating, 16
      OpenAPI files, exposing, 16–17
      UI, 17–19
   tags, listing, 129–130
   testing, 51–53
   updating, 105, 110–112, 127–131
   usage limits, 173–176
   web API, 15–16
performance (HPA), load-testing, 177–179
permissions, key vault, 110
persistent volume claims, 117
physical and software container comparisons, 23
physical machines, declarative configurations, 21–22
pipelines, CI/CD
   branches, building, 142
   declarations, Terraform, 228–233
   Helm integration, 190
      chart/value files, 191–194
      deployments, 194–196
      Git branches/chart files, 190–191
      GitHub Actions, 199–201
      helpers, 198–199
      HPA, 197–198
      services, 196–197
      testing workflows, 194–196
   IaC integration, 221–222
   testing, Terraform, 233–235
Pods
   Cluster Autoscaler, 177–179
   descriptions, 80–81
   HPA, 170
      applying, 172–173
      configuring, 170–172
      load-testing, 177–179
   Kubernetes, 74–75
   listing, 77–78, 131
   load balancing, 132
   manual scaling, 137
   names, retrieving, 127–130
   ReplicaSets, checking status, 130–131
   resource requests/limits, 173–176
   usage limits, 173–176
   volumes, building for Pods, 117
Portal, Azure
   clusters
      alerts, 119–120
      metrics, 120–121
      monitoring features, 119–125
   commands, running, 119

Portal, Azure (continued)
  Container Insights, 121–125
  container registries, building, 56–59
  namespaces
    accessing, 115
    building, 115
    listing, 115–116
    removing, 115
  services
    ingresses, 116–117
    listing, 116–117
    viewing, 116–117
POST method, adding people to databases, 17–19
previewing, Azure SQL Database, 106–107
provisioning multi-container solutions, Docker Compose, 46–47
pulling containers with Docker, 26–28
pushing images
  Docker images, automated image builds, 143–147
  local images to container registries, 65–68

Q

queries
  data queries, People.WebApp example, 106–107
  KQL, 123–125

R

rapid deployments, declarative configurations, 21
registries
  ACR, 92
  Azure Container Registry
    Azure CLI, building container registries, 56–59
    Azure CLI, Help, 60
    Azure CLI, invoking commands with Azure Command Shell, 65
    Azure CLI, output formats, 61–63
    Azure CLI, overview, 59–61
    Azure CLI, removing resource groups, 65
    Azure Cloud Shell, accessing, 64
    Azure Cloud Shell, building container registries, 64
    Azure Cloud Shell, displaying resource groups, 65
    Azure Cloud Shell, removing resource groups, 65
    Azure Portal, building container registries, 56–59
    defined, 56
    deploying, Terraform, 208–209

    listing images, 68
    listing repositories, 68
    pushing local images to container registries, 65–68
  container registries
    building with Azure CLI, 56–59
    building with Azure Cloud Shell, 64
    building with Azure Portal, 56–59
    pushing local images to container registries, 65–68
  Docker Hub, 25
releases, defined, 182
remote backends, 209–210
removing
  containers with Docker, 30–31
  namespaces, 115
  resource groups, 65
  volumes, 36
ReplicaSets
  listing, 130–131
  Pods, checking status, 130–131
repositories
  building Secrets, 150
  Helm, 182
  importing, 141–142
  listing, Azure Container Registry, 68
  running updated workflows, 157–158
  workflow statuses, 152
resource groups
  displaying in Azure Cloud Shell, 64
  listing, 88–90
  removing, 65
resource requests/limits, 173–176
retrieving
  web browser data, web API, 16
  lists of
    Pods with kubectl, 77–78
    Web API users, 53–54
  Pod names, 127–130
  Secrets, key vaults, 108–109
Review tab, Azure SQL Database, 102
rollbacks, 135–136, 187–190
rollouts
  deployments
    anotating, 135
    listing, 130
  Helm charts, 187–190
  histories, 134
  load balancing, 132
  status, checking, 130–131
  strategies, 132–134

rules, alerts, 120
running
   apps, 14, 50–52
   clusters, 81–82
   commands, from Azure Portal, 119
   containers
      listing running containers, 44–45
      load tests, 167–169
      multiple containers, 31–32
      People.WebApp example, 42–46
      with Docker, 28–29
      with Docker Desktop, 31
   People.WebApp example, 14, 50–52, 109
   updated workflows, automated image builds, 157–158
   viewing running apps, 14
runtimes, containers, 74

S

scaling pods, manual, 137
Secrets, 117–118
   building
      GitHub, 150
      Visual Studio Code, 149
   configuring, automated image builds, 147–150
   key vaults
      displaying, 108
      retrieving, 108–109
serverless Azure SQL Database, 98, 103
servers
   Azure SQL Database servers, building, 100
   Kubernetes API Server (kube-api-server), 75
   Microsoft SQL Server, 15, 48–50
   vCore, 97
services
   building, 81
   clusters
      AKS clusters, Terraform deployments, 213–216
      listing in clusters, 116–117
      viewing in clusters, 116–117
   deploying, 81
   Helm and CI/CD pipeline integration, 196–197
Services, Kubernetes, 75
setting up
   local Kubernetes clusters, 75–77
   workflows, automated image builds, 141–143
showing volumes with Docker CLI command, 32
software, physical and software container comparisons, 23
source code, cloning in automated image builds, 142

SQL Database, Azure
   Basics tab, 100–101
   building, 98–103
   configuring, 99
   connecting to, 106
   connection strings, 97, 103–105
   dashboard, 98–99
   database deployments, Terraform, 216–219
   DTU, 97
   elastic data pools, 98
   Networking tab, 101–102
   overview, 103, 106
   People.WebApp example
      modifying deployments, 104–105
      querying data, 106–107
      updating people, 105
   previewing, 106–107
   pricing options, 97–98
   requirements, 97
   Review tab, 102
   serverless, 98, 103
   servers, building, 100
   vCore, 97
SQL Server, 15, 48–50
state files, managing, 209–210
status checks
   rollouts, 130–131
   workflows with GitHub Action extension, 151–152
stopping multiple containers, 53
storage, clusters, 117–118
subscriptions, Azure, 9
Swagger
   generator, activating, 16
   OpenAPI files, exposing, 16–17
   UI, 17–19
      adding people to databases, POST method, 17–18
      containerized People.WebApp example, 44–45
      GET method, accessing, 17
      Try It Out button, 17

T

tags, listing, 129–130
Terraform
   Azure Container Registry deployments, 208–209
   CI/CD pipeline integration, 221–222
   CI/CD pipelines
      declarations, 228–233
      testing, 233–235

Terraform *(continued)*
    declaration files, 222–227
    deploying
        AKS clusters, 213–216
        Azure SQL Databases, 216–219
        infrastructures, 210–213
        key vaults, 219–221
    Helm files, 227–228
    introduction to, 206–207
    remote backends, 209–210
testing
    apps, 51–53
    CI/CD pipelines, Terraform, 233–235
    Helm and CI/CD pipeline integration workflows, 201–203
    People.WebApp example, 51–53
    POST method, 19
    workflows, 151–152, 201–203
triggering workflows with GitHub, 151
Try It Out button, Swagger UI, 17

U

UI (User Interface), Swagger UI, 17–19
    adding people to databases, POST method, 17–18
    containerized People.WebApp example, 44–45
    GET method, accessing, 17
    Try It Out button, 17
uninstalling apps, Helm, 189–190
updating
    apps, 127–131, 159
    deployments, AKS, 153–157
    images, 129–131
    People.WebApp example, 105, 110–112, 127–131
    workflows, running, 157–158
upgrading apps, Helm, 188–189
usage limits, 173–176
users (Web API), retrieving lists of, 53–54

V

vCore, 97
viewing
    container identifiers, 32–33
    ingresses in clusters, 116–117
    running apps, 14
    services in clusters, 116–117
Visual Studio Code
    Command Palette, 38
    Dockerfiles, building, 38
    GitHub Action extension, workflow statuses, 151–152
    installing, 9
    repositories, building Secrets, 149
VM (Virtual Machines)
    containers vs.23–24
    declarative configurations, 21–22
volumes
    attaching to containers, 33
    building
        for Pods, 117
        with Docker, 32
    listing contents of, 33
    name conflicts, 33
    persistent volume claims, 117
    removing, 36
    showing with Docker CLI command, 32
Volumes tab, Docker Desktop, 27

W

web API (Application Programming Interfaces)
    accessing, 15
    data retrieval, web browser, 16
    People.WebApp example app
        accessing web API, 15
        retrieving data, 16
        Swagger, exposing OpenAPI files, 16–17
        Swagger UI, 17–19
    retrieving lists of users, 53–54
    testing methods, 19
workflows
    automated image builds, 141–143
    declaration files, 142–143
    Helm and CI/CD pipeline integration, 201–203
    modern app development and deployment, overview, 4–6
    modern app workflows, 55
    testing, 151–152, 201–203
    triggering with GitHub, 151
    updating, 157–158
workspaces, adding Docker Compose files to, 47